You Girls Stay Here

You Girls Stay Here:

Gender Roles in Popular British Children's Adventure Fiction, 1930-70

By

Elizabeth Poynter

Cambridge
Scholars
Publishing

You Girls Stay Here:
Gender Roles in Popular British Children's Adventure Fiction, 1930-70

By Elizabeth Poynter

This book first published 2018

Cambridge Scholars Publishing

Lady Stephenson Library, Newcastle upon Tyne, NE6 2PA, UK

British Library Cataloguing in Publication Data
A catalogue record for this book is available from the British Library

ISBN (10): 1-5275-0773-4
ISBN (13): 978-1-5275-0773-9

To my mother, who taught me to read and introduced me to so many
of these authors

TABLE OF CONTENTS

LIST OF ILLUSTRATIONS

LIST OF TABLES

INTRODUCTION

During the twentieth century, critics tended to treat children's literature like adult literature in terms of what they expected of it. Frank Eyre's *British Children's Books in the Twentieth Century*, for example, is very clear and informative, but I was greatly disappointed, to say the least, by his summing up of children's adventure books in the first half of the century:

> "A few authors overcame these difficulties and produced books that have stood the test of time, but the majority were produced by writers who were either under-paid hacks or over-paid formula-mongers. The commercial and practical difficulties of the period created an infertile soil for the growth of the genuine writer for children." (Eyre 1972, 78)

There is a kind of intellectual snobbery about this.

John Rowe Townsend in 1990 never even mentioned popular writers for girls Elinor Brent-Dyer, Elsie Oxenham or Dorita Fairlie Bruce (his chapter on school stories is mostly about boys), and generally seemed to feel that the period 1915-45 was a poor one for children's literature, too many potential authors having been killed in the Great War; he devoted a mere thirty seven pages to that period, as compared with a hundred and sixty to that following, up to 1989. Mary Cadogan and Patricia Craig in *You're a Brick, Angela!* did cover popular girls' stories, but were generally extremely negative in their judgements on Angela Brazil and the above three; reading their later book *Women and Children First*, which looks at fictional portrayals of women and children in the two world wars, I found their criteria for determining what was "literature" and what was merely fiction very subjective. Yet Harry Hendrick in his 1997 study of *Children, childhood and English society 1880-1990* quoted Townsend's judgement of "second, third and tenth rate school and adventure stories" (Hendrick 1997, 87) as if that were the last word on the subject.

To my mind, children's fiction should be judged by children; if they like it, it's good, in the sense that it fulfils its purpose. And to be frank, if it manages to be good literature, as determined by adult critics, as well, that is pretty rare. It is true that others have advocated this way of assessing the quality of children's literature (Grenby and Reynolds 2011). Yet I am not sure that anyone has gone so far as to say the opposite, that if most children's reaction is "that's boring", then a book is NOT good literature, no matter what the adult critics may say, although Peter Hunt comes fairly close when he says "We might well argue ... *real* children's books are the ones read *only* by children - ones that do *not* have anything to say to adults, and which are not, therefore, subject to adult judgements." (Hunt 2009, 21).

All in all, it seemed to me more valid, as well as more enjoyable, to examine popular fiction. At the very least, these are the books which parents and schoolteachers bought for children at the time. With the advent of (cheaper) paperbacks, in particular, they are also the books which children bought for themselves. Popular fiction, because by definition it is more widely read than other books, critically acclaimed or otherwise, represents the principal models provided for children to emulate. One of the criticisms levelled against such books is that they reflected prevailing attitudes and beliefs. Is a good book necessarily one which challenges prevailing morality and mores? Good literature is intended to make the reader think, so perhaps. However, I would take issue with the view that if a book does not challenge society in any way it must be badly written, which does seem an assumption by many literary critics. I also feel that in reading a book written for an earlier generation, one should not assume that if it falls short of what is currently an acceptable view of society, that means it must have done so when it was written. Such a book may contain elements distasteful to many modern readers, but should like or dislike come into it? If you read with your mind already made up, you will see what you expect to see.

I also feel that some surveys of children's literature cover so many texts that, inevitably, they skim the surface of some of the authors. An example would be Gillian Avery's very good *Childhood's Pattern* (1975), which many later critics refer to. On pages 241-2 she says of Biggles:

"He is square-chinned, grey-eyed; he speaks laconically, nods curtly, his face is usually expressionless. Here is the boy's ideal, a man of deeds, not words, and no silly nonsense about him thinking."

Here is a description of Biggles from *The Rescue Flight*, set during World War I:

"Slight in build, his features were as delicate as those of a girl, as were his hands, which fidgeted continually with the throat fastening of his tunic. His deep-set hazel eyes were never still, yet held a quality of humour that seemed out of place in a pale face upon which the strain of war, and the sight of sudden death, had already graven little lines (28).”

It is true that in at least one book he has grey eyes, and he often speaks curtly−Monty Python sent that up years ago−but he certainly thinks, and he is no simple stereotyped hero.

For these various reasons, I wanted to take a look for myself at some of the books I loved as a child. I read most of them over and over (twenty or thirty times at least), and they must have had some impact on my view of life. At the time the only aspect I was aware of having appropriated was the concept of “honour” as expressed in both girls' and boys' school stories, and in the *Beau Geste* trilogy which I also loved. If the authors I read most were indeed sexist, racist and middle-class, I should have imbibed these attitudes. Gender continuing to be a contentious subject well into the twenty-first century, I decided I wanted to examine some of these books as an adult, setting them in their historical context, and see how gender roles were actually portrayed in them, rather than relying on my memory and the somewhat sweeping generalisations of many critics. As Eyre (1972, 27) pointed out, “By 1950 British children's books were entering a new phase…Almost overnight writers who had seemed on a pinnacle of commercial success became disreputable.” It is largely such authors in whom I am interested.

This book presents the results of that study. I have chosen to look at adventure stories because they mostly involve both girls and boys, and many of them were aimed at both genders rather than only one. Also, by their very nature they provide opportunities for action and danger which may (or may not) be used by the author to distinguish the genders. I have not included historical adventures, such as those by Geoffrey Trease, or Rosemary Sutcliff, because if they are true to their period they would necessarily give little weight to female characters, although I have read a few in order to gain that perspective. Nor have I considered the very considerable array of fantasy adventures for which British authors were justly famous, as I felt this would have made this study too unwieldy, although I was tempted to include the Narnia books as otherwise very much fitting my criteria, being a short series involving both boys and girls.

I am focusing on the period long derided by critics, although recently there have been some reappraisals (Ray 1982; Reynolds 2016). All the authors selected feature white middle-class protagonists: while it is understandable that later critics were concerned that children's literature did not reflect the diversity of British society, in fact this makes a focus on gender more meaningful. In today's Britain, class and ethnicity interact with gender to create a complex web of cultural identities; the culture represented in these books is more homogeneous, and gender may more easily be isolated as a factor.

Chapter one gives brief information about the authors I have chosen to study and my rationale for choosing the particular books I have looked at. Chapter two then outlines the development of gendered children's literature up to World War One, and some of the socio-cultural changes during the lifetimes of the authors studied, such as the impact of feminism and changing views of childhood, in order to set a context for the study. The themes which emerged from the primary texts were: female agency or share of the action; types of activities and skills assigned to the different genders; adult gender roles; leadership and power relations; courage and sensitivity. These are examined in chapters three to seven. Then, since I am by training a linguist, chapter eight analyses some of the language used by and about the two genders. Finally chapter nine examines the concept of gender identity and how these books might have contributed to its development in their readers.

CHAPTER ONE

WHO, WHAT AND WHY?
AN OUTLINE OF THE AUTHORS
AND TEXTS IN THIS STUDY

Whilst I have tried to take into account a wide range of authors, I chiefly considered: Arthur Ransome, Captain W.E. Johns, M.E. Atkinson, Enid Blyton, Gwendoline Courtney, Malcolm Saville and Elinor Brent-Dyer. Because I wanted to see what large numbers of children were reading, I have focused on popular authors rather than on authors acclaimed by the critics, although Ransome is both, in fact. In the case of Brent-Dyer I was not looking at the girls' school stories for which she is best known, except for purposes of comparison, but at her adventure stories involving both boys and girls. With Johns, I was interested to compare the *Biggles* books for boys with the *Worrals* books for girls; Cadogan and Craig (1992) acknowledge that the latter have some superficial feminist remarks but otherwise dismiss them. Since Johns' protagonists are adult, I thought it would be useful to include not only the *Lone Pine* books by Malcolm Saville but also his *Marston Baines* series with older characters. Overall, I wanted approximately equal numbers of texts by male and female writers, and some texts by writers who also wrote in other genres or for two different readerships, to enable comparisons. These principal primary texts comprise 126 books, 65 by female and 61 by male authors (see Appendix A for a full list).

I have concentrated largely on "series" books, with some or all of the same characters running through several volumes, partly to see if there was any development in the author's ideas or portrayal of gender over a long period of time. Although the critics include the 1920s as part of the doldrums of children's literature, these various series did not begin until 1930 or later, so that is where my focus begins. And by the early 1960s, the critics are agreed that a "second golden age" of children's literature had begun (Eyre as mentioned in the introduction placed it as early as 1950: Eyre 1972, 27), but since several of these authors were producing work in their main series during the 1960s, I have chosen to end my study in 1970. I was born in 1962, so it makes sense to continue into my lifetime.

Below is a brief outline of the work of each of the above authors, which is intended to serve both as an introduction for any reader not familiar with them, and an explanation as to why each has been included. I have arranged them in chronological order of first publication studied, and noted the time span of the books of each author which I have studied. These books vary considerably in the nature of "adventure", and I have outlined this for each author. If one were to include only tales with danger to life, involving guns and serious villains like smugglers or spies, some of these authors would have to be omitted; I have looked at some books which are more family adventure than thriller, but which were identified in the blurb and / or in the constant use of the word "adventure" as adventure genre.

Arthur Ransome (1884-1967)
Publications 1930-47

Ransome stands out among the authors I have chosen in having been granted various awards such as an honorary Litt. D. and an honorary M.A., and of course winning the inaugural Carnegie Medal for his writing for children (Ransome 1930; Ransome 1976). None of the other writers examined here was as critically acclaimed, and some, as I have mentioned, were quite savagely attacked in the 1960s and '70s. However, Ransome was undoubtedly also popular with children, and as one of the early exponents of the mixed-gender adventure genre, he can hardly be excluded. As a literary critic himself, and for years a professional journalist, with a wide experience of the world (having travelled for the *Manchester Guardian* in Russia, China and Egypt, following a wartime post as a war correspondent on the Russian front), it can be expected that he would write rather differently than a female near-contemporary like Elinor Brent-Dyer, for example. I should note here that he profoundly disagreed with me as regards children's literature, stating in his autobiography: "Any book worth reading by children is also worth reading by grown-up persons" (Ransome 1976, 35). His mother used to read aloud to the family, and only read those books she felt were worthwhile.

I have looked here only at his *Swallows and Amazons* series: twelve books (the thirteenth was unfinished at his death) featuring boys and girls in boats on lakes (Cumbria), rivers (East Anglia) and the sea. We do not have precisely the same group of children in every book, but there is sufficient overlap to get some sense of development. The youngest children (Roger aged seven in the first book, Bridget aged two) quite clearly grow older, but the ages of the older children are deliberately left vague, and they do not seem to age quite as rapidly, since they (John Walker captain of the *Swallow*, and Nancy Blackett captain of the *Amazon*) must be at least twelve in the first book and should therefore be at least sixteen in the last, where they are still being identified as children, in an age when many left school at fourteen. They do however develop in terms of experience and in what adults trust them with (camping on an island more or less in view of the house in *Swallows and Amazons*; being "marooned" without adult supervision and with the addition of five-year-old Bridget in *Secret Water*).

The adventures in Ransome's books are mostly imaginary. The children engage in holiday activities such as sailing and camping, but dress them up by being pirates and raiding each other's ships, or explorers mapping uncharted territory. They are rarely in serious danger except occasionally when they do something silly like sailing at night or being caught in a fog on a moor. There are no gunrunners or drug smugglers here. The exceptions to this are the two books which are metafictional, telling stories imagined by the child characters of their exploits in foreign lands: *Peter Duck* which takes them treasure hunting in the Caribbean, and *Missee Lee* in which they meet a Chinese pirate. In the former they are shot at and in the latter threatened with beheading. However, since the characters behave much as usual (not unduly heroic, young Roger always hungry and Nancy suffering from seasickness), apart from the exotic setting the metafictional nature of these tales is not, in my view, clearly flagged up and they may well have been read at face value by many children.

Capt. W. E. Johns (1893-1968)
Publications 1932-67

William Earl Johns left school at fourteen and trained in a surveyor's office, but joined up in 1914 and saw the end of the Gallipoli campaign and the equally disastrous one in Salonika before transferring to the Royal Flying Corps with a temporary commission. In fact he saw very little active flying service as he was made an instructor after training, and then two months after going out to France was shot down and taken prisoner. He stayed in the RAF, as it had then become, for several years but eventually set up as an aviation illustrator and in 1932 became editor of a new magazine, *Popular Flying*, where the first *Biggles* stories were serialised. During the 1930s the enormous popular interest in aviation gave rise to a range of books and periodicals: Johns edited two of the latter until the Spanish Civil War and the rise of Fascism generally caused him to produce outspoken editorials attacking the government's policy of appeasement, resulting in his dismissal. He repudiated accusations of being a warmonger, claiming he hated war but did not want Britain to lose one, or to end up appeasing the Fascists (Berresford Ellis and Williams 1985).

Johns' personal life was also potentially controversial, although he managed to keep it from his public. In 1914 he had married a woman eleven years his senior, who bore him a son, Jack. However, when he returned from the war they became estranged and he eventually formed a liaison with Doris Leigh, who was known thereafter as his wife, while his son became his "nephew". It is not really known whether it was his first wife or her father, a vicar, who opposed a divorce, but Doris' family, though naturally not delighted, accepted the situation and her younger brother trained with Johns as an artist (Berresford Ellis and Williams 1985).

Johns was a prolific writer, producing ninety-six *Biggles* books, eleven *Worrals* books, nine *Gimlet* books (about a group of Commandos), ten science fiction adventures, five *Steeley* books aimed at slightly older readers and quite a number of other novels, including some adult thrillers. For this study I have focused on the first two series mentioned above. Biggles started off as the hero of short stories set in the RFC in World War One, based on Johns' own experiences and those of people he knew. The first stories were collected in book form within a few months, and the next year the first full-length tale came out. Biggles and his cousin Algy, soon joined by the teenage Ginger Hebblethwaite, enjoyed a variety of adventures set in the 1930s, Ginger presumably being introduced to give young readers someone to identify with, once Biggles himself ceased to be a teenager. In the Second War Biggles commanded a special squadron, then post war he and his two friends, augmented by Bertie Lissie from the squadron, formed the Air Police at Scotland Yard. Worrals, alias Flight Officer (later Squadron Officer) Joan Worralson, was created in 1941 at the request of the Air Ministry to aid recruitment to the WAAF. She and her friend Betty "Frecks" Lovell enjoyed six wartime adventures and a further five post-war.

I felt it would be fruitful to compare these two series by the same author. They differ from most of the other books in this study in that *Biggles* is aimed only at boys (though girls certainly read him; I inherited my first *Biggles* book from my mother) and the protagonists are all male, and mostly adult, indeed in most of the books professional rather than amateur adventurers, serving in the air force and then the police. *Worrals*, similarly, is aimed at girls, although the two heroines are always assisted by a number of male characters. The nature of the adventures is much more dramatic than in those series featuring largely children: people are shot and sometimes die, they are attacked by crocodiles and lions, bitten by venomous snakes, threatened with executions and lynch mobs, not to mention natural disasters such as hurricanes and sandstorms; the settings take us to every continent including Antarctica; and the villains, when not the enemy in wartime, are serious criminals or, often, spies.

Since there are eleven *Worrals* books, I decided to study specifically the same number of *Biggles* books, though I have read most of the ninety-six. If we discount one-line appearances of, for example, chambermaids, waitresses and the housekeeper Mrs Symes, only sixteen of the ninety-six *Biggles* books have one or more female characters. From these I selected ten, plus one other for reasons which will become apparent: one set in the First War, five in the 1930s (though two of these were published in 1940), one from the Second War and four Air Police tales. The later books became pretty formulaic so although there are far more of them, I would not in any case have included more than that.

M. E. Atkinson (1899-1974)
Publications 1936-50

Mary Evelyn Atkinson was a fairly prolific writer for children. Her works include several typical genres including pony books and family adventures. Like those of some of the other authors here, they have been severely criticised for being serenely middle-class and not merely ignoring the lower classes or making them amusing caricatures, but actually sneering at them. Possibly this is one reason why her works are more or less unknown to today's children, but more likely in my view is that the adventures are so realistic as to be not terribly exciting to a generation brought up with video games and Harry Potter. With the exception of the occasional moorland fire and swimming accident, most of the adventures occur in the children's heads, but unlike Ransome's children, who knowingly create imaginary worlds, Atkinson's imagine smugglers and villains where there is nothing but a minor mystery. Like Ransome's, her books were published through the war without mentioning the conflict, another source of criticism, but Ransome apparently commented that his publishers wanted him to "Steer clear of the war at all costs", and this fits with the widespread view at the time that children should be protected from certain subjects, quite apart from the technical difficulties of writing about current events in book form, given the necessary delay in publication. Clearly some of the other authors here did manage it, however.

Whatever these shortcomings to modern eyes, Atkinson's books were popular in their day: *August Adventure*, the first in the *Lockett* series, was described on its cover by the Yorkshire Post as "Streets ahead of anything in this class besides the Ransome books", and obviously sold well enough for her to produce another thirteen featuring the same group of children. I have focused on this series, which starts with the three Locketts, then aged thirteen, twelve and ten and a half respectively, and their friend Anna and her little brother Robin. The Locketts age gradually throughout the series, as they continue to have an adventure per school holiday, and other friends and rivals are introduced and feature in some of the books. There is an interesting twist in that, although written in the third person, the books are supposedly produced by the Locketts themselves, with the help of a writer aunt. As a result, in the later books they frequently meet people who have read about their adventures.

Enid Blyton (1897-1968)
Publications 1938-63

One cannot look at adventure stories for children without considering Enid Blyton. Not only was she enormously popular in her lifetime, dominating the field of children's literature in the 1940s, when wartime paper shortages meant that many authors struggled while she continued to produce several books a year, but she has continued to be read. Two different TV series were made based on her *Famous Five*, and the current spoofs such as *Five on Brexit Island* suggest many of the adult population of Britain are sufficiently familiar with the characters to appreciate a parody. Yet in the 1960s and '70s critics began to write her off as insufficiently literary, librarians, while perhaps not banning her works as urban myths suggest, at least ceased to encourage children to read them, and we probably all have a friend whose parents forbade her books. Nonetheless in 2009, forty years after her death, Rudd (2009, 168) was able to state she still sold eleven million copies per year and was the only children's author to have outsold J.K. Rowling.

It is true that her tales have a more limited vocabulary than most of the others in this study. They lack quotations from the classics and their geographical references are vague. One would not gain much general knowledge from them. Nor are her plotlines particularly probable, especially with protagonists of ten to fourteen or so. However, that raises two questions: firstly, to what extent are most adult thrillers either realistic or of great literary merit? And secondly, what is the purpose of children's literature? There has been and probably still is considerable debate about this. If you feel that it is to educate, and children should only read carefully-selected texts which develop their vocabulary and steer them towards views acceptable to their (middle-class liberal) parents and teachers, then Blyton probably doesn't fill the bill. If you feel it is more important to get people reading something fun, in the hope they will move on to more serious literature, then she does. I shall not debate this further as it is really a matter of opinion anyway, but it needs to be borne in mind that among the criticisms were racism, class-ism and sexism.

Blyton was a trained teacher who worked both in a school and then with a group of children privately before becoming a full-time author. Her works include many tales for younger children, the school series *St Clare's* and *Malory Towers*, and many non-fiction educational and religious books, but she is probably most famous for her various adventure series, particularly the *Famous Five*. I have looked at that series, the *Adventure* series which starts with *The Island of Adventure*, the *Secret* series (*Secret Island, Secret of Spiggy Holes*) and the *"R" Mysteries* (*Rilloby Fair, Rockingdown* etc.). These all feature either two boys and two girls, or in the case of the *R Mysteries* three and one, of one family or two, aged between ten and fourteen or fifteen (Barney in the *R Mysteries* is probably the oldest). All but the *Adventure* series are set in various parts of rural Britain, never with real place names. They all tend to involve serious criminals such as kidnappers or gun-runners, although no-one ever gets killed or seriously hurt; Barbara Stoney in her biography presents Blyton's view as "The 'best writers for children' did not deal in murders, rapes, violence, blood, torture and ghosts - these things did not belong to the children's world" (Stoney 1986, 148)

Gwendoline Courtney (1911-96)
Publications 1940-56

Unlike most of the other writers studied here, Gwendoline Courtney was neither a teacher nor a journalist. Illness forced her to abandon plans for university, and she worked for her father in his office before the Second World War, then during it in Lord Goodman's office, being the only civilian to work on Operation Overlord. Like many female authors, she never married, living with her sister until the latter died (Cridland and Mackie-Hunter 2004). Her books were all published between 1935 and 1956, although she lived for another forty years, and they contain many of the elements typical of the period, featuring middle-class families, generally with a servant or two, and children often at boarding schools. However she had an excellent sense of humour which enabled her to portray teasing among her characters very effectively, which in my view sets her apart from many other writers, for children or otherwise.

Gwendoline Courtney published eight "family" stories and seven adventures (one, *Mermaid House*, only in instalment form in the *Salisbury Journal* until Girls Gone By brought it out as a book). Three of the adventures are set in a girls' boarding school: *The Denehurst Secret Service* is a blend of genres, with only six whole and two part chapters of twenty-one actually about the spying, the rest being typical school-story themes, although the *Wild Lorings* books contain very little that is typical of a school story, (nothing about lessons, sport only mentioned as giving some people alibis) and are really thrillers in a school setting. The second *Denehurst* title, *The Grenville Garrison* and *Mermaid House* all involve a mixture of boys and girls, mostly teenagers, (and in fact mostly one family in each case), during the summer holidays, the first being another wartime spy tale, the second a "Ruritania" novel and the last a gang of thieves reminiscent of Elinor Brent-Dyer's *Chudleigh Hold* (see below). Nearly all of the adventure books have equal numbers of boys and girls or more girls (*The Grenville Garrison* is the exception), and this together with the fact that the author is clearly female, that the majority of her books are typical girls' stories, together with the girls' school setting of three of them, suggests the adventures would have chiefly been read by girls rather than boys.

Her books are interesting in the degree of danger they contain: there are guns which do get fired, villains actually get wounded, torture is threatened, a prefect gets bopped over the head and knocked out, in addition to the usual hazards of being captured and tied up. The degree of independence shown by the children in each is more plausible than in Enid Blyton, for instance, since Courtney's protagonists are older, the eldest in each book being generally sixteen or seventeen, the youngest twelve (*Mermaid House*), thirteen (*The Grenville Garrison, Denehurst Secret Service*) or even fourteen (*Wild Lorings*), although obviously the plots are somewhat unlikely. The children mostly win through by quite possible means such as overhearing something crucial and calling on an appropriate adult, or being able to read Morse, only *Grenville Garrison* really departing from this and ending with an armed attack on the "garrison" on its island in the river, which the children hold off until the cavalry arrives. I decided to include her, despite the fact that her books are not a series (although the six include two pairs with the same, or nearly the same, characters), and she was not very prolific, partly because the ages of her protagonists compare well with Saville's *Lone Pine* series, and partly because she also wrote in the family genre, enabling some comparison there.

Malcolm Saville (1901-1982)
Publications 1943-[78]

Malcolm Saville was a very successful children's author, producing over ninety books, most of which were reprinted and some of which were popularised by Armada's paperback editions. He wrote part-time, with a "day job" in publishing, which gave him insight into the market, but he still came in for criticism in the 1960s and '70s for being "middle-class". This is not the focus of this book, so I shall not consider it in detail. I imagine this impression arose from the fact that some of his protagonists go to boarding school and they mostly come from nice unbroken homes. However, the facts that Tom Ingles in the *Lone Pine* series seems to have left school and be working full-time for his uncle at age fifteen when we first meet him, Jenny Harman's father runs the village shop, and in their London home anyway the Mortons have no maid, cook, gardener etc., make Saville far less middle-class, surely, than some of the other authors in this study. While it is understandable that critics were concerned that children's literature did not reflect the diversity of British society by the 1960s, it is also understandable that writers tend to write about what they know. Daughter of two teachers and university educated myself, I would not feel particularly comfortable writing a novel with a hero from a very different background; I would get too many details wrong, for a start. But this question really lies outside the scope of this book.

I decided to include Saville for the above-mentioned reasons, namely that he was popular with his child readers and that he came in for some flak from the critics, but also because I felt I needed at least three male writers in the study, one aspect of which was to see if there were any differences in the writers' attitudes which could be ascribed to gender rather than individuality. I have studied his twenty *Lone Pine* books, published between 1943 and 1978 (the last couple are admittedly out of the period I had set myself, but most of the series falls within it), and his seven *Marston Baines* books, published 1963 to 1978 (again, the last falls strictly outside the period). The *Lone Pine* series features children aged nine to fifteen (in the first book), who age to become nearly twelve and eighteen respectively in the last, which makes them reasonably comparable with Brent-Dyer and Courtney, and since the young Morton twins play a large role in every book, it is also possible to compare him with Blyton and Ransome, whose heroes are younger than the older Lone Piners. The *Marston Baines* books are aimed at the Young Adult market, with main characters who at first are students and then starting off on their professional lives, while Baines himself is a middle-aged professional Intelligence agent. This provides two advantages: it is interesting to compare the two series, and it is valuable to have another series with older characters to set against those of Captain Johns.

The adventure in the *Lone Pine* series ranges from quite serious villainy such as attempted wartime sabotage (*Mystery At Witchend* 1943), a gang hijacking lorries (*Man With Three Fingers* 1966) and gunrunners (*Where's My Girl?* 1972) to rather amateurish attempts to find a stolen necklace (*The Secret of the Gorge* 1958) or possible Roman treasure (*Treasure at Amory's* 1964). Note the dates given here are those of first publication (see Appendix A); in some cases I have used other editions and quotations are from those editions (see References: primary texts). The children quite intentionally seek out adventure (the fifth rule of the Lone Pine Club states that it is for "exploring and watching birds and animals and tracking strangers": *Mystery At Witchend,* 59) and are frequently captured and locked up, and occasionally genuinely hurt by the villains.

Danger also comes from a number of natural disasters, generally involving water: high seas break through flood barriers or excessive rain leads to a landslide, or indeed in the first book, the saboteurs succeed in blowing up a reservoir (not strictly natural!). They tend to be in danger of their lives only from the water, while the criminals rarely do more than lock them up; usually they are rescued rather than able to escape by their own ingenuity. Sometimes they are actually rescued by the police! Thus it might be said that, although it is highly improbable that so many adventures would happen to the same group of people, however avidly they sought them, each specific story is reasonably possible. The same cannot really be said of the *Marston Baines* plotlines, which include international anarchist gangs, mysterious new drugs being used to undermine Western society, and the European student activism of the late 1960s being provoked by China. This kind of thing was common in earlier adult thrillers such as those of John Buchan, but by the 1970s writers for adults were becoming more sophisticated (Hammond Innes started publishing in the 1930s, Desmond Bagley in 1963, Frederick Forsyth's *Day of the Jackal* was 1979).

Elinor M. Brent-Dyer (1894-1969)
Publications 1950-55

Gladys Eleanor May Dyer, to give her her baptismal name, was born and brought up in South Shields. She shared Enid Blyton's experience in that her father deserted her mother and the family hid the fact for the sake of respectability, though in Elinor's case when she was probably no more than three. Luckily for the family Mrs Dyer had inherited a small income from her father, and there may have been maintenance payments from her husband as well, so Elinor grew up in a house with a maid. She attended small private schools like so many of her future heroines, worked for a time as a "pupil-teacher", then entered the City of Leeds Training College before continuing as a teacher, still living with her mother and, now, stepfather. In later years she ran her own small school in Herefordshire (McClelland 1981). With this background it is not surprising that the first stories she wrote were girls' school stories, and she is most famous for the *Chalet School* series, which ran to 62 volumes in the Armada paperback versions. Published over four decades, these sold well and continue to sell.

Most of her non-*Chalet School* books were either also school stories or domestic / family stories, clearly aimed at girl readers. However, in the 1950s she also produced five adventure tales, which I felt it would be interesting to compare with her other works. The first of these in reading order is *Chudleigh Hold*, published in 1954 but clearly conceived much earlier, as a boiled-down version appears in *Gay from China at the Chalet School* in 1944. This and *Fardingales* (1950) are a kind of hybrid genre, combining the large families and domestic details of her family books with a thriller plotline pursued by a small number of the characters. These are both set in rural England. *The Susannah Adventure* is a sequel to *Fardingales*, with the same protagonists and a great deal of sailing about the Channel trying to evade the villains, *Condor Crags Adventure* blends these protagonists with two brothers from *Chudleigh Hold*, and is set mainly in South America with adult male heroes, while *Top Secret* abandons all but one of the Chudleigh brothers, who, en route to Australia with some secret papers, has to outwit those who are trying to kill him and seize the papers. Here again the protagonists are chiefly male, the exception being an elderly spinster. My impression is that the first two books were aimed at presenting a new genre to her readership of girls, but the last two have many more characteristics of adventures written for boys.

Almost all these writers were born in late Victorian or Edwardian times. As children, they would have read the books available for children in the 1890s and 1900s (many of which were published considerably earlier than that, of course). Their views and ideals were likely to have been formed, in many cases (Gwendoline Courtney is the real exception) before the First War. The following chapter, therefore, looks at the development of children's fiction prior to the 1920s, by which time most of these writers were adults, with a particular focus on genres aimed at one gender rather than the other. It tries to set this in the wider context of sociocultural changes during the late nineteenth and early twentieth centuries, particularly ideas about gender and about childhood. Only when we understand the world which formed these writers and the world in which they were living when they wrote can we assess their work effectively.

CHAPTER TWO

IN THEIR SHOES
THE SOCIAL CONTEXT OF THE AUTHORS

"What adults read is their own affair, but what children read is *our* responsibility." These words of Boris Ford, quoted in Rosemary Auchmuty's excellent study of girls' school stories (Auchmuty 1992, 10) reflect a fairly consistent attitude among adult critics of children's literature. Since the development of a literature aimed specifically at children, and indeed earlier, parents, teachers, writers, philosophers and self-declared experts have tended to unite in this, if in nothing else. The development of more liberal views of childhood and the desirability of children being encouraged to evolve in their own way has not necessarily changed this, although childist criticism, taking account of the child-as-reader, has grown as an approach in recent decades. It is widely agreed that the child is father to the man, that events and influences when we are young shape the person we become, and the books we read or have read to us are one of those influences. During the period this book is examining, reading books or magazines was indeed a bigger part of most people's lives than now, since television was in its infancy and video games unknown. In particular, the portrayal of gender roles in early fiction has been shown to be of great importance in the shaping of our gender identity (Foster and Simons 1995).

Why do we have books written for children? What is their primary purpose? There are essentially two possible answers to this question: to give pleasure and entertain, or to educate and instruct. Of course, these are not mutually exclusive, but the weight you give to each will tend to determine how you evaluate a text. If it is popular, it is presumably succeeding in the former goal, but it seems to be the nature of critics to regard the popular with suspicion. If too many people like something, it cannot be good quality. This is a kind of middle-class intellectual snobbery, and I am hardly immune, I confess. When *Star Wars* first came out and there were huge queues outside cinemas, I turned up my nose and refused to go because "real" science fiction was in books, and something everybody liked couldn't be good. Twenty years later I finally watched the first film on television and discovered it was actually quite good science fiction, although it didn't have any particularly thought-provoking message. Probably most people who watched it just had a jolly good time, but there must by the law of averages have been some who were brought through that enjoyment to more serious science fiction, which examines human society through the lens of the Other, or who perhaps even decided on a career in science. Having fun does not necessarily lead to learning, but without enjoyment learning is that much less likely.

This point has been recognised about children's literature. Instructive writers began to coat the medicine of their message in a dollop of jam, and critics began to realise that perhaps any book which encouraged children to read was a good thing. Enid Blyton is one author who has been justified on that account (Ray 1982). It is impossible to ignore her enormous and enduring popularity, but equally it is true that she wrote with quite a limited vocabulary, two-dimensional characters and in a nice, safe world with no sex or violence and very little poverty. These facts led to her being heavily attacked in the 1960s by those who felt children's books should stretch children's minds, and reflect the real world. Either children were discouraged or even forbidden from reading her, or it was permitted with a shrug and the attitude "Oh, well, at least they're reading something. They'll grow out of her and move on to better stuff". This is perhaps to ignore that Blyton herself fully intended to write as she did. If you look at her books for different age-groups, the vocabulary is as carefully graded as a reader aimed at learners of English as a Foreign Language, and she herself said she concentrated on plot and on giving each character just one or two recognisable traits, and avoided unpleasant issues: her goal was to keep children within their comfort zone, not take them out of it (Stoney 1986). This leads me to the point that the "meaning" of a book is always a blend of the author's intention, the actual text, the reader's interpretation and the context. Since the latter two will change (every reader is different, and the context in which the book was written will be viewed differently by later generations), books change their meaning over time.

I am concerned here to look at the texts for what they say and don't say about gender in the light of present-day feminist expectations, but also to look at the world in which they were written, and even further back, the world in which their authors grew up. I feel that some criticisms of the period are based on unreasonable expectations; we cannot expect someone writing in the 1930s to see the world as we do today, or even as the most progressive thinkers in their own day did. And perhaps by focusing on how they fell short of what we would consider acceptable ideas about gender, we fail to see the places where they did *not* fall short. As Johnson once wrote: "To judge rightly of an author we must transport ourselves to his time," (quoted in Grenby and Reynolds 2011, 102). In this chapter I shall begin by outlining some of the changes in the status of women and ideas about gender; move on to ideas about childhood and the status of children; then give a brief overview of the development of children's literature as a genre and how it reflected attitudes to both women and childhood; and finally put this together and examine the context in which my selected authors were growing up and that in which they were writing.

The "little woman" to the "modern woman"

Most human societies have been and are patriarchies: that is, women have been excluded from political authority, from cultural authority (including education), have been exploited economically and, often, sexually (LeGates 2001). Philosophy and religion bring forward arguments to support this: the ancient Greeks explained that female biology made women less intelligent and therefore less able for public life, while the Abrahamic religions hark back to Eve and original sin. In the modern West, science has taken the place of religion and been invoked to demonstrate that women are less intelligent because they have, on average, smaller brains (nineteenth century), or more recently that men and women have different brains and therefore should have different roles, based on brain scan images whose significance is as yet little understood, plus a lot of preconceptions (Fine 2011). This isn't just about women, of course: if women have their assigned role, then so do men, and they may be equally uncomfortable with it. However, because patriarchy privileges men even if it also restricts them, until very recently it is feminism which has had the loudest voice on gender issues.

There are many different shades of feminism, but one great distinction may be identified: between the liberal or equal-rights feminists, who originated in the eighteenth century and gained strength in the nineteenth, and who stress the similarity (equality) of the genders; and the cultural or maternal feminists, who emphasise the differences and celebrate feminine values over the male ones of traditional societies. This is not the place to go into the various feminist movements in any detail, but we need to bear this distinction in mind and not simply assume that for an author to uphold feminist values s/he must assign equal and similar roles to male and female characters, which I feel is how feminism has largely been rewritten in the popular mind.

Some cultures stress the role of the father as the head of the family, but Victorian Britain saw women as the heart of a family, and as families were the bridge between the individual and society, woman's role was crucial. The negative side of this view was that it emphasised woman's role as a mother at the expense of her individuality, but the positive side was that it gave weight to arguments in favour of female education, since an educated woman could better prepare her children for their future role in the world. In 1850 Frances Buss established the North London Collegiate School for Girls, and in 1858 Dorothea Beale became the principal of Cheltenham Ladies' College, a post she retained until shortly before her death in 1906. During the 1870s the High School Movement for Girls spread rapidly, and at Cambridge and Oxford the first women's colleges were founded in 1872 and 1878 respectively, although it was decades before women were actually allowed to graduate with a degree. Girls' schools, instead of concentrating on social skills like sketching and playing the piano, began to teach geography, maths and science, although most female educators recognised the different roles girls and boys would play in the future and did not advocate total parity. There was also a strong class bias, which I shall return to.

Not only were Miss Buss and Miss Beale enormously influential in developing standards of excellence in girls' education, in 1865 they joined leading feminists in a women's discussion group called the Kensington Society, and a year later the London Suffrage Committee which petitioned Parliament to grant women the vote. Women's suffrage has been viewed as the most radical idea put forward by early feminists (LeGates 2001, 222); it certainly aroused fierce opposition. Later in the twentieth century some felt that it had taken up a disproportionate amount of time, when there were other aspects of women's lives to worry about, but if the traditional division between the sexes is that women belong to the private, domestic sphere and men to the public, it is understandable that a move to give women a public role would be deeply controversial. Most Western governments finally extended suffrage to women in the aftermath of World War One: Denmark in 1915, the Soviet Union in 1917, Germany, Austria and Great Britain in 1918, the US and Belgium in 1920, although in Britain the extension only applied to married women over thirty, the rest having to wait another ten years.

While the vote might be regarded as a landmark, other things were probably having greater impact on individual women's lives. The 1882 Married Women's Property Act ended the legal assumption that a wife had no separate existence from her husband, enabling married women to own land and property (and also making them responsible for their own debts).

Journalism and office work opened up to women, and the job market expanded again with the 1914-18 war, as young women who had previously been in domestic service went into factories and public transport. The war saw around 800,000 more women workers in industry, 400,000 in offices, 200,000 in government jobs and over 50,000 more in banks (Marr 2009). After the war it was considered unpatriotic for a woman to hold on to a job which could be done by a returning soldier, but in the meantime some women farmworkers had begun wearing trousers and everywhere skirts were shorter, the bra had started to replace the camisole, cigarettes were now popular among women as well as men, and by 1919 every village chemist had begun selling contraceptives, even if only to married couples.

Many women rejected a return to domestic service and preferred to be unemployed, although this was not accepted by the authorities; essentially married women were not expected to work, and if they claimed unemployment benefit their claims were frequently rejected. For example, in the first three months after the 1931 Anomalies Act, which tightened the law, 48% of women's claims were rejected as against 4% of men's (Pugh 2008). And of course women were paid less, effectively being paid as though they were single while men were paid as though they had a family to support, even though in the 1921 census 39% of men had not, in fact. Women teachers and civil servants routinely lost their jobs when they married, despite the Sex Disqualification (Removal) Act, which should have prevented this. Nonetheless there were more opportunities than ever before: in Britain by 1935 116 women were practising as solicitors, 79 as barristers, and 1914's 477 female doctors had become 2,830 by 1931, though mostly GPs rather than consultants. This is particularly significant because these are professions, normally entered by the middle class, and these were the women who in Victorian times had definitely been expected to stay at home and provide an example of radiant motherhood. Working class women had been part of the workforce in one way or another all along. Moreover, the books in this study featured and were aimed at children of precisely this class.

The Second World War brought another wave of job opportunities. The women's services might seem more glamorous to public imagination, but there was also industrial conscription of women from 1941, to meet the country's shortfall of two million workers, and by 1943 46% of all women aged fourteen to fifty-nine were doing paid work for the war effort (Pugh 2008). This reinforced the small change in attitudes towards acceptance of married women working outside the home, even though there was a similar post-war backlash to that of the 1920s. Even two steps forward and one back means that you are one step forward.

Changes in the workplace were not only down to two world wars. There was a chicken-and-egg relationship between female education and the late-Victorian increase in unmarried women, who needed to work. In the second half of the nineteenth century, nearly one in four women "failed" to marry, and early feminists used this as an argument in favour of both education and job opportunities for women, to enable them to support themselves. Equally, once educated, women had an alternative to marriage which seemed to some more attractive (Auchmuty 1999). This trend was exacerbated by male deaths in the First War, and the 1921 census saw an unprecedented 37% of adult women unmarried. However, a combination of official worries about the falling birth rate (it had been falling since the late nineteenth century) and a general desire to return to normal after the war meant that actually in the 1920s the popularity of marriage increased (Pugh 2008). This may have been partly due to legislation which improved women's property, divorce and custody rights, (the 1923 Act, passed with a large majority, made divorce equal, in that both sides only had to prove adultery, where previously women had additionally had to prove cruelty), yet it is also true that marriage was still seen as the chief goal of a girl's life, and maintaining a successful marriage the chief responsibility of the wife rather than the husband. *Woman's Own* in 1932 could cheerfully print that "any girl worth her salt wants to be the best housewife ever - and then some" (quoted in Pugh 2008, 174). My first thought on reading this was that "men-only" magazines means pornography, while *Woman's Own* clearly isn't the female equivalent.

Many women, especially but not exclusively unmarried ones, put their energy and enthusiasm into female institutions such as the Girl Guides (founded 1910), Girls' Guild and the Women's Institute (not the cosy organisation we think of today but viewed in the 1920s as rather subversive), but this began to be called into question as more people became familiar with lesbianism as a concept. In late Victorian times deep emotional friendships between women were widely accepted, and were by no means necessarily sexual in nature, but once psychoanalysis gained some credence, and key works like Havelock Ellis' sexual studies (published between 1894 and 1910, though only available to men and then only with difficulty) began to impact on the medical profession, ideas changed (LeGates 2001). Nineteen twenty-one saw an (unsuccessful) attempt to criminalise lesbianism in Britain, and in 1928 the prosecution of the lesbian novel *The Well of Loneliness* brought much publicity and a great deal of negative reaction; close female friendships began to be seen as latently if not actively lesbian, and a threat to patriarchal society (Auchmuty 1992; LeGates 2001). Nonetheless the 1920s and '30s are the golden age of girls' school stories, which tends to indicate that children's literature lags somewhat behind social trends.

Gender identity was becoming recognised as problematic by Edwardian times. This was not just because of a superfluity of bicycle-riding, bloomer-wearing career women, but also because the early setbacks Britain faced in the second Boer War (1899-1902) called into question the British confidence in their empire and led to worries that the great days of the British hero were over. Boys needed to be encouraged to become "real men" as much as girls to become wives and mothers. In mid nineteenth century literature, a male demonstrating "feminine" characteristics such as sensitivity was viewed in a positive light as something pure and noble, but this gradually became suspect, fuelled by highly-publicised trials such as those of Oscar Wilde, and boys were encouraged to be frank, bold, good at sport and generally hearty (Nelson 1991). Other factors involved were the fact that a longer education (see below) meant that adolescence was now recognised as a stage in human development, and with it the need for clear role models in literature as regards sexual identity. There was also an increase in commuting made possible by rail networks, and hence fathers generally spent less time with their sons and were less available as role models (Reynolds 1990). Probably also the rise in feminism and higher levels of female education led to male defensiveness and a perceived need to emphasise gender differences. The use of different colours to mark gender started in the late nineteenth century, as a new way to give clear signals (Fine 2011), although initially pink was for boys and blue for girls. (At this point I am taking the position that sex is a matter of biology, while gender is a cultural construct; I shall return to this in chapter nine.)

In the 1920s, although many women cut their hair and cultivated a boyish figure, there was more interest in personal fulfilment than in wider issues, and feminism did not make enormous progress. Women's magazines were aimed at the "modern woman", but in practice this meant largely fashion tips; while female sexualisation could be perceived as giving women agency (the good middle-class Edwardian girl did not wear makeup or revealing clothes, because she had to suppress her sexual self in public to meet the expectations of society; her counterpart in 1925 did), yet it was also titillating to men. The nineteen thirties brought a return of more "feminine" looks in terms of hair and dress, and further tensions as regards working women as the Depression put large numbers of men out of work; it was felt women should not take jobs from men, but at the same time, sometimes they had to work because they were able to find a job and their husband was not.

The Second World War was quite different from the First, in that instead of being largely fought by males on foreign soil it had a major impact on the Home Front (LeGates 2001; Marr 2009). Women learned to develop their skills and independence. Afterwards the number of divorces increased, but many of those who divorced remarried; early marriage was in fact increasingly fashionable over the period 1951-71, and marriage as an institution had not lost its popularity. In 1911 552 out of a thousand women aged twenty to thirty-nine were married, while the 1951 census had 731 out of a thousand. As Arthur Marwick (2003, 47) states: "The basic assumption in all classes was that girls would become wives and mothers, and should therefore be treated accordingly". This meant fewer girls than boys would go to university or be encouraged to have a career as opposed to a job. The 1961 census showed that 90% of nurses, 20% of journalists and 12.5% of sales personnel were female, but often in practice doing fairly menial work assisting males. Over a quarter of all working women were secretaries or typists, and only one in ten in the professions (Auchmuty 1999). The proponents of unequal pay explicitly acknowledged that by paying women less they hoped to discourage them from working in order to encourage them to have more children.

It is not surprising that Betty Friedan's book *The Feminine Mystique*, published in 1963, had an enormous impact on women who read it and realised that their feelings of dissatisfaction were shared and not a failing to be hidden. In 1968 the Miss America Pageant drew protesters to New Jersey and a year later over five hundred delegates met in New York City at the Congress to Unite Women. In Britain, the Labour government brought in a raft of liberalising laws under Home Secretary Roy Jenkins: the NHS (Family Planning) Act enabling GPs to prescribe the Pill; the Sexual Offences Act legalising homosexuality and the Abortion Act in 1967, and in 1969 the Divorce Reform Act allowing the grounds of "irretrievable breakdown" (Marr 2008). Germaine Greer published *The Female Eunuch* in 1970. So-called Second Wave feminism was taking off, and feminist ideas became increasingly mainstream. With the Second Wave as with the first there were two main strands, those who were concerned with social equality and rights, and the radicals who saw patriarchy as the root of all evil and wanted to change society completely. Yet over three decades later Lamb and Brown (2006), studying children's clothing, books, TV, movies and music in America, found gender stereotyping to be depressingly pervasive. A couple of examples: T-shirt logos "Math Never Spells Fun" for girls but "Math Rules" for boys, and a report from Children Now in 2005 that "71 per cent of lawyers, 80 per cent of CEOs, 92 per cent of officials, and 80 per cent of doctors on TV are men" (Lamb and Brown 2006, 92). If this is true of popular fiction in the twenty-first century, what should we expect of the mid-twentieth?

The "century of the child"

If we look beyond the definition of mere biological immaturity, the concept of childhood is a social construct, different in different societies and in different eras. Just as ideas about women's role changed, this construct also saw considerable changes in the nineteenth and early twentieth centuries, so much so that the twentieth century has been dubbed "the century of the child" (Cunningham 2005). To generalise somewhat, the medieval Christian idea that children were filled with original sin and needed bringing to God was gradually replaced by a secularisation of attitudes to childhood in the eighteenth century. John Locke and Rousseau were key figures here; Rousseau's advocacy of allowing the child to develop naturally was very influential in Continental Europe and to some extent in Britain. The nineteenth century saw the "sacralisation" of childhood (term coined by Vivian Zelizer, cited in Hendrick 1997, 10) with children being seen as somehow closer to God, pure and angelic, an idea propounded by the Romantics and exemplified in many Victorian novels. Prior to about 1830 concern had been either with children's souls or with the future manpower needs of the state, but the Romantic view of childhood as a separate period of life to be enjoyed, to be protected and dependent, then began to influence public action (Cunningham 2005).

This resulted in enormous social changes. In the late Middle Ages, the vast majority of children began gradually learning to work from the age of around seven, but still had plenty of free time as their work was likely to be helping their parents, part-time or seasonally. The Industrial Revolution changed that pattern; in factories, children worked full-time, often from an early age. This focused the attention of philanthropists on their lives, particularly as at this point Britain still had an overwhelmingly young population: a third to a half were under fifteen, and around 20% of these would have lost at least one parent, so towns were full of children, often in gangs on the streets (Cunningham 2005). In response to this situation most Western countries began to introduce laws to protect children and to provide for their education.

Some European countries (mostly the Protestant ones, following Luther's advocacy in 1530) passed laws on the compulsory provision of schools in the sixteenth and seventeenth centuries, but it was not until the later nineteenth century that most succeeded in making schooling compulsory. In England and Wales the first government grants for elementary education came in 1833, 1870 saw an Act to establish a school in every neighbourhood, the1880 Education Act made it compulsory to attend up to the age of ten, and 1891 saw the abolition of fees at primary school. The Acts were not popular with everyone. In the 1880s there were nearly 100,000 prosecutions for truancy annually, and this problem was reduced but did not disappear with the removal of all fees, because children who were in school were not able, or were less able, to contribute to the family income. The proportion of children aged five to fourteen who were regularly in school increased from 24% in 1870 to 48% in 1880 and reached 70% in 1900 (Cunningham 2005). Statistics for that year have 97.2% of adult males literate, and 73.2% of women (Altick 1957, cited in Bristow 1991, 32). In 1918 the leaving age was raised to fourteen, in 1944 to fifteen and 1972 to sixteen. Making education compulsory meant children were transformed from wage earners to pupils, which helped to create childhood as a distinct phase, but at the same time deprived them of socially significant activity which had given them a sense of self-worth (Hendrick 1997).

Schools were intended to teach not only the three Rs but morality, patriotism and good behaviour. There was still considerable division on class lines, with the upper class attending public school which trained them for government, the middle classes attending fee-paying high schools or lesser public schools in preparation for the professions, and the lower classes mostly learning the basics and then moving into work. Social mobility was possible but not encouraged. This continued to be true between the wars, and many village schools suffered from large classes and inadequate resources. Grammar schools were required to offer some scholarships in order to qualify for a government grant, but not until the 1944 Act was secondary education made free for all. Of course, there continued to be (and still continue to be, many would argue) many inequalities in the system. From the point of view of gender rather than class, the state system became largely co-educational in the 1920s, but many private schools were single sex long after the Second War. The drive to get women back in the home between the wars resulted in the Domestic Science movement (during the 1920s and '30s the government required girls to spend two afternoons a week learning cookery (Pugh 2008), but the better girls' schools were able to focus on academic achievement and develop girls' abilities in a nurturing environment.

It was not only the state's attitude to children which changed in this period. The falling birthrate from the late nineteenth century meant smaller families, which in turn meant parents were able to devote more time to each child. (The rate fell from 35.5 per thousand population in 1871-5 to

29.3 in 1896-1900, and initially that was coupled with a rising infant mortality rate, but in the early twentieth century this began falling (Hendrick 1997)). Children in a family were valued as individuals more, and for emotional reasons rather than, as they had been, partly for their contribution to the family income. At state level, concern with the low birthrate led to an emphasis on mothering and child care, which meant the development of local authority clinics. Paediatrics emerged as a discipline between 1880 and 1918, and the fate of the children in the defeated countries after the War led to a declaration of children's rights which was adopted by the League of Nations in 1924. Although the traditional strict approach to bringing up children continued quite widespread until the 1940s at least, from the 1920s there began to develop also a new relationship, more intense and less strict. Nonetheless, oral testimonies suggest corporal punishment was also still common although it varied regionally as well as with class (Hendrick 1997), and schools used it plentifully as part of a regime designed to teach, as much as anything, one's place in the world. A more child-centred approach developed, and prospered particularly after the Second War, but corporal punishment was not abolished in state schools until 1986.

A "Little Pretty Pocket-Book"

How did children's literature develop as a genre, and how did it incorporate / respond to changing ideas about childhood and gender roles? In medieval times, there were instructional books for children and fiction for everyone, but in 1693 John Locke published *Thoughts Concerning Education*, and as described above there developed the idea of a child as a child, and not merely an immature adult (Rowe Townsend 1990). John Newbery's *Little Pretty Pocket-Book*, published in 1744, is generally regarded as a landmark; the following year he established a children's bookshop. This book came with a free gift of a ball for "Little Master Tommy" and a pincushion for "Pretty Miss Polly", but although toys were evidently already gender-specific, the book itself was not.

Books now regarded as classics such as *A Pilgrim's Progress, Robinson Crusoe* and *Gulliver's Travels,* which were not written for children, came to be regarded as children's books; books written for children tended to offer quite a simplistic moral, namely work hard and you'll get rich, in other words, virtue is rewarded, but virtue consists of hard work and the reward is material. The eighteenth century was rationalist, seeing the world as it is. The division tended to be not between the genders but between the well-brought-up and the poorly, the sensible and the foolish, with rewards for the former and punishment for the latter (Nelson 1991). As teachers, moralists and parents took an interest, while this kind of tale continued to be available, a more serious literature developed for the middle classes in particular. Fairy tales and fiction were rejected, and novel-reading considered dangerous, especially for girls. As Gillian Avery put it, "The corrupting power of the novel over the young female mind seems indeed to have preoccupied the authorities much as drugs and promiscuous sexual habits do in the 1970s." (Avery 1975, 35). In this period the goal of education was paramount, that of entertainment despised.

The Evangelical belief, held over from the medieval, that children were naturally sinful, led to tale after tale of naughty children dying young or reforming on their deathbeds. By the mid-nineteenth century, moralists had begun to realise they needed to entertain as well as instruct, however, and this was the age of the great Victorian women writers: Elizabeth Sewell (1815-1906), Charlotte Yonge (1823-1901), Mrs Molesworth (1839-1921) and Mrs Ewing (1841-85). Their works featured the close-knit middle-class family circle, where the mother imparted virtues to her children and the father was loved and respected but remote. The virtue most encouraged in girls was selflessness, the abnegation of one's own desires for the good of others. There was also a strong condemnation of tale-bearing even if one were wrongly accused of a crime, and telling lies was the supreme crime: these values continued to appear in tales for both boys and girls right through to the Second World War and beyond.

Adventure stories developed through the nineteenth century, influenced by *Robinson Crusoe* and Walter Scott's novels. In 1847 Captain Marryatt produced *The Children of the New Forest*, which with its family of boys and girls living alone in a cottage after their home is destroyed by Roundheads in the Civil War is a prototype for so many twentieth-century adventure books. Ballantyne's *The Coral Island* and Stevenson's *Treasure Island* and *Kidnapped* focused more on plot than moral lessons, and eliminated most female characters, taking boys into dangerous and exotic locations. In Stevenson's account of how he came to write *Treasure Island* he said: "It was to be a story for boys; no need for psychology or fine writing; and I had a boy at hand to be a touchstone. Women were excluded." (Stevenson 2009, 55). In the later nineteenth century G.A. Henty produced novel after novel featuring manly, athletic heroes in various parts of the Empire, with narratives heavily interspersed with accounts of famous battles; the didacticism was still there, but the Christian morality of earlier writers had been transformed into the virtues of the all-British action hero, frank, patriotic, courageous and bold.

These books were aimed at boys, but there is considerable evidence that they were also read by girls, who were rather bored by the anaemic domestic dramas produced for them. In 1884 a survey of boys' and girls' reading (Salmon 1888, 124-6) with over two thousand respondents from schoolchildren aged eleven to nineteen (therefore presumably not including working class children as schooling was only compulsory till age ten) found that girls read most of the same books as boys plus some by female writers. Girls were quoted as saying girls "don't care for Sunday-school twaddle; they like a good stirring story, with a plot and some incident and adventures"; and

> "People try to make boys' books as exciting and amusing as possible, while we girls, who are much quicker and more imaginative, are very often supposed to read milk-and-watery sorts of stories that we could generally write better ourselves" (ibid, 129).

By the 1880s, the proliferation of cheap papers with "blood and thunder" style stories, the so-called "penny dreadfuls", had aroused a storm of criticism; a self-proclaimed "cultured" minority attempted to control the reading of the working class. Here was the problem with educating them: they used their literacy skills to read "trash", filled with violence and vulgarity, which would surely lead them to commit crimes in emulation of the heroes of these tales. There was a widespread belief that with the lower classes, as with children, reading was tightly bound to the development of the person, so to control reading matter was essential for the future of society (Bristow 1991). One is reminded of Mary Whitehouse's attempts to impose her personal morality on television and other media in the twentieth century. One result of the concern with the penny dreadfuls was that in 1879 the *Boy's Own Paper* was begun by the Religious Tract Society, to try to provide stories equally exciting but with a measure of morality. So successful was it that the paper ran until 1967, managing both to entertain boys and to convince their parents and schoolteachers that it was morally sound. In 1880 the *Girl's Own Paper* followed. While many of the stories and articles in the *GOP* reflected and reinforced the ideal of the domestic young woman, the paper did become slightly more progressive with the second (female) editor from 1908 onwards, and it was this magazine which published the first *Worrals* book by Captain Johns in 1941.

In 1906 Angela Brazil published *The Fortunes of Philippa*, and quickly became enormously popular. These were not the first school stories ever, but hers set a new trend by being optimistic and lively rather than pious and moralising (Cadogan and Craig 1976). Brazil herself longed to have gone to a modern girls' school with clubs, societies and team sports and she infused her readers with the same enthusiasm. The other major writers of girls' school stories, Elsie Oxenham, Elinor Brent-Dyer and Dorita Fairlie Bruce shared some of her ideals but unlike Brazil they all developed the series story, which drew in a devoted fanbase and still does today. Within the female world of a girls' boarding school they were able to create an array of roles and models far more appealing to the average girl than the dutiful Victorian daughters of earlier girls' fiction. They also picked up some of the ideals of the boys' school story: honour and team-spirit.

The 1920s when the above writers became popular were the great period of the "Reward" books, cheap books mass-produced as Sunday school prizes or Christmas presents. They were printed on thick paper which made them look fatter and therefore better value, and often written to a formula much as Mills and Boon are. Many of these were either adventures or school stories, and many do deserve to be forgotten, what Marcus Crouch has called "characterless conventional writing" (Crouch 1962, 39), but the better ones have survived to be reprinted in the twenty-first century and sought in the second-hand market; if they do not appeal to the modern child, they still have something to say as social documents.

In a sense the family adventure stories of the 1930s to 1960s were a fusion of the late Victorian and Edwardian adventure tale for boys with the girls' school story, which frequently involved extra-mural adventures, such as Princess Elisaveta being kidnapped by her wicked cousin from the Chalet School (*Princess of the Chalet School* 1927), or art thieves pursued in an illegally-driven car by Dimsie and Pamela (*Dimsie Moves Up Again* 1922). Many of the ideals of these genres such as the value of honour and of telling the truth are present: in *Swallows and Amazons* John is deeply upset to have his word questioned by "Captain Flint", and in *Well Done, Denhurst*! the German spy accepts sixteen-year-old Avice's parole that she will not cry for help and refrains from gagging her. Many of the girls' schools have Girl Guide companies, and it is not surprising to find girls in the family adventures who are competent at tying knots or Morse Code. I shall explore this more fully in chapter four.

Once childhood was perceived as a distinct phase of life, books aimed specifically at children began to be written. As long as children were seen as full of original sin there was considerable emphasis on weeping, praying and repentance, plus an inordinate number of heart-rending death scenes, then as the idea of nurturing children took hold, the scope of children's literature widened somewhat. Boys' books were more exciting, partly because this reflected the more active role males played in society, and partly because it was early recognised that boys are more reluctant readers than girls and need to be enticed into it. God came to play less and less of a role in adventure literature, being replaced by ideals of duty, honour and patriotism, reflecting changing definitions of masculinity in British society. Some girls' books, such as *Little Women* and *What Katy Did*, transcended their genre, were full of life as well as the message that girls may be tomboys but young women must conform, and survived at least into my childhood. However, it must be noted that these were both by American authors, American girls being brought up to more independence than British girls at this time. British authors for girls were less successful on the other side of the Atlantic. As girls' schools became more academic, more respected, they became a suitable setting for all-female plots, but by the 1930s some real-life schools were co-educational, and although in Britain husband-and-wife roles were still fairly stereotyped an idea of marriage as companionate was fairly widespread, especially among the middle classes, and the separate spheres of males and females were less clear-cut as more women entered the workforce. The time was right for children's books to be aimed at both sexes, with a mixture of characters and roles.

Autres temps, autres moeurs: growing up in 1890-1910

With the exception of Gwendoline Courtney, the principal authors in this study would have been growing up in the 1890s and/ or 1900s. This was a very different Britain from our own. The poorer people did not have enough to eat. Every town had some shoeless children. Many homes had no bathroom or indoor toilet, and one would be accustomed to the smell of unwashed bodies (Marr 2009). Much transport was still horse-powered, contributing its own smells as well as sounds to the cities. Every middle-class household had a maid, probably a cook and possibly a gardener. Elinor Brent-Dyer grew up in South Shields in a terrace house with an outside toilet and no hot running water, but nonetheless (and despite the fact that her father deserted her mother when she, Elinor, was a toddler) they had a maidservant (McClelland 1981).

Children of middle-class households were likely to have attended private schools as a matter of course, whatever the state provision; Courtney has this continuing in her family books well after the Second War, by which time grammar schools were free, but the 1944 Act seems to have passed her by as she continues to have families scrimping and saving to send bright children to (fee-paying) high schools (*Sally's Family* 1946). Arthur Ransome's children go to boarding schools, Oliver Lockett in M.E.

Atkinson is at public school, Blyton's boys and girls go to separate boarding schools: this is probably one reason for the development of the "holiday adventure", as the school holidays were the only time the family would be together.

What would these authors have read while they were growing up? The novels of Walter Scott, Dickens and Hardy enjoyed enormous popularity and were likely to have been read by anyone who was fond of reading, which we can assume to have been the case with a future author. Adventure yarns from Captain Marryatt through Stevenson to Henty, Ballantyne, Fenimore Cooper and Rider Haggard were available for boys, and as we have seen were also popular with girls. Since *Tom Brown's Schooldays,* (1857) and *Eric, or Little by Little* (1858) there had been a plethora of boys' school stories, famously those by Talbot Baines Reed (1852-93), most of which were first serialised in the *Boy's Own Paper*. This and the *GOP* came out regularly and were hugely popular with the middle classes and, unlike the penny dreadfuls, generally approved by parents. Girls' fiction was more domestic and sentimental, although Bessie Marchant was writing adventures with female protagonists in the 1890s.

At the turn of the century Edith Nesbit produced her *Treasure Seekers* (1899), *Wouldbegoods* (1901) and *Railway Children* (1906), featuring believable boys and girls in credible and highly entertaining adventures; Crouch pointed out that "Stories so true, so funny, so free of moralising - though based on sound values - were a new experience for children in the first years of the century" (Crouch 1962, 13-14). We know that Blyton enjoyed *Alice's Adventures in Wonderland, The Coral Island, Black Beauty* and *Little Women* (Stoney 1986). It is quite likely that Brent-Dyer, Blyton and Atkinson, born in 1894, 1897 and 1899 respectively, read Angela Brazil's school stories. In her *Chalet School* series Brent-Dyer has her heroine Joey reading Dickens, Buchan's thrillers and Elsie Oxenham's books for girls, among other things. The others reference books less, perhaps because the adventure genre focuses on action, rather than sedentary activities. Ransome, for instance, refers to *Robinson Crusoe* (and indirectly to *Treasure Island* by having the Blackett girls' uncle nicknamed Captain Flint), but otherwise if his children read at all it is non-fiction such as books on sailing, navigation or birdwatching. Yet we know from his autobiography that he was both a precocious and a voracious reader: he received *Robinson Crusoe* as a fourth birthday present as a reward for having read it through unaided, and as a young man regularly went short of food in order to buy books (Ransome 1976). As a child he read Lear, Carroll, Ballantyne, Stevenson, Kipling and Scott, not to mention several of the women writers such as Charlotte M. Yonge and Mrs Ewing, and folk tales from Grimm and Andersen.

In the last decades of Victoria's reign there were numerous different suffrage societies, each with a slightly different membership and agenda. Probably the most famous, the Women's Social and Political Union led by the Pankhursts, was founded in 1905 in frustration that nothing seemed to be changing and with the motto "Votes for Women, Liberty or Death!" This group's sometimes violent methods, breaking windows, cutting phone wires and even planting bombs, did not endear them to the majority, however, whatever the righteousness of their cause, and their demonstrations frequently turned ugly, with women being mauled or injured by police or by hecklers with police complicity (LeGates 2001). The mere fact that feminist organisations existed does not mean that most people belonged to them, or even agreed with them. When we look at how in 1923 Parliament readily passed the bill making grounds for divorce the same for both sexes, and compare this with the long and ferocious opposition to giving women the vote, it is clear that this was an extremely divisive issue. A large proportion of the population, male and female, regarded the Suffragettes if not all suffragists as monstrous and unnatural. We have to remember that most people resist change, and if there are still those today, over a century later, who claim that certain socio-cultural differences in gender roles are "natural" (and therefore not to be altered), how much more was that true in Edwardian times?

These authors grew up in a society, or at least a social class, which still largely expected women to be home-makers and mothers, even though more women were in fact entering the workplace and a wider range of jobs was now available to the middle-class spinster. Elinor Brent-Dyer's mother Eleanor (Nelly) married at twenty-four and she and her husband lived in her childhood home with her mother. When Charles Dyer deserted her she was fortunate in having a small inheritance from her father which enabled them to live (McClelland 1981). Brent-Dyer herself became a teacher, not a radical choice, although in an article in 1947 she suggested banking, medicine, the law and the church as possible career paths to girls (Auchmuty 1999), in addition to more orthodox office work.

In Enid Blyton's family, one of her father's sisters was a professional musician and another an elocutionist, but her parents moved where her father's work took him and her mother concerned herself with home and family, and indeed clashed with the teenage Enid, who had no interest in the domestic (Stoney 1986). Captain Johns' mother is described in his biography as "the daughter of a master butcher" (Berresford Ellis and

Williams 1986, 11), and his wife was the eldest daughter of the Reverend John Hunt; neither had a profession.

Most of my selected authors came from a background of respectable tradespeople and had one servant rather than a plethora; they were on the whole not separated from their parents by nannies and then boarding schools, although in Ransome's family there was both a nurse and a cook, and he was sent first to prep. school and then to Rugby, despite his father's early death which put an extra strain on the family finances (Ransome 1976). Malcolm Saville, too, son of a bookshop owner, went to boarding school (O'Hanlon 2001). Whatever each individual's circumstances, they nevertheless grew up in a world where children obeyed parents, bedtimes were early and regular, and many adults still believed that children should be seen and not heard.

1930-70

By the 1930s, when Ransome, Johns, Atkinson and Blyton all started publishing adventure books for children, Britain was in some ways very different from the world in which they had grown up. There was still poverty, of course, but in 1911 Lloyd George had successfully introduced old-age pensions, and the general standard of living for most people had risen (Pugh 2008). However the NHS and the rest of the Welfare State did not come into being until after the Second War, and women's health in particular prior to that was worryingly poor. Although younger women were having fewer children and antenatal care was improving, there was still a good deal of poor hygiene, women still died of puerperal fever, and as in many developing countries today, the woman of a family tended to prioritise her husband as the breadwinner, and her children, when it came to getting medical treatment (normally to pay for).

This is indicative of the basic gender inequality which was very much a part of British society. As noted above, women were routinely paid less for the same work, and marriage was still the accepted goal for a woman, rather than a career. When the flier Amy Johnson got divorced in 1938, and despite the fact that this was on the grounds of her husband's adultery, women's magazines "took it as proof that no good could come of tactless attempts by women to pursue equality in roles for which Nature had not designed them" (Pugh 2008, 320). Many men were offended at the idea of their wife working, as it would suggest they were unable to provide for her. Yet marriages were becoming more companionate, and the growth of interest in decorating, home improvement and gardening gave couples more common interests. However, it was not until 1937 that rape was made legal grounds for divorce, and not until 1970 that Britain saw an Equal Pay Act.

The 1930s were in some senses a golden age of childhood. Modern worries about paedophiles were a thing of the future (occasionally in books girls worry about meeting "tramps" when they are out at night on some adventure) and children were given a great deal of independence, allowed out for hours without supervision. There was a great boom in childcare literature, with two main approaches, the behaviourists influenced by American psychologist John B. Watson, who believed in habit training and no demonstrativeness from parent to child, and the more liberal "new psychology" suggesting mothers should have fun with their babies, which throve. However, corporal punishment remained normal practice, and as young people tended to live at home until they married, parents retained a great deal of control over their lives, including their "courting". This was reflected in the legal situation too, with the age of majority only coming down from twenty-one to eighteen in 1968. To a child of the twenty-first century this might seem stifling, but over-protection is the obverse of a positive safeguarding of children such that those of the middle-class, at least, had nothing more serious to worry about than forgotten homework until they were in their late teens.

There was still an enormous disparity among the social classes, notably as regards education. Working class fathers generally wanted their sons to do a "real man's job", i.e. manual work, and viewed too much education negatively in consequence. It was relatively easy to get a university place but the problem was cost, so many people did not go; even many grammar school scholarships were not taken up because of collateral costs like shoes and books, and loss of potential earnings. Upper and upper-middle class children, by contrast, still had nannies when small and then went to boarding school; even after the Second War this way of life lingered on, as Stephen Fry's autobiographical works illustrate (Fry 1997). Several of my selected authors were actually, and perhaps ironically, childless, but Blyton employed a nanny for her daughters, and Saville's four children also had one for a year or two, until the war sent her to work in an aircraft factory. All four went to public schools, even though this was a financial stretch for the family (O'Hanlon 2001).

Books were still comparatively expensive in the 1930s, the paperback revolution in children's books really coming post-war, although Penguins were introduced in July 1935 and sold seventeen million books in the first four years, including Hemingway and Agatha Christie. However, there was growing concern for children and what they read, as evidenced by the appearance of W.C. Berwick Sayers' *Manual of Children's Libraries* in

1932 and the establishment of the Carnegie Medal by the Library Association in 1936. The following year came an Association of Children's Librarians, and meanwhile publishers were increasingly aware of the potential profit in the children's market. This gave opportunities to new writers in the field such as Ransome, winner of the first Carnegie Medal, but the Reward market continued to flourish and, as at any time, there were many more professional writers turning out books to a proven formula than experimenters breaking new ground.

Although most leading literary figures such as W.H. Auden, Stephen Spender and Cecil Day-Lewis were left-wing, the adult reading public preferred middle-brow writers like Daphne du Maurier and John Buchan, or the humour of Waugh and Wodehouse. The inter-war years saw many people turning to escapist literature as the real world grew darker. Hunt (2009, 73) says that:

> "[B]etween the world wars, children's books were about protection - ostensibly protecting the child, actually protecting the adult. Out there was civil war in Spain, the Wall Street crash, the rise of Nazism. In children's-book land there were worried stuffed toys, a mystic nanny, and a Hobbit trying not to be a hero".

In the same way, many children's writers ignored the War, despite its impact on civilians (60,000 people killed by German bombing, children buried alive for days next to their dead parents, Coventry, Plymouth, Birmingham, Hull with gutted centres and thousands of homeless, to mention only some of the more brutal aspects). Most realistic wartime stories were published much later, such as Ian Seraillier's *The Silver Sword* (1956) and Jill Paton Walsh's *The Dolphin Crossing* (1967), about Dunkirk. More socially realistic stories for children, i.e. ones not confined to middle-class white protagonists, and addressing issues such as teenage pregnancy or divorced parents, did not really begin to flourish until the 1960s or later.

In the 1931 election 55% voted Conservative, and the 1935 National Government got nearly as much support. The Church was still strong; indeed, even as late as the early 1950s, when only 11% of women and 7% of men were regular churchgoers, 50% of parents still sent their children to Sunday school (Marwick 2003). In the thirties idealist movements such as socialism remained a quite small minority, at odds with the growing materialism as more consumer goods became available and prices went down in the Depression. Even the famous hunger marches were well-behaved (Pugh 2008). The majority of the population were loyal to the monarchy, (witness the grief when George V died in 1936), and conservative with a small "c" if not with a capital one. It is important to remember this when starting to look at the portrayal of gender roles in mainstream children's literature.

In conclusion, these authors would have been brought up in a world of clear-cut gender roles, reflected in most if not all the fiction they read and indeed the non-fiction, a clear child-adult divide for the middle class at least, and by parents who were born in the 1870s and '60s, even the 1850s, the height of the Victorian era. When they came to write the books in this study, the world had changed and was still changing enormously: Europe endured two major wars, Tsar Nicholas (cousin of George V) had been murdered and a Bolshevik regime set up in Russia, Fascism came to power in Germany and Italy and had many supporters in Britain, there was a General Strike in 1926 and Wall Street crashed in 1929. After the Second War, India gained independence and other colonies followed suit in the next two decades. Some people embraced change, others hid from it. Women had begun to take a much greater role in public affairs and had more opportunities than previously, but feminism was not a majority viewpoint during most of these authors' lives. Childhood was seen by most as a privileged period, sheltered from the world's nastier realities. Within that context, what kind of gender roles did these authors offer to their readers?

Table 2-1: A timeline of key events

Decade	Authors born	Children's Literature
1860		1868 publication of *Little Women*
1870		1879 *Boy's Own Paper* began
1880	1884 Arthur Ransome	1880 *Girl's Own Paper* began 1883 *Treasure Island*
1890	1893 Captain Johns 1894 Elinor Brent-Dyer 1897 Enid Blyton 1899 M.E. Atkinson	1899 E. Nesbit's *The Treasure Seekers*
1900	1901 Malcolm Saville	1904 Angela Brazil began publishing 1908 *The Wind in the Willows*
1910	1911 Gwendoline Courtney	
1920		"Reward" books popular
1930		proliferation of "air" adventure stories, some with girl pilots 1936 first Carnegie Medal 1937 *The Hobbit*
1940		1949 Geoffrey Trease published *Tales Out of School*, a critical survey of children's literature
1950		1950 *The Lion, the Witch and the Wardrobe* OUP dropped Captain Johns
1960	1967 death of Ransome 1968 deaths of Johns and Blyton 1969 death of Brent-Dyer	

Socio-political events (Britain)	Decade
1867 Second Reform act extended male suffrage; a section proposing giving the vote to women was defeated	1860
1877 Britain officially became an Empire, as Queen Victoria was made Empress of India 1878 London university admitted women to degrees	1870
1880 compulsory education introduced	1880
1891 compulsory education made free 1897 National Union of Women's Suffrage Societies formed	1890
1903 Women's Social and Political Union ("suffragettes") founded by the Pankhursts	1900
1914-18 World War I 1918 franchise extended (married women over 30)	1910
1924 first Labour government 1928 universal franchise	1920
the Depression 1930 Amy Johnson flew from England to Australia 1932 Amelia Earhart flew the Atlantic solo	1930
1939-45 World War II in Europe 1944 Education Act ensured all children had some secondary education (up to 15) 1945-51 creation of the Welfare State under Attlee	1940
1950-53 Korean War 1956 Suez Crisis	1950
1967 NHS (Family Planning) Act; Abortion Act; Sexual Offences Act 1969 Divorce Reform Act	1960

CHAPTER THREE

YOU GIRLS STAY HERE?
A SHARE OF THE ACTION

Having outlined the social context in which the authors studied, grew up and wrote, I shall now turn to the books themselves. Most of these books were already familiar to me, but I tried not to begin with impressionistic preconceptions based on previous readings, and indeed sometimes I was surprised not to have my impressions confirmed by the evidence. I concentrated on one author at a time, and, where I was considering more than one series by that author, one series at a time. Each book was read and relevant points noted, then general points about each author determined. Once I had looked at several authors, some themes began to emerge, and these were then expanded or modified as I continued to read.

Many human societies have assigned action "outside", in the external, the public world, to males, and "inside", the domestic and private, to females. While Britain the 1920s and '30s was a long way from, say, Classical Athens, where the men walked the streets, debated politics and philosophy, ran the state and went to war, while their sisters and wives rarely left the home and never alone, there was nonetheless still, as we have seen, a strong feeling that women belonged in the home rather than the workplace. This in turn fuelled differences between male and female education. Yet these differences were far slighter than they had been a century before. Girls played sports, including team sports; they wore shorts and light swimsuits in order to facilitate activity; if women's magazines held up catching and holding on to a man as the shining goal of a girl's life, there were other models available in the real world: female racing drivers, pilots and MPs.

This chapter addresses the roles the girls (and / or women) play in the action, whether this is contested by the males, and the degree of initiative they show. Adventure stories lend themselves to this particularly, because by their very nature they are plot-driven and the action is of the category which would traditionally be assigned to males: going out at night to investigate mysteries or follow strangers, exploring secret passages or empty houses, attempting to outwit criminals or spies. If these authors were mainstream products of their time, one would expect there still to be a fairly clear division of gender roles here. Yet other ideas were in the air, so this is by no means a foregone conclusion.

Not getting the girls into danger

Enid Blyton does tend to be predictable in this respect. Her boys are mostly older than her girls: of the *Famous Five*, though Dick and George (Georgina) are the same age, Julian is the oldest (and seems to get older in later books) and Anne the youngest; while Snubby is the youngest in the *R Mysteries*, Roger and Barney are both older than Diana; Jack is the oldest in the *Secret* series and in the *Adventure* series the ages run Jack - Philip - Dinah - Lucy-Ann. This introduces an element of protectiveness into their taking over the action. For example, in *The Castle of Adventure* Jack says "But you can trust us not to fool about on any landslides, Aunt Allie. We shouldn't dream of getting the girls into danger," (22) and again in *The Mountain of Adventure* the boys notice that they have left the track in the mist but agree not to tell the girls because "they'll be scared" (58). Similarly when Snubby in *The Rat-A-Tat Mystery* sees someone outside the window Barney tells him "It's only the snowman, ass... Don't scare Diana." In *Five on a Hike Together* at the showdown with the villains "Julian felt sure that Timmy would go for Dirty Dick and bring him to the ground, and he didn't want Anne to see dog and man fighting savagely" (181).

This attitude is reinforced by the adults, especially adult males. In *The Sea of Adventure* when the children have rescued Bill (a police officer) from the gun-runners and bullets are flying, he tells them all to lie flat in the boat with the boys on top of the girls (162). And in *The River of Adventure* he reprimands the boys for running to help Oola, the little native boy who was being beaten, while they were out in the city: "Even if your feelings run away with you, you have ALWAYS got to think of your sisters first. If you want to jump into a brawl, do it when you're alone" (52). This sense of responsibility is sometimes extended to adult women, notably mothers. Philip in the *Adventure* books several times takes on the role of "man of the house", perhaps partly because his father is dead, checking that his mother is not seriously hurt in *Mountain* before the children go off without her (she has caught her hand in a banging door), and in *Sea* when she has measles that she doesn't want one of them to stay with her rather than all go off on holiday with Bill.

It is hardly surprising, in view of this, that there are situations where the boys go off and engage in action while the girls sit waiting at home. In *The Secret of Spiggy Holes* it is the boys who go to try to rescue Prince Paul, not the girls (84), and later the boys who perform the rescue up the secret tunnel, while the girls stay behind and get food ready for the escape to the secret island (107). In *The Island of Adventure* the boys insist that they should row out to the Isle of Gloom without the girls the first time, as they don't know the way through the rocks and it could be dangerous: "I don't mind any risk myself - but I won't risk anything with the girls." The *R Mysteries* begin more positively, with Diana joining in the midnight explorations in the first book, but by *The Ring O'Bells Mystery*, published only two years later, she is most reluctant to go down the well and through the secret passage, which is just as well since Barney forbids it (146).

There are many similar situations, and often the girls are quite happy to be left out, but not always. The obvious exception is George in the *Famous Five*. The phenomenon of the tomboy is an interesting one and will be returned to in chapter nine. Blyton apparently suggested that George (Georgina) was based on herself (Stoney 1986, 153), and she herself was certainly a strong character, who hated domestic chores and carved her own path in life. One would therefore expect George to be a positive model, and to some extent she is, often being the one whose actions resolve the case, and yet there are many ambivalences in her presentation, which will be explored later. Whenever Dick and Julian plan to go off into action she tries to insist on coming too; for instance, in *Smuggler's Top* when they are going to search for her father, who has been kidnapped, she says "Aren't I as good as a boy?" and Julian admits she is, but she should stay and keep an eye on Anne and Marybelle, the two "girly" girls. This argument is repeated in other books, and George usually gives in, but sometimes merely pretends to do so and pre-empts the boys by taking action on her own, as in *Five Are Together Again* when Julian is planning to be the one to row over to Kirrin Island at night to hide the secret papers and George simply gets up before him and goes off in her boat (and succeeds in trapping the villains on the island by setting their boat adrift). The gipsy girl Jo who appears in some of the *Famous Five* books is likewise forbidden from accompanying the boys to rescue George (*Five Have Plenty of Fun*), but follows them secretly and ends up rescuing them when they get caught.

Dinah in the *Adventure* series is less successful at joining in. In the first book, although she fights her brother Philip, she is otherwise not much of a tomboy, and she and Lucy-Ann are portrayed as equally scared, so that it is easy for the boys to assume the lion's share of the action. However, in later books she becomes a stronger character, with remarks like "You're not going to keep all the excitement to yourselves, I'm coming too" (*Valley,* 84), but these protests are always overridden. The other girls, Anne and Lucy-Ann in these series, Diana, Peggy and Nora, mostly seem quite content to be left out of the action. In *The Ring O'Bells Mystery,* Snubby is scared and Barney tells him "Well, don't come then [on a midnight adventure]. Stay with Diana. I'm not letting her come" (156). Diana is relieved. "She had thought she really *ought* to come, but she didn't want to in the least." Blyton also frequently has one child alone having part of the adventure, and with the exception of George, as in the example above, this is invariably a boy. In both *Island* and *Mountain* Jack gets separated from the others looking for his parrot Kiki, and ends up having an adventure alone; Philip stows away on the villains' plane to escape from the *Valley*; Barney sleeps in the old hall in Ring O'Bells village and witnesses some mysterious goings-on.

Overall, while some of her female characters challenge the male right to hog all the excitement, Blyton leaves one with a strong sense of traditional roles intact, and this used to annoy me when I was a child. Elinor Brent-Dyer has a similar ethos of males protecting females, but more equality when it comes to share of the action, although there is a great deal of variation in her five thrillers. For example, in *Fardingales,* when Anstace and Humphrey meet the villains in the secret passage Humphrey "yanked her up to his own stair and shoved himself below her" (154), reflecting the attitudes of his father and uncle to their respective wives: "The two women were bidden take Lettice and go and see about something to eat; and then, accompanied by Jill, the two men went down to look for the entrance to the hidden stairway" (165). In *Condor Crags Adventure,* Humphrey's uncle approves him going off into danger but says they mustn't tell his mother or aunt, only his father.

This kind of treatment of women as objects of chivalry (to put it kindly), or as something akin to children, to be protected from life's problems, also appears in Brent-Dyer's books for girls. Despite her oft-repeated desire for girls to grow up "strong, helpful women" rather than "jellyfish", we still have situations like the one which shocked me when I first read it in *The Chalet School Goes To It* when her heroine Joey, now married and mother of triplets, is to be evacuated from the Channel Islands to mainland Britain ahead of the German invasion; this decision is taken by her older sister, her brother-in-law and her husband, without consulting her. Granted that her husband is probably much of an age with her sister, who is twelve years her senior and used to mothering her, this doesn't speak of a very equal marriage.

Whatever Humphrey's chivalrous intentions, however, in fact he is knocked unconscious and Anstace ends up looking after him while they are kept captive in a cave. In an early chapter of *Chudleigh Hold* the boys decide it is no problem for the girls to come with them to explore the Cavern (which means swimming into it) as "It's calm enough" (46), showing a similar assumption of a protective role, but the chief focus of the book is twelve-year-old Arminel, known as Crumpet, who realises there is something odd going on and had planned to follow her mysterious "cousin" down the secret passage; once she has shared her story with her older brother Hawk he tries to take over the action: "I'm in this now and I'll handle it myself", and "'Tisn't a thing for a girl to be mixed up in", but she objects that "I *am* mixed up in it and you can't unmix me!" (203) In the end the highlight of the adventure is shared between Crumpet, Hawk and their intrepid great aunt Merrill, a delightfully feisty old lady who picks up a revolver and tells Hawk to take the other, and once down the passage takes charge and goes off on all fours round a bend to spy on the villains, assuring the children: "I've got my revolver, and if they spot me, I'll shoot at once" (214).

In both *Fardingales* and *Chudleigh Hold* the actual action is fairly equally shared by boys and girls, with the girls taking the initiative as much as one would expect from Brent-Dyer's other works. Think of Joey aged fourteen taking off at night to follow Elisaveta and her kidnappers over the mountain (*Princess*), or Joey and Grizel pursuing the madman who has abducted Cornelia into a network of salt-caves at night (*Head Girl*). In a girls' school story, if there is action it is naturally undertaken by the more adventurous of the girls, because there aren't any boys, though admittedly most school stories don't include quite so many dramatic events as Brent-Dyer's. *The Susannah Adventure* has Anstace and Humphrey on a sailing trip together, without the younger members of their family, and they take an equal share of the worry and attempt to follow clues, though in actual fact they don't really *do* very much.

The last two books, however, are very different. Anstace appears in *Condor Crags* married to Roger, the naval officer who helped save them in *Susannah,* and her chief role is to supply food and drink to the men as they discuss what to do to rescue Godfrey Chudleigh who has been taken prisoner by a tribe of "Indians" in South America. Godfrey's brother Hawk, Humphrey and Tom from *Fardingales* and a Brazilian friend with a convenient helicopter go off to perform the actual rescue. The only woman featured in *Top Secret* is another feisty elderly spinster, Aunt Freda. Several times the men express a desire to get her, the boy Archie and the injured Walter away before the villains arrive, but they don't succeed and she plays her part in the final action. Hawk points out that if she is still there when the villains arrive, they may torture her to make him speak (they are after secret documents he was carrying, and have already tried to murder him to get them). This is a valid point (it actually happens), yet it is also telling that torturing her is seen as more effective than torturing any of the equally innocent young men.

Kindred spirits

Gwendoline Courtney and Malcolm Saville both also have moments when the male characters suggest it is their role to protect the female ones, yet in both cases the girls resist this quite effectively. Courtney tends to have more female than male characters (three girls, then three girls and a boy in the *Denehurst* books, a whole school full of girls and one boy in *Wild Lorings*, three of each in *Mermaid House*, though four boys, including the prince, and only two girls in *The Grenville Garrison),* which enables her to have a good range of female personalities, some bolder than others. Nick Loring not only accepts girls sharing the action but criticises his older sister Elspeth for losing her nerve "You'd have jumped at anything like this once" (82), and the boys in *Mermaid House* are well aware of their sister Fay's skill as a swimmer and consequent right to be involved, and laugh at other people who are fooled by her fragile appearance, although there is one point where Giles, the eldest, wishes the girls were not involved (137). The prince in *Grenville Garrison* is constantly trying to protect the girls; initially he refuses the Grenvilles' help because "you have girls with you, and there might be - in fact I'm afraid it is a case of there *will* be - danger" (68), and when the eldest boy Edward allows Helen to go to rescue her twin Roy from the enemy (with a gun) he accuses Edward of cowardice. However, the boys assure him that "in these days in England the girls prefer to take their chances with us" (68), and Edward is portrayed as showing great maturity in accepting that he needs to stay on the island to protect the prince, whom the enemy are trying to abduct, rather than keep going off on expeditions like the rest of the family, girls and boys both. In the *Denehurst* books, far from trying to keep them away from the action, the girls' help is enlisted by their cousin, Deryk, who is in British Intelligence, though admittedly he does not foresee the danger they actually run into.

Many of Courtney's heroines positively relish action and danger. In *Mermaid House* the whole family, girls and boys, is determined to solve the mystery (37), and Agnes Morvyn even more so as it is her father who has disappeared. In the *Denehurst* books, Moira the younger sister and

Bob are "kindred spirits with a decided love of fun and a reckless disregard for danger" (19), and Moira, who ends up the only one not captured by the enemy, is happy because in the first adventure the two older girls had most of the excitement "but this time she was going to have it - and she'd give the enemy a run for his money if she could manage it" (136). In *The Wild Lorings at School*, half the school would have plunged down the secret passage if they had been allowed, and when it comes to the final fight with the villains up in the attic Pamela, the female criminal, bites, kicks and scratches while Elspeth twists her male accomplice's ears and Joan sits on his legs after Nick and his father have wrestled him to the ground. Helen in *The Grenville Garrison* might be seen as acting out of a sense of duty; she volunteers for a daylight reconnaissance because the enemy will be less suspicious of a girl, and she goes to rescue Roy because he is her twin and there's a special bond between them, but her younger sister Audrey is quite definitely in it for the excitement: "I've been kept out of everything so far, and I'm not going to miss any more of the fun". Even when the older ones point out it isn't a game and if the baddies find them they'll shoot, "Audrey gave a gasp at this plain speaking, but it was more of excitement than fear. 'Do you really think so?' she demanded, her eyes lighting up at the prospect of further thrills" (169). She is in fact sent off with a sports bag to fetch some guns and ammunition from the big house so that the "garrison" can defend itself. The butler is somewhat surprised.

Malcolm Saville almost always has an equal balance of boys and girls. The Lone Piners come in pairs: David with Peter (Petronella), Tom with Jenny, Jon with Penny, and the twins, Mary and Dickie, all but these last developing into boyfriend-girlfriend, though as Jon and Penny are first cousins Saville drew back a little from that one, not sure whether they should end up together or not. It is rare for all eight (later nine with Harriet Sparrow) to appear in the same book; we always see the three Mortons, sometimes with Jon and Penny Warrender and perhaps Peter, sometimes with Peter, Tom and Jenny, this largely depending on the location as Tom is tied to working on his uncle's farm and Jenny won't go off without him. We do have incidents where the boys go off together (in *The Secret of Grey Walls* they go to scout round the mysterious house, Grey Walls, and get captured; in *Mystery Mine* Jon and David are hiking together) or the girls do (they set off to rescue the boys from Grey Walls, but we also have Peter and Jenny going off for a girls' day out in *Where's My Girl?* - and getting captured). However, it is more common for them to set out in boy-girl pairs if they are not in a group.

In each pair (except for the twins) the boy is about a year older than the girl (though their relative ages don't stay exactly the same throughout the series, somewhat oddly as each book begins with a list of characters, so it would have been easy for Saville to check). There are occasions when David acts protectively: in *Not Scarlet But Gold* he tries to cover Peter's body with his when the roof of the cave they are in falls in (207), and in the first book, published and set during the war, he has been left in charge of the family by his father who is in the RAF "Take care of Mother for me, old chap, and look after those awful twins as well" (11). In general, however, he not only assumes Peter will join him in action, he clearly admires her abilities and courage. In *Mystery at Witchend*, the first *Lone Pine* story, when he and Tom are going to see what is going on near the reservoir (which is due to be blown up by saboteurs) he asks Peter to come too: "You're the one who knows the valley best" (155). In the event, she is the one who takes action, grabbing him and pulling him to safety when the reservoir blows, and doing her "circus trick" whistle to stop her pony when the saboteur tries to escape on it: "'Yes,' David interrupted, 'but she wasn't feeble. She was just splendid.'"

Penny Warrender also insists on being part of the action, rails at being left behind, and sometimes turns out to be the one to act, as in *Saucers over the Moor*, when they have all been locked in their sitting room on the first floor to keep them out of danger; they succeed in making a rope with curtains, and she is the one to climb down to try and let them out, being lighter than the boys and good at gym. Jenny is less proactive, portrayed initially as "about twelve", i.e. midway between the nine-year-old twins and fifteen-year-old Peter, and full of fears. As time goes by she becomes more or less the same age as Peter, less talented and amusingly garrulous but all the same never left behind and sometimes showing unexpected sang-froid, as in *Wings Over Witchend* when she keeps her cool up the watchtower much better than Tom, who has a poor head for heights.

As for the twins, they almost always do things together, usually taking off on their own when they feel the older children are ignoring them. For instance, in *Seven White Gates* they follow Peter's Uncle Micah, on whose farm they are staying, when he goes for a mysterious midnight walk, and get trapped in a disused mine; in *Wings over Witchend* they go off in dudgeon, locate where the stolen Christmas trees are being stored and are captured, but after a miserable time are left, locked up but not tied up, in the derelict cottage where two foresters are also being held prisoner (the twins help them escape); and in *Lone Pine Five* they very enterprisingly kidnap the boy, Percy, whose parents are the villains of the piece (he likes his kidnappers so much he refuses to be rescued). The twins do everything together, and there is no question of Dickie going off without Mary because she is a girl.

Interestingly, the first *Lone Pine* story was published in 1941 and featured the enterprising Peter who easily holds her own with David and Tom, while the first *Marston Baines* book, *Three Towers in Tuscany*, came out two decades later in 1963, yet its hero is male (Simon, Marston Baines' nephew), most of the action being undertaken by him and two undergraduate friends, Charles and Patrick, while the female interest, Rosina, is pretty, impractical, flirtatious and not very brave. She is captured by the enemy and the young men go to rescue her; to be fair, she does try to escape by herself by tricking her jailor, but fails (198). She also manages to give them all away at a crucial moment by screaming in surprise (209).

Why did Saville create such a character? It seems to be a step backwards rather than forwards. He was trying to break into a new market (the *Marston Baines* books are aimed at Young Adults, although according to Sheila Ray (1972) they were usually read by younger children) and possibly felt, or had been advised, that this kind of traditionally feminine heroine was appropriate. In any event, by the second book he had evidently changed his mind somewhat; Rosina is not in evidence (though she resurfaces later in the series and Simon gets engaged to her). *The Purple Valley* features Kate, a complex character recovering from drug addiction, and Annabelle, who is most unwilling to be left out of anything. After they have all been rescued from the master criminal the police are going after him and tell everyone else to go home, to which she meekly agrees, but in fact she and Simon head off to watch "the end of the hunt" (204), mostly on her initiative. The pair encounter the villain, Bonvet, before the police catch him, and she tells Simon to "Rush him!" (206) because he has recognised their car - in other words, to drive straight at a pedestrian on the edge of a cliff! When he then shoots the windscreen and Simon has to stop, Bonvet grabs Annabelle as a hostage but she fights "like a cat" and bites him until Simon hits him with a torch and puts him out of his misery.

In general, in the *Marston Baines* series there is quite a lot of male protectiveness, which is usually resented. In *Power of Three* Annabelle tells the two young men "And don't either of you try this 'mustn't tell the little woman' business" (41), and later in the same book when Charles tells Kate "I know you don't like being reminded that I'm responsible for you, in an old-fashioned way, to your parents, but I am" she is furious: "Don't dare talk to me as if I'm about six" (122). Of course, this could be partly because of her history of drug-abuse, which makes her a somewhat unstable character in *The Purple Valley*. We get a number of remarks like Simon's "And I'm not keen on either of you two girls being left alone here or wandering about the country without us, until we've settled this business" (*Dagger,* 61). This is in definite contrast to the *Lone Pine* series, where the girls are accepted much more as equal partners, and as often rescue the boys as vice versa. Feminism was obviously not less potent a force in the 1960s and '70s than in the 1940s, and in any case, Saville was writing the later *Lone Pine* stories at the same time as the *Marston Baines* ones, so this looks like a conscious choice.

The authors I have looked at so far all contain some element of "You girls stay here", although for most of them it is an attitude expressed by some of the male characters but not actually a policy realised in practice. Blyton is the real exception to this; her girls usually do "stay here". Arthur Ransome, however, stands out in never even expressing the idea. If there is any division it is between older and younger children, or sometimes more and less experienced (at sailing, which comes into every book), and since unlike Blyton he does not make the boys necessarily the oldest, this does not result in a gender split.

Firstly, Ransome has, perhaps surprisingly, more girls than boys in general. The Walker family (Swallows), who are the focus of most of the books, consists of two boys and two girls, of whom the eldest and youngest are boys; in *Swallows and Amazons* Roger is only seven and there is doubt whether he will be allowed to go camping on the island with the others. In several of the books there is a split between John and Susan, the older, more responsible pair, and Titty and Roger, who owing to her active imagination and his small-boy intrepidity often end up in trouble. When we add in the Amazons, the two Blackett sisters, the gender balance is actually in favour of the female (and later the Walkers are supplemented by their little sister Bridget). The addition of the "D's", Dick and Dorothea Callum, does not alter this, and in *The Picts and the Martyrs* we only have the D's and the Blacketts, leaving us with three to one in favour of the female. Even in *Coot Club*, although there are five boys and three girls, in fact the three youngest "Coots" play relatively small roles, so that the main focus is on Tom, Dick, Dorothea and the twins, so again, more girls than boys. This is not of course just a matter of numbers, though I think that in itself is important: many action films, going back to Deborah Kerr in *King Solomon's Mines*, feature the odd female for glamour, or as the object of male chivalry, but it is rare for the genders to get equal billing in this genre, on screen or page. This is still true of TV shows today, and of course of the ubiquitous Harry Potter. However, having several girl characters enables them to be distinct individuals rather than some generic female, and this is what Ransome certainly achieves.

I have found absolutely no examples in Ransome of any of the males, boys or adults, suggesting any of the females should stay behind or not join in. Of course, in most of the books the adventures are not actually dangerous; in the metafictional stories, *Peter Duck* and *Missee Lee*, the Blackett's Uncle Jim (alias Captain Flint) does at times express remorse at having brought the children into danger, although in point of fact it is they who rescue him in both books. However, they are certainly involved in activities which in Blyton would probably have resulted in Julian or Jack and Philip telling their respective girls to "stay here". In *Swallows and Amazons* the Walkers attempt a night assault on the *Amazon*, in which John, Susan and Roger take part while Titty stays on the island to manage the "lighthouse". This division of labour is decided by the facts that John and Susan are the only competent sailors at this point, so they have to be in the action which will need both of them, that Roger is too young to be left alone on the island, and finally that Titty actually really wants to be left, in order to play at Robinson Crusoe. As things turn out, she proves to be the hero of the day, as the Amazons sail past the waiting Swallows by a ruse and assault the island, and Titty succeeds in capturing their boat single-handed while they are ashore.

This example is typical, and it would be tedious to describe plot after plot in order to expand the point, so I shall only mention a couple more. In *Great Northern?*, the last completed book, when it is vital for Dick to take photographs of the eponymous birds without being followed by the villainous egg-collector or stopped by the local gamekeepers, John and Nancy head off in one direction as "decoys" for the former, and the rest: Susan, Titty, Roger, Peggy and Dorothea; in another as "red herrings" to distract the latter. In *Peter Duck*, everyone goes off to dig for treasure, and later after the storm they all sail the ship *Wild Cat* round the island to rescue Captain Flint, who is in danger of capture by the villains, and it is John and Nancy together, as the best sailors, who take the little *Swallow* in through the rocks in the dark to pick him up. In general, each child's role is determined by a combination of what s/he wants and what s/he is good at. I shall return to this in the next chapter.

M.E. Atkinson in her *Lockett* series also created a group of individual children. In *August Adventure* Jane Lockett is thirteen, Oliver twelve and Bill ten and a half, but the first two are small so Bill is actually physically the biggest. They are supplemented by Anna Angel who becomes Jane's best friend, and her little brother Robin, aged five. Over the course of the series the children get gradually older (Oliver starts Public School, for example) and they meet various other friends who appear in one or more books. There are certainly instances of the girls doing things together and the boys doing other things, but not generally when it comes to the actual action. For instance, in the first book when they take refuge from a storm in a disused house it is Jane and Oliver who wake in the night, wander around and discover the house is supposed to be haunted. In *Smuggler's Gap* the Locketts get an SOS from Robin because Anna has disappeared, and as they don't have enough money for three plane tickets, Jane and Oliver fly over to the Scillies to look for her (though Bill manages to get across anyway). If boys are involved in an adventure without girls it is normally Bill, whose impetuous and restless character sends him charging into action where his siblings' common sense holds them back.

We do, in fact, have more than one example of girls being more adventurous than boys. *Chimney Cottage* barely includes the Locketts, being more about little Evelyn and her friend Veronica, who deeply admire the Lockett family and are determined, Evelyn especially, to emulate them. In order to do this they need two boys to play the Oliver and Bill roles, but fail to find anyone really suitable and in the end embark on the kidnapping of a doctor with the help of another girl friend. They are assisted in this by advice from Fenella, one of a rival family who appear in several of the books. Fenella is tall, active, and extremely enterprising; while the Locketts fall into adventure, she makes adventure happen. When she first meets the Locketts she orchestrates a battle between the "Ancient Britons" (her family) and the "Picts and Scots" (the Locketts), in *Going Gangster* she blackmails Jane and Bill into helping a little girl abscond from her boarding school, and in *The Monster of Widgeon Weir* she not only organises a hoax "monster" à la Nessie but also a plot to get rid of the actress she is understudying in an amateur production of *Antony and Cleopatra* so that she can perform. Her brothers are very much in the background in all this.

It is possible, of course, that Ransome and Atkinson felt able to give their girl characters a good share of the action partly because they were not, as I have said, usually in serious danger (though this would not apply to Courtney's girls), and partly because they are very definitely children. Was it perhaps more acceptable for girls to be active than grown women? I will come back to the adult roles in their books in chapter five, but I can say here that, although they both feature some strong and interesting female characters, traditional gender roles are fairly marked among their adults. In the case of Captain Johns, my final principal author of study, the dangers are manifold and the characters are adult, so neither of these reasons would apply. What part do females play in the action in his works?

Princesses and pilots

If we look first at the *Biggles* books, the answer is, very little. As I have already indicated, of the ninety-six books, only sixteen have any kind of significant female role, but even most of these are quite minimal. In *Biggles Flies Again*, for instance, a collection of short stories involving Biggles and Algy between the wars, of thirteen stories only three have a woman in, of which one doesn't actually speak, one is the beautiful daughter of the president of Bolivia, whose kidnap necessitates a rescue (essentially an updated Perseus and Andromeda tale), and only one, an apparent senorita in distress, demonstrates any brains or initiative - she persuades them to give her a lift in their plane out of the country, but her place is taken by her husband in drag, he being "wanted" by the authorities, so our heroes unwittingly aid him to escape. This degree of participation is fairly typical: if there is a woman character, she may be the driver for some of the action but her role is normally quite small.

Three clear examples of this are two princesses and one rich young woman with her own plane. In *Biggles and Co.*, published in 1936, the friends are asked to transport gold to the Continent, previous shipments having been hijacked. Stella Carstairs, the "remarkably pretty" daughter of one of the owners of the bullion company, appears in five of thirteen chapters, sometimes quite briefly. Aside from moving the narrative along by giving the men information in her role as her father's assistant, her main function is to leave her plane conveniently on their aerodrome so Ginger can "borrow" it to go the rescue of Biggles and Algy, who have each in turn been captured by the enemy. *Biggles Goes to War,* published two years later, deals with an imaginary Central European country being threatened by its equally imaginary neighbour. The princess of the former is young and beautiful: "She was rather pale, but he thought that her features were the most perfect he had ever seen. With a sudden movement she threw back the hoodlike garment that covered her head, releasing a halo of golden curls" (42). She appears in four of twenty-one chapters, and does very little except make a personal appeal for help to Biggles. The Italian princess in *Biggles "Fails to Return"* is equally beautiful, though rather than golden curls she has "dark, flashing eyes", but she is somewhat more proactive; she holds both Algy and Bertie up at gunpoint on different occasions, not knowing who they are, and before the book begins, when she and Biggles were being picked up by plane from Vichy France, he was wounded and she jumped out of the plane, shot two Italian soldiers who were firing on them, and managed to get him away to safety. Nonetheless she is only in five chapters of nineteen. These women, the princesses especially, are the archetypal heroines of fairy tale and nineteenth-century adventure yarn: beautiful, passive, virtuous, occasionally showing a flash of spirit but essentially there for the hero to serve dutifully and/ or rescue. Beau Geste did this *par excellence.*

Before moving on to the one exception to the above, I have to mention Marie Janis, the beautiful German spy with whom Biggles fell in love in one of the short stories in *The Camels Are Coming*, a collection of tales originally published in Johns' magazine. Apparently merely an object of desire, "a vision of blonde loveliness", "a slim blue-clad figure" (177-8), she is in fact tasked with locating Biggles' airfield, which is too heavily camouflaged to spot from the air, and passing the information to German High Command so they can bomb it. Her carrier pigeon has been killed so she persuades Biggles to drop a message for her, supposedly to her old father who is trapped behind enemy lines. British Intelligence is watching her, however, and substitutes her house for the airfield on the map in the message; the house is bombed, but she escapes because she was not at home but trying to save Biggles from the bombing raid she thought was going to hit his squadron. She misses him and has to flee, and Johns makes this episode the reason why Biggles was never afterwards interested in women; actually he had been advised by his editors to avoid love interest (Berresford Ellis and Williams, 1985).

Years later, in the 1950s, Marie is trapped in Czechoslovakia behind the Iron Curtain and Biggles goes to rescue her (*Biggles Looks Back*); she only appears in six of seventeen chapters, but she has at least aged realistically, and demonstrates considerable fortitude in refusing to tell the authorities where her family treasure is. In the final escape they have to ford a river and Biggles is worried if she falls she will get swept away, so they are all roped together, but in fact it is Von Stalhein (Biggles' former arch-enemy, in this book a colleague) who falls and "As his full weight fell on the rope Biggles nearly went in head first. He dug his heels into the bank. The bank began to slip under his feet. Marie ... added her weight by clutching him round the waist" (182). And again, when the plane lands to pick them up Biggles is shot and tells them to get away, "[B]ut Marie and Von Stalhein had jumped out again. As they reached him he slumped. With bullets flying they dragged him into the cabin" (186). Marie is not merely the motivation for male action, but a player herself.

The female character who really stands out in the *Biggles* series, however, is Full Moon, a fifteen-year-old from the Marquesas, who with her boyfriend Shell Breaker joins Biggles, Algy, Ginger (also a teenager) and their friend Sandy in a pearl-diving expedition which is dogged by giant octopuses, sharks, a typhoon and a villain named Castanelli who wants the pearls for himself (*Biggles in the South Seas*). Full Moon is of course pretty, but she also probably does more than any of the other characters to ensure the good guys win this particular adventure. When Castanelli is trying to ram their flying boat she swims very fast to cut the cable, which no-one else could have reached in time. When they are bothered by a shark, it is she and Shell Breaker who dive in with their knives to kill it. When the typhoon hits the island she lashes herself and Ginger to a palm tree with great efficiency, so they don't get blown away. When Castanelli has captured Ginger and drops him overboard weighted with lead, it is Full Moon who rescues him before he drowns, having meantime casually retrieved the pearls, which the villain had grabbed. The pair hide in a cave in the coral reef and when Castanelli sends a man after them she hits him on the head with a lump of coral and kills him. As she says (in her unfortunately, to modern eyes, pidgin English) "Me no run away when plenty trouble" (131). This is a formidable character, brave, skilful and acting with initiative; nor is she the object of anyone's love/ lust, since she already has a boyfriend. And interestingly, when the men are saying how wonderful she is, they do not make an issue of her gender. It is not amazing that she does what she does despite being a girl, it is simply amazing full stop.

I have no idea why Johns did not follow up Full Moon with other similar characters. That book was set in the '30s but not published until 1940, by which time he had started writing war stories. In 1941 he was asked by the Air Ministry to write something with a WAAF heroine, to encourage recruitment, and the result was *Worrals of the WAAF*, which was followed by a further five wartime stories and then five more post-war. The heroines are Joan Worralson ("Worrals") and her great friend Betty Lovell ("Frecks"), who in the first book are eighteen and seventeen respectively, although thereafter they feel older than that, fully adult.

Unlike Ransome, Johns does not have his heroines dominate the action without comment. The books are full of men being surprised at what these particular girls can do, or trying to protect them. "Wars aren't for women" is the view of their commanding officer, but "'He means well, poor brute,' murmured Frecks condescendingly. 'The old damsel-in-distress stuff dies hard in some of these whiskered warriors'" (*Islands*, 7). And over and over, the women, especially Worrals, challenge this attitude. When the major in *Worrals Goes East* wants to post them home after two attempts on their lives, because they are female, Worrals responds: "And in just what way, may I ask, does that make any difference? Are men to have a monopoly of the risks? If we've to start fighting male prejudice as well as the Nazis, then we *are* in for a tough time" (75-6). Moreover, when in

Worrals Flies Again Squadron Leader Yorke suggests "'in view of your previous exploits, we suspect that it is possible for a girl to evade suspicion where a man -' 'Just a moment, sir,' interrupted Worrals coldly. 'Are you suggesting that any useful work I may have done in the past was due entirely to the fact that being a girl I enjoyed privileges that would have been denied to a man?'" (10). These moments are particularly striking because she is talking to a senior officer, and Johns having been in the RAF was of course familiar with military discipline.

In fact, whatever Worrals says, there are numerous instances in the books of the heroines getting away with something simply because they are female, and men either find it hard to suspect them, or just assume that spies, saboteurs and pilots will be male. Later in that same book she is walking down a road in France, having landed her plane, and there are German troops out looking for the pilot; two different groups ask her if she has seen a strange man about. In *Worrals on the Warpath* there is a similar situation, and she also pretends to be her colleague Lucien's fiancée in order to rescue him when he is caught by the local police, who do not suspect her until she holds them up at gunpoint. In *Worrals Flies Again* her services are actually enlisted by the Gestapo for the same reason Squadron-Leader Yorke employs her; as a woman she can get away with things a man could not.

Writing a wartime adventure about young men would not necessarily require them to demonstrate much personal initiative; their normal military activities would provide enough of a plot. With women or girls it is different, because the sort of jobs the women's services were in reality asked to do were fairly routine: paperwork, transport, radar tracking and the like. Worrals however plunges into adventure on her own account. In the first book, she spots something suspicious while transporting a plane, reports it to her C.O. who pooh-poohs the idea, so she and Frecks decide to spend their weekend leave investigating, and uncover a nest of spies. Something similar occurs in the next book, also partly set in England. After that she is sometimes asked to carry out a particular job because she has shown her abilities, but she also continues to volunteer, and indeed to come up with her own ideas, such as setting up a refuelling station for fighter planes in France, despite the German Occupation, to help them get through to Malta (*Worrals on the Warpath*), thus showing a grasp of strategy as well as tactics. Frecks does not come up with the ideas herself, but she always insists on being involved.

Nor are they volunteering simply out of a sense of duty, although that comes into it in the wartime books, certainly. The fact is, they both enjoy action. In the first story while they are escaping from the spies in a stolen car, Frecks comments:

> "D'you know, I'm beginning to enjoy this ... I've seen it scores of times on the flicks, but I didn't dream I'd ever get a chance of doing it myself. I wish we had one of those howling sirens they use on the police cars in America. Phew! would I make it howl!" (160).

At the beginning of *Worrals Flies Again* she is bored, missing the action and restricted to normal female duties, and in the last book, *Worrals Investigates*, Frecks declares "I'm so bored it'd be a pleasure to dig my own grave" (8).

Together with this enthusiasm for action and excitement is a combination of optimism and determination which means that whatever happens they rarely contemplate defeat. In the first book the girls have to get a message to HQ that a bombing raid is planned, and the only telephone is in the enemy's house, so they break in and use it, while the German spies are talking in the next room. In the second, *Worrals Carries On*, they are following a "Belgian" (actually German) pilot who has been behaving suspiciously through blacked-out London with an air-raid going on, and when he takes to a boat on the Thames they steal another boat to stay on the trail. In these books it is the men who get despondent when things go wrong. For instance in *Worrals Flies Again*, they are staying in a chateau with a couple of elderly "caretakers" who actually turn out to be the Count and Countess who own the place, but while she is reasonably alert and optimistic, he is a picture of gloom throughout the book, convinced girls cannot achieve anything. In *Worrals on the Warpath*, when Lucien is captured his friend Raoul immediately gives up, but Worrals just focuses on working out a plan to free him. The male role is often either to offer a solution to a problem which simply won't work, so Worrals can point out how stupid they are, or to give up in despair so she can step in and present her own (daring) solution.

This leads me to my final point: Worrals is intelligent. Yes, she sometimes gets physical. In the first book when they grab the plane from the enemy Worrals flies it and Frecks fights the men in the back. In *Worrals Carries On* they need transport and the only thing available is a German army lorry full of troops; Worrals decoys the troops away, jumps into the cab and kicks the driver out into the road. But this is unusual: she is no Lara Croft or Modesty Blaise. She more often uses a gun than her fists or feet when she fights, but more often still it is her brain and her tongue. Over and over she keeps her cool and tells a good lie to get out of trouble, as when she persuades Von Brandisch, the Gestapo agent, to let her question Bill Ashton, her friend and fellow pilot who has been captured (*Worrals Flies Again*), or in *Warpath* dresses as a local girl (complete with sheep) in order to convince the Germans that their pilot, who has landed on her secret airfield by mistake, has gone off to find a telephone (rather than being currently her prisoner).

It might be assumed that this was because Worrals and Frecks are young women, not particularly large and muscular, and realistically they would not have been likely to win many fist fights with men. However, a brief look at the *Biggles* books shows rather that this is Johns' preferred type of hero. Perhaps a couple of times in 96 books Biggles hits someone with his fist. Most of the time he rejects this option. In *Biggles Goes to School*, set before the First War but not published until 1951, his method of dealing with the school bully is to arm his victims with sticks, rather than slogging it out in fair fight like a normal schoolboy hero. In *Biggles takes a Holiday* his arch-enemy Von Stalhein says:

> "Bigglesworth doesn't strike anybody - at least not with his fists ... He isn't one of these super-men who go about hitting people on the jaw. I doubt if he could do it anyhow. He has no weight behind him and his hands are more like a woman's than a man's ... What he lacks in brawn he more than makes up for with brain, plus sheer nerve" (127).

In my view this is refreshing, and more interesting anyway.

Other adventure books I have looked at were more likely to be read by girls, even when they include male characters. Jane Shaw (Jean Bell Shaw Patrick, 1910-2000) published among other things the comedy adventure series about "Susan" between 1952 and 1969, which featured three girls and a boy, and was billed as "for girls". The two sisters Midge and Charlotte are lazy, and it is their cousin Susan who instigates most of the action, abetted by their young brother Bill, who is a traditionally typical boy, always hungry and keen on adventures. Susan is actually not so much keen on adventures as keen to help people and right wrongs, and incurably curious. For instance, in *Susan Pulls the Strings* (1952) she becomes convinced that their charming neighbour is a smuggler of watches (she is right), and cannot simply tell the police but must go and get the evidence herself, while in *Susan Interferes* (1957) the family is on holiday in Switzerland and manages to help the son of a Czech scientist who has defected to the West to join his father, mainly because Susan will not ignore a minor mystery.

Mabel Esther Allan was also known as a "writer for girls", and many of her books were more about girls growing up than adventures, but some do involve spies or criminals, kidnapping and secret passages. Her

Adventure Royal (1954) is a Ruritania novel to be compared with Blyton's *The Secret of Spiggy Holes* and Courtney's *Grenville Garrison*; however, *Adventure Royal* is set in "Zaronia" not in Britain. A brother and sister, while on holiday there, get to know the Crown Princess and successfully rescue her from the Duke who has abducted her as part of a planned coup. The rescue is initiated by the girl, Katharine, and her brother agrees to join in because otherwise she will go alone.

Antonia Forest wrote a series of books about the Marlow family, six girls and a boy, who are all realistic and individual characters. Some of the books are school stories set in the girls' boarding school, one (*Falconer's Lure* 1957) is an animal story, and two are holiday adventures (*The Marlows and the Traitor* 1953, and *The Thuggery Affair* 1965). In both of these the children battle with their own weaknesses (seasickness, fear of heights, fear of the enemy, fear of being thought a coward) as much as with the villains. If one read *The Thuggery Affair* without having first read any of the other books, one might feel the roles were somewhat gender-determined, with the girl Lawrie playing her part reluctantly and not very competently, but in the other books she is contrasted with her twin Nicola, who is brave and jumps into action; Forest deliberately excluded Nicola from *The Thuggery Affair* because "This would be a boy-dominated book ... and if Nicola made up the numbers, that meant another brave, resourceful child helping to cope. So Nicola must go visiting. Lawrie, not over-brave nor especially resourceful, must be brought in instead" (Forest 2002). Overall her books do not present a picture of helpless females and active males, but a mixture of personalities with different strengths and weaknesses.

One interesting situation occurs in the final Dimsie book by Dorita Fairlie-Bruce, a contemporary of Brent-Dyer. Most of the Dimsie books are school stories, but the final volume, *Dimsie Carries On* (1941), features two girls from one of her other school series, now grown up, and Dimsie herself, now a wife and mother, getting involved with spies at the start of World War Two. It turns out that the young woman Dimsie has hired as a governess for her children is really a German agent; she and heroine Anne hide this fact from her (Dimsie's) husband because they think he won't be able to handle it, while they keep watch on the spy to find out what she's up to. Husband Peter is a doctor and a strong and kindly character, but the women seem to feel he needs protecting and try to keep him out of the action. Possibly this is an extension of the way these very independent females behaved at school towards their mistresses?

It might be expected that adventure books aimed at girls would make the female characters active and full of initiative, just as girls' school stories were doing. However, it seems that the male writers were doing the same thing in this period. Although some of these authors have males being, or trying to be, protective, the females are generally proactive, and often the initiators of the action. This is definitely different from adventure yarns of earlier ages. For example, *The Coral Island* features three boys aged eighteen, fifteen and thirteen respectively, and female characters are limited to a "native" woman and mention of the narrator's mother, whom he had promised he would say his prayers every day. G.A. Henty's *By Sheer Pluck* sees its hero Frank through heroic rescues of schoolmates, managing to find a job in London when poverty forces him to leave school, accompanying a famous explorer to Africa and getting involved in the Ashanti War, but apart from some "Amazons" he has to fight in the war, the women characters consist of his mother (who dies) and his friend's sweet little sister, who is waiting patiently for him when he finally comes home, and whom he eventually marries. Henty did admittedly among his prolific output write one or two books with a heroine instead of a hero, such as *A Soldier's Daughter*, where Nita is a "regular tomboy" who can shoot and fence, and who takes the initiative in most of the action; yet in the end this is weakened by having her "finished" at school and coming back to marry her comrade in action. In the *Beau Geste* trilogy, Aunt Patricia and her illegitimate daughter Claudia, while traditionally beautiful are at least interesting, but Isobel is a nice golden-haired English rose, and none of the three does much except provide a reason for the male characters to go off, join the Foreign Legion and have lots of adventures. Of course, there is also a beautiful half-caste harlot who threatens to put one hero's eyes out, and in Rider Haggard there is She, the immortal Ayesha, but these are challenges the heroes meet in the course of their adventures, rather than comrades sharing those adventures.

Although the three male writers in this study have different approaches: Ransome never mentions gender as an obstacle to action, Johns harps on how other people see Worrals and Frecks, and Saville has some gender distinctions in behaviour, but shares the action fairly equally; they all give agency to their female characters. Atkinson, Brent-Dyer and Courtney do likewise, the two latter in quite similar ways to their other genre of books for girls. Only Blyton really makes her girls "stay here". Even when her girls are involved in the action, they rarely take the initiative, with the exception of George in the *Famous Five* books.

CHAPTER FOUR

AS GOOD AS ANY BOY
SKILLS AND ACTIVITIES

In the mid-nineteenth century women on both sides of the Atlantic were campaigning for more practical clothing than corsets, heavy petticoats, and sleeves which made it difficult to raise one's arm above shoulder height. The long loose trousers, worn under a skirt, which were named after Amelia Bloomer (actually designed by Elizabeth Smith Miller in 1850), gave rise to much ridicule; in England the Rational Dress Society fared no better with a combination of skirt and knee-length trousers. Although educators were advocating physical exercise for girls and young women, usually gymnastics, it was not really until bicycling took off as a sport that dress reform really began. Yet over a century later, Lamb and Brown's survey of popular clothing stores in America in 2005 found that clothes aimed at little girls were designed for fashion rather than for activity. "Whether it's T-shirts, pants, or sleepwear, according to marketers boys live for action and girls live to look cute." (Lamb and Brown 2006, 18). They point out that whereas adults nowadays tend to put on special clothes for sports or the gym, small children should be able to play actively in their normal outfits, "[b]ut how active can a girl be in shorts that promise to reveal half her butt or fall away below the navel...?" (ibid, 36).

The period of this study falls happily between these two fashion situations: some women were wearing trousers in the 1930s and a lot more by the 1960s, and girls as well as boys wore shorts during the summer holidays. Ransome, for instance, has the Amazons in "knickers", later called shorts, although the Walker girls seem to be in skirts judging by the illustrations, which were by Ransome himself. Even the "girly" girls Anne and Lucy-Ann in Blyton wear shorts, and in a time when children were being protected from sexuality rather than bombarded with it, these would be the kind of shorts you could indeed be active in. How physically active were they? And what kind of skills did they demonstrate?

Mermaids and squirrels

A wide range of skills, physical, technical, cerebral and even artistic, is to be found in children's adventure books. The ones perhaps most to be expected are the physical: swimming, climbing, rowing and so on. All the authors I studied included these to some extent, though some more than others. A good proportion of the stories take place by the sea, or on a lake or river, and swimming is much to the fore. In *Swallows and Amazons*, Roger is very much learning how to swim, Titty is a little better, and John and Susan are both competent; in other words, age is more of a factor than gender in determining ability. The Blackett girls (the Amazons) are both good at all water-related activities. In Gwendoline Courtney's *Mermaid House* it is Fay and Agnes who are the really good swimmers, and who therefore get to swim into the sea-cave at night to spy on the villains (when the others first see Agnes, Peggy is convinced she's a mermaid). Captain Johns tends to prefer air and land environments, but I have already talked about the Marquesan girl Full Moon in *Biggles in the South Seas*, who swims better than any of the men except perhaps her boyfriend Shell Breaker. M.E. Atkinson's Locketts can all swim well but there is an interesting episode in *Going Gangster* where Fenella and a friend go swimming in a cove where the currents are dangerous and the friend gets into trouble; Bill Lockett rescues her but then gets cramp and has to be rescued himself by Fenella, who is portrayed as very athletic. The point of this is to place Jane Lockett under an obligation to Fenella, necessary to the plot, but it could have been done by having Jane the one to be rescued, rather than her brother. Add this to a fight between Bill and Fenella which the former barely wins (*The Compass Points North*), and an occasion in *Widgeon Weir* when she boards their boat unasked and it takes all three of the Locketts to remove her (she then steals the boat while they are out of it), and it can be seen that her physical prowess is remarkable.

Blyton's *Famous Five* adventures nearly all take place by the sea, and George is an excellent swimmer. In most of the books this is contrasted with Anne's much lesser abilities: "George tried a dive off one of the rocks, and went in beautifully. 'George can do anything in the water,' said Anne, admiringly. 'I wish I could dive and swim like George. But I never shall'" (*Five Run Away Together*, 106). In other words, there is an implication that George is good at swimming because she is like a boy. However, in *Five Have Plenty of Fun* George is scornful of Berta, who has come to stay, because she is pale and weak-looking, and says she doesn't like adventures, but it later emerges Berta is a really good swimmer, as good as George. Even Blyton is not completely black-and-white.

Climbing is to some extent a matter of strength, so it is perhaps reasonable that Anne has to be helped up a rope by her brothers (*Five Have a Mystery to Solve*, 170). However in *The Secret of Spiggy Holes* the boys say that the ladder is "too dangerous" for the girls, who have to wait for a boy to climb into the empty house and let them in through the door (21). Jane Lockett climbs a tree to hide from pursuers: "She did not rival the squirrel for speed, but she would have shamed many a boy" (*Going Gangster*, 138). Here there is still an assumption that tree-climbing is something boys can be expected to be good at, whereas if girls are, it is remarkable. However, in Courtney's *Wild Lorings* books, it is the three Lorings who possess notable physical skills as compared with other characters, due to their upbringing. Elspeth dives into a lake to save a junior who has got caught in a dangerous current, and she and her sister Maud climb out of a second-floor window to rescue a Fourth former who has got stuck on a ledge outside in a dare that went wrong. Maud later demonstrates how a thief could have escaped from the prefects' room via the window (this time on the first floor) using the ivy.

The ability to throw straight was often popularly considered to be restricted to boys. It is probable that until sports became part of the curriculum at girls' schools, there was considerable truth in this; if you get no practice and moreover wear restrictive clothing, you are unlikely to be very skilful. Many girls' school stories of the 'twenties and 'thirties feature cricket, and frequently stress that actually girls *can* throw. In Courtney's *Grenville Garrison* Audrey throws turf at Nigel when he is teasing her, and catches him "neatly on the mouth" (33); rather more seriously, in *Worrals of the WAAF* Worrals throws the package she has grabbed from the spies to Frecks, who "made a brilliant catch" (93) and managed to elude the enemy and escape with the documents; by contrast, in *The Picts and the Martyrs*, Dorothea remarks that Dick is "no good at throwing", and he agrees with her: "I know" (203).

In the heyday of the Girl Guide movement there were many stories for girls featuring Guides, including the school stories of Elinor Brent-Dyer. Therefore girls were accustomed to reading about heroines who could tie knots, read Morse code and send semaphore messages (and presumably many of the readers belonged to the movement and were similarly able). The characters in this study are none of them, apparently, in the Guides or Scouts, (except Missee Lee, who had been a Guide), but Morse and semaphore do come up quite a lot. The Locketts can all do semaphore, and for instance in *Smuggler's Gap* Oliver and Bill exchange information by signalling; Jane can read the message, and the skill is just taken for granted. On another occasion, Jane warns Bill not to talk about the smuggling by giving him S-M-U-G in Morse dots and dashes in the middle of a sentence, the assumption being that their landlady will *not* understand. In Courtney's *Denehurst* books, Avice can read Morse, but this is because her brother was very keen on it and built a transmitter, and wanted someone to practise with him; there is an implication that this is more of a "boy thing". Avice uses the skill to read the signals being flashed by a German girl to a submarine, and in the second book to send an SOS when she is captured by the enemy. The Swallows and Amazons can of course all do both Morse and semaphore, although the D's, Dick and Dorothea, are only learning and are conscious of their lack of skill. Again, in Ransome the division is between the less and more experienced, not between the sexes.

Sailing is of course the most important skill involved in Ransome's books, and is described in a great deal of detail. The two captains, John (*Swallow*) and Nancy (*Amazon*) are the most skilful sailors, and Nancy more than John is held up as a model, perhaps because although we are sometimes given John's point of view, we never get Nancy's; she is always seen through others' eyes, and they are often admiring or envious. In *Swallowdale* when she is helping John retrieve the *Swallow* after the shipwreck, she thinks of practicalities he does not: "Nancy really was a sailor. That was something he ought to have thought of himself" (85). In *Coot Club*, when the D's are learning to sail, they often refer to Nancy's skills as something to emulate, and in *Great Northern?* she is swinging the lead to check the depth of the water as they negotiate into harbour because "Nobody aboard could do that as well as she" (29). At no point does anyone comment that her skill is remarkable in a girl, they simply admire her.

There are boats of one sort or another in quite a few of the books in this study. In Brent-Dyer's *Fardingales* the older children are taught to sail and the two eldest, Humphrey and Anstace, have been allowed to take the *Susannah* off on their own in the eponymous *Adventure*. They share the actual handling of the boat fairly equally. The Locketts enter for a range of events in a regatta in *The Monster of Widgeon Weir*, and are all competent at rowing. The interesting character here when it comes to physical skills is Anna, who is not sporty but desperately wants to pull her weight in the team; in the first book she plays cricket for the first time in her life, because they are a person short, and manages to stand her ground and help win the match, and something similar happens in the regatta. However, her relative lack of skill does not appear to be connected with gender: firstly it is perceived as a positive thing, the way she overcomes her fear of failure in particular and always does her best (though the fact that this always miraculously leads to victory is somewhat unrealistic), and secondly Fenella in the same book is extremely skilful with oar and punt pole, and beats Bill in one race. Not only that, for Fenella in many ways is the archetypal tomboy, but there is also Brenda, who has lovely frocks and beautifully-cut hair, so that she makes Bill, who is used to his sister's bobbed hair and utility Kirby grip, feel uncomfortable, but who wins her first heat and very nearly beats Fenella in the final of the punting. Atkinson has a range of characters with a range of skills and interests which are not, on the whole, primarily related to their gender.

Shooting by the protagonists, as opposed to the villains, really only comes into Courtney's *Grenville Garrison* of the books featuring children rather than adult heroes. In that, all of them can shoot and it is actually Helen who is the best shot. When her twin Roy has been captured by the enemy she rescues him by holding them up at gunpoint through an open window, and does in fact shoot one of the men, though she doesn't kill him. Helen is fifteen. Hawk Chudleigh also carries a gun, as I have mentioned, in *Chudleigh Hold*, a gun given him by his great aunt, who is the only one actually to fire. He is sixteen.

Only really the *Marston Baines* books, Brent-Dyer's last two thrillers and those of Captain Johns feature driving or flying, for the obvious reason that they are the only ones with adult protagonists. Saville generally has the male characters driving; even the feisty Annabelle, determined to be in at the death of the police pursuit of the villain in *The Purple Valley*, is a passenger while Simon drives, although to be fair it is his uncle's car. Brent-Dyer has a male pilot in both *Condor Crags Adventure* and *Top Secret*, in both cases a minor character. Johns tends to have the leader flying the plane, i.e. Biggles and Worrals rather than Algy or Frecks, though realistically on long journeys they would surely spell one another. Biggles learned to fly in the war and was posted to the Front with less than fifteen hours' flying time, dual and solo, (think how you might feel after fifteen hours' driving lessons being told to drive off alone into, say, war-torn Syria with no satnav, and you get some idea), and learned not merely normal piloting skills but aerial combat. He was of course lucky to survive. In later books he frequently demonstrates his skill by landing or taking off in difficult circumstances, such as taking off in a seaplane as a typhoon is beginning or an enemy ship sails across his bows; he is no run-of-the-mill pilot, but then if he had been, he would not have lived very long and there would have been far fewer books about him.

The Women's Royal Air Force actually came into being in 1918, at the same time as the RAF, but the women were known as "Penguins" because they did not fly. In the *Daily Express* this was explained: "As a matter of fact flying is not a woman's job . . . they always lost their head in an emergency" (quoted in Pugh 2008, 318). However, by the late 1930s the vogue for flying stories included a number featuring girls or women, for example those by Eileen Marsh such as *Lorna—Air Pilot,* where Lorna flies her mother, a talented photographer, so that they can take aerial shots for newspapers to make money to take Lorna's father for some expensive medical treatment (nothing so mundane as merely earning a living). In the first *Worrals* story, we learn that she and Frecks have both learned to fly privately just before the war, but they are still teenagers and don't have much experience. Indeed, when Worrals flies a machine of a type she hasn't flown before she struggles realistically with the controls. However, before long they are making a night landing in a field in France (*Worrals Flies Again*) and then flying over Pacific islands searching for some missing servicewomen (*Worrals of the Islands*). She rarely ends up in actual combat but her technical skills are not in doubt.

Science, art and animal magic

Flying of course is not just a matter of the aircraft controls: you have to know where you are and where you're going, and if you are flying "off the map" you have to have some rudimentary mechanical knowledge in case of breakdowns. Worrals and Frecks are both capable navigators and radio operators, and do manage to deal with minor repairs, such as a spot of sabotage in *Worrals Down Under*, when Frecks has flown into a town called Oodnadatta with their friend Janet, leaving Worrals at Janet's house in the Australian outback. The villains who are trying to drive them off the property, where there is an opal deposit, take the opportunity to damage the plane on the airfield by ramming it "accidentally" with their car, so as to deprive the women of transport; Frecks succeeds in fixing the problem, a torn-off longeron, although it takes her several hours. Worrals at least is not merely competent but interested in technical matters; in *Worrals Carries On* she confirms her suspicions of the supposedly Belgian pilot by testing the petrol in his tanks, having paid attention to a lecture about the visible difference between German and British aviation spirit (they are different colours due to different additives), and proving that he must have refuelled in Occupied France.

In the early days of flight, a lot of navigation consisted of following rivers or railway lines, and there is still a certain amount of that involved in flying by Visual Flight Rules today. However, to plot a course requires mathematics, and the same is true of navigating a ship, of course. In most of Ransome's books the children are on a lake or river, but in *Peter Duck* they sail to the Caribbean and in *Missee Lee* they are in the China seas. The navigation is in the hands of Captain Flint (the Amazons' uncle Jim), but John Walker works with him. This is really the one skill related to sailing which Nancy does not possess. It fits with her dislike of school and general array of outdoor rather than cerebral talents, but it does also match the stereotype of "girls can't do maths". However, this is never made explicit. John wants to go in the Navy, so he has worked at navigation because it is knowledge he will need. He is quite a serious, focused person, where Nancy is frequently described as "cheerful", and laughs a lot; it is plausible that she would not apply herself to something she found difficult. In *Missee Lee* the eponymous pirate leader has studied in England and desperately wanted to pursue a Cambridge degree and a career as a bluestocking, but had had to return home when her father was dying. She keeps the children prisoner because she wants someone to study Latin with: John is not good at it, because it isn't something he will need when he goes to Dartmouth College, and the girls haven't studied it at all (suggesting Ransome was a little behind the times as regards girls' schools), so only Roger, the youngest, manages to please her. Nancy in particular absolutely hates the lessons they are obliged to take.

Susan Walker is also not naturally good at maths, but she does overcome this in *Peter Duck* when it becomes imperative that they sail directly to the Caribbean rather than calling at Madeira, in order to escape the attentions of Black Jake who is pursuing them. Susan and Peggy are in charge of the stores, and do a lot of arithmetic to check their water consumption so that they can be sure they have enough for the voyage. This is interesting in that Susan is working at a skill she does not enjoy and finds hard, for the good of everyone. It is reminiscent of Anna in the *Lockett* books, always forcing herself to play cricket or take part in a regatta because her friends need her to make up the numbers. It looks like the self-sacrifice which was praised and encouraged in so many girls' books of the nineteenth century. The classic example I suppose is the March girls giving up their breakfast to a poor family on Christmas morning in *Little Women*, but while that could be seen as an act of Christian charity, there are other examples in other books of girls giving up what they want for their brothers' sakes, which are less about charity and more about male selfishness. Even the powerful Missee Lee has given up her desires to take over her father's role when he died; she has authority over other, lesser pirate chiefs, but it is not the life she wants. I have not found any clear examples of boys behaving like this, although Tom in the *Lone Pine* books has doubts about becoming a farmer like his uncle and wants to go off and do something more exciting, but eventually is reconciled to his fate. This is portrayed as adolescence clashing with the older generation, and both sides give way to some extent.

Most of the skills in these books tend to be physical ones like swimming and climbing, but there are other more cerebral ones like navigation, and the Latin of Missee Lee. One of the key points in Courtney's *Denehurst* books is that the sisters Elspeth and Moira, because their father is a diplomat, speak fluent French and German; in these wartime tales it is the latter which is important, as they understand what the spies are saying. Similarly in *The Grenville Garrison* all of them speak French and German, both of which languages are used by the multi-cultural villains, and Nigel, whose father is the ambassador to Czaravia, also speaks that language, and is able to eavesdrop on the enemy. Biggles is also a talented linguist, speaking several Indian languages from his boyhood, and rapidly picking up German when he pretends to be a traitor and joins the German air force in *Biggles Flies East*. Worrals, like Courtney's characters, had a diplomat father and speaks French and German well enough to play a Frenchwoman when her life depends on it, and to understand what the Germans are saying to one another. This is logical if the adventure has international ramifications; Marston Baines the Intelligence agent is also fluent in Italian and French. Blyton, however, who could have given her characters linguistic skills (several of the *Adventure* series and two of the *Secret* series are set abroad), did not do so. Languages are often seen as a female subject at school, and more girls than boys tend to opt to specialise in them, but in these books there does not appear to be any particular gender bias in this area. Of course, there would be a difference between a girl being good at, say, German at school, because "languages are a girls' subject", and her being able to understand the enemy and therefore having a power not shared by the boys. Perhaps this is one reason why Blyton does not enter this territory.

It seems to be assumed by most of the authors that children do not enjoy lessons, even if they like school. Saville has only Jon Warrender of all the Lone Piners interested in books and a good student. At one point he talks about going to Cambridge, but he ends up at Sussex University. Oliver Lockett is also brainy, but most of the other characters in Atkinson's books are not bookish. Ransome's Walker family do their holiday homework because they must, but don't enjoy it; however, the D's, Dick and Dorothea, are both keen on reading, and Dick in particular learns things from books. It's a telling point that the pair have bought a book on sailing to help them learn, where all the others learn by doing and being shown. When they are given a rabbit to cook in *The Picts and the Martyrs,* their response is to buy a recipe book in order to find out what to do with it. One distinction, though, is that while Dick reads up on sailing and birdwatching, Dorothea obviously spends a lot of time reading fiction, to judge by the stories she makes up - she wants to be a writer. Titty also lives a great deal in her imagination. All the children imagine themselves pirates or explorers, but it seems most important to Titty, and she is the one who keeps the character Peter Duck alive when the others might have forgotten him. This creativity seems to be a feminine characteristic: Jenny of the Lone Piners, Jane Lockett, and Lucy-Ann in Blyton are all very imaginative, in contrast to more prosaic boyfriends or brothers. I shall return to this in chapter nine.

Creative skills do not tend to be necessary to the action (unless one includes the ability to tell lies under pressure), but are sometimes part of the background. Fenella in *Widgeon Weir*, having got the leading actress of her company out of the way by a ruse, proves herself very talented in the role of Shakespeare's Cleopatra. The Locketts' various aunts include the professional writer who polishes the books they supposedly write about their adventures, and a professional artist. Blyton several times has artist characters, and hers are usually men; indeed, in at least one *Famous Five* book Julian expresses the intention of becoming one. In one adventure the Five meet a boy called Martin who is a very talented artist, but his father despises this ambition and forbids him to paint: "He thinks it's a weak, feeble thing for a man to do" (*Five on Kirrin Island Again*, 114). The Five are shocked at this, and the "father" turns out to be nothing of the sort, and a criminal to boot, so at the end Martin gets his wish to train at art school. Courtney's adventure books do not feature the creatively talented particularly, except that one of the (male) suspects in *Well Done, Denehurst!* is an artist, but her family books have a number: in *Stepmother* Elizabeth is a talented actress, her friend Oswald wants to be a writer, and her new stepmother's brother is a famous actor; in *The Girls of Friar's Rise* the eldest girl does wonderful illustrations and gets a children's book published; in *The Chiltons* Brian writes a melodrama for the family to perform. This creativity seems to be shared out fairly evenly between the genders.

Some of the skills in these books are unusual and not necessarily predictable from the context. Snubby in the *R Mysteries* is extremely good at playing imaginary musical instruments, such as a Jew's harp and a zither. This adds nothing particularly to the mystery plot, it is just amusing. More integral to the plots is Philip in the *Adventure* series, who is able to tame any kind of animal, including reptiles and insects. Sometimes these play a role in the adventure, such as in *The Castle of Adventure* when the children, captive in the castle, send the fox cub he has tamed out with a message, or in *Ship* when the monkey Micky and Kiki the parrot get into a fight in his cabin and break the ship-in-a-bottle, revealing the secret treasure map. Philip is one of the four main characters in this series, and every book features a different animal, so we are constantly reminded of his skill. In *Five Have a Mystery to Solve* the Five meet a boy, Wilfrid, who has a similar talent, and in the *R Mysteries* Barney the circus boy has a pet monkey, Miranda, who sometimes helps and sometimes hinders the adventures. In Blyton it is normally a boy who has the special skill. An exception perhaps would be *Mr Galliano's Circus* (not one of my primary texts), where Lotta the little circus girl can do trick riding and walk a tightrope, while the boy Jimmy comes from an ordinary home and envies her. However, the point here is to take the reader into circus life from the outside, so Jimmy is the hero, and in the end he teaches his dog Lucky to do tricks even the circus people had not imagined possible.

Saville also has a character with power over animals, namely Peter (Petronella), the vice-captain of the Lone Piners. In the first book when her pony is being used for a getaway by the saboteur she halts it with a special whistle, and on two occasions she stops a large dog from attacking. This is more believable than Blyton, with her range from beetles to fox cubs, because the horse has been trained, and dogs do behave differently with different people. It is logical that it should be Peter, the country girl, who has this skill, but it is also notable that she uses it to save David, the club captain, from being bitten by an alsatian (*The Neglected Mountain),* that is, girl-saves-boy rather than the reverse. Gwendoline Courtney has the Lorings all able to handle wildlife, though they are not portrayed as having any extraordinary powers, it is simply that their father is a naturalist. Maud cheerfully picks up frogs and grass snakes when the other girls are screaming and shuddering; it emerges that it is her brother Nick who has been putting them in people's beds and desks, as a joke.

To sum up so far, most of the authors feature individuals who are good at particular things, such as swimming or painting or taming animals. Blyton tends to make these individuals male, with the notable exception of George in the *Famous Five*, but the other authors spread the talent out, and may indeed have a girl being better than the boys, as with Fenella in the *Lockett* stories and Peter in the *Lone Pine* ones. Many of the skills concerned would have been considered unsuitable for girls, especially in British books, a few decades earlier. Johns tends to make his hero, male or female, multi-talented, and just as we never go inside Nancy Blackett's head, but always see her from others' viewpoints, Biggles in particular is usually shown from the outside except in the first few (World War One) stories, when he often muses on the tragedy of war. Chapter three suggested that for most of these authors, girls had a fair share of the action, and it now appears that they also had a fair share of the talents. What about the more mundane tasks and activities? Were they divided, and if so, how?

Cooking and carrying

The obvious division of labour in the adult world of the 1930s and indeed to a large extent today is between domestic chores such as cooking, laundry and sewing, and more mechanical tasks such as repairing vehicles or other machinery. Girls as I have said were required to study domestic science in state schools, and this is reflected in many girls' school stories. Elinor Brent-Dyer frequently has comedy incidents occurring when someone adds the wrong ingredient, such as garlic cloves instead of cloves to an apple pie, and also published *The Chalet School Cookbook*, where some of the characters present their favourite recipes. I attended an independent girls' school in the 1970s, and although the focus was very much on academic lessons, we had to do a year of DS, unlike my brother at the equivalent boys' school. However, by the 1960s and '70s state schools were often offering cookery and woodwork to both sexes, though in the days before a National Curriculum that would have depended on the individual head teacher; my mother as a primary school teacher shocked her headmistress by making the boys in her class learn to sew.

Most of the authors I studied have the girls doing the catering. From what has already been shown of Enid Blyton, it comes as no surprise that her girls cook, and if her boys help at all it is to wash up, or sometimes do jobs like podding peas, which they enjoy and which enables them to eat a few. In most of the *Secret* series the children are staying with adults, and the catering is managed for them, but in the first, *The Secret Island*, when they run away to the said island and live on their own for months, it is Peggy who is in charge of the commissary. She is actually older than the twins, but with the *Famous Five* it is the youngest, Anne, who takes on this role whenever they go camping. In the early books she is very much a little girl, but she soon develops a motherly streak. For instance, in *Five Have a Mystery to Solve* (*Famous Five* number 20) when they arrive at the cottage where they are to stay, Anne immediately starts planning who will sleep where and what food she is going to buy. Julian sees her and says "Acting "mother" to us, as usual? " (40). In the *Adventure* series they mostly eat out of tins, however, and the choice of which tin to open is communal; one of the boys has charge of the tin-opener. The *R Mysteries* all take place in a house or hotel rather than camping, so although as usual in Blyton there are many descriptions of meals, it is not normally the children who have cooked them; however, Diana in the first book especially is portrayed as careless and untidy, quite unlike the domestic Peggy and Anne.

The Lockett children are camping in some form in several of the books, and the girls (usually Jane and Anna, but if Anna is not there, Jane alone) are responsible for shopping and cooking. Jane sees this as a chore and does not particularly enjoy it, but is nonetheless proprietorial about it, referring to "my shopping" (*Widgeon Weir,* 29). Oliver Lockett may dry the dishes after the girls have washed them; Bill is more likely to be off doing something more congenial. Blyton's Dick and Julian do at least always help in some way, but jobs are nearly always assigned by gender, as for instance in *Five on a Hike Together* when the boys go and get heather and bracken for bedding while the girls wash up. Similarly in *The Island of Adventure* the boys do heavy jobs like fetching water from the well and wood for the fire while the girls do "household tasks". Even when there is no traditional gender role involved, her children tend to form gender pairs: in *The Secret of Spiggy Holes* there is one torch for the boys, one for the girls, for example.

Saville's Lone Piners also often camp, sometimes in a barn or caravan. Peter is the official cook, when they are all together, but if she is not there Tom or David is likely to put potatoes to roast in the fire, they all fetch firewood, and quite often "they" cook or wash up, with no clear indication as to who does what. Certainly David sometimes makes the shopping list. This is much vaguer than Ransome's camps, where Susan is quite explicitly in charge. Susan and John in fact increasingly as the books progress take on roles akin to mother and father, especially noticeable in *Secret Water* where little sister Bridget is with them for the first time, and they are extremely protective of her. (Nancy wants them all to become blood-brothers and -sisters, but Bridget is scared so John and Susan oppose the idea.) Susan's cooking skills also include the ability to build a campfire and keep it going better than anyone, and this is acknowledged and praised by others. Is this about gender or about individual character?

She is a prosaic and methodical person, a contrast to the imaginative Titty, and managing the stores suits her temperament. On the other hand, when they join with the Amazons, and especially on board ship, Peggy shares the cooking with her, and Peggy is otherwise casual, feckless and nearly as tomboyish as Nancy. They all have naval ranks, Susan and Peggy each being a "mate", i.e. second-in-command. They take the ranks quite seriously and obey orders according to the chain-of-command, so if it were standard practice for the mate also to be the cook on board ship, this would offer an explanation; however, I do not believe this to be the case. So although at no point does Ransome say anything so explicit as Blyton about girls and domesticity, the same assumption seems to be there. Brent-Dyer also has Anstace doing the cooking on the *Susannah*, and the grocery shopping, though when they are cooking outdoors Humphrey does the sausages, rather like a modern man taking charge of the barbecue. In view of the sharp differentiation of roles in her family stories, this is not surprising.

An exception to the above is in all-male households. In *The House on the Moor*, after having their car stolen by an escaped convict, the Locketts with their aunt are helped by an elderly widower sea captain; his house is spick and span and Jane thinks his manservant must have been a sailor too, because sailors are good at keeping things clean and tidy. Presumably therefore she believes most men are not. Somewhat similarly, in *The Susannah Adventure* Tom does the housework on Mr Pratt's barge, by assumption because there are no females on it. Boats are often all-male environments, and in that context men need to do jobs which on land would fall to the women. In Ransome's *Coot Club* the twins (girls) hitch a lift on a wherry, whose mate teaches them how to peel potatoes, and then how to cook bacon properly after they have overcooked it: "and then when you get husbands they'll have a good word for yer cookin'" (265). In *Top Secret* Hawk Chudleigh is cast adrift in a lifeboat with an injured boy when their ship is blown up by a Japanese mine left over from the war, and he nurses the boy with great care, and then when they finally make landfall he also prepares the food, again because there is no-one else. Once they are joined by others, it is Aunt Freda who does the cooking; one could argue that this is because actually it is her house, rather than because of her gender, but the rest of Brent-Dyer's work would not support this interpretation.

In the first *Marston Baines* book, the agent actually requests the visiting Rosina to make a cup of tea even though they are in his house. This could have been in order to get a quiet word with Simon while she is out of the room, but the same could have been achieved by asking Simon to accompany him to the kitchen, and anyway later in the chapter he asks her to make a fresh pot. In default of useful female visitors, Baines cooks for himself, and when Simon is staying with him, for both of them. In this he is handier than Biggles, who employs a housekeeper. There is very little about food in Johns' books, but Biggles and his friends share rooms in Mount Street and do not even seem to make cups of tea for themselves, though when, as they frequently are, they are camping out in the desert or jungle somewhere off the beaten track, they obviously have to do so. In the *Worrals* books there is no mention of a housekeeper, and indeed although they do not ever seem to have a regular job as they are always available to take on missions for Scotland Yard after the war, they do certainly talk about having to earn their own living. Cooking however apparently consists in opening the occasional tin, much as it does for their male counterparts.

Despite this exception, there does seem in general in the books to be an expectation that domestic chores and in particular cooking are a female preserve. Although the girls take their share of the excitement, and demonstrate a range of skills, some of which are traditionally masculine, they are also expected to take charge of traditional female activities. This may not apply to all the girls in a particular set: George in the *Famous Five* and Nancy in the Ransome books do not enjoy such activities, and Nancy definitely isn't very good at them; when their mother is away in *The Picts and the Martyrs* the cook wants her to order the meals for the day, and her response is "Oh, bother. I won't start housekeeping until tomorrow. Ask Peggy. Or, you do just as you like" (14). However, unlike their share of the action, they do not challenge this expectation. Even Nancy does not question that she needs to take her mother's place in some sense. When the males suggest they should stay behind because something is too dangerous, they are up in arms; when the males sit back and eat the food they have prepared, they are happy to have their cooking skills praised.

CHAPTER FIVE

MOTHERS AND FATHERS AND AUNTS
ADULT GENDER ROLES

If the children in adventure books did not always conform to stereotypical gender roles, what about the adults? What kind of men and women were the children expected to grow into? In the books with child protagonists, adults tend to play a minor role, of course. Parents conveniently visit America or mothers have to go and look after a sick relative, leaving the children free to have their adventure unsupervised. Even this can be quite informative; it is always the mother who is looking after the relative, and the father whose work calls him to America (or India, or Scotland) and who needs his wife to look after him.

Penny Warrender in the *Lone Pine* books lives with her aunt because her parents are in India where her father works. The Locketts' parents are also out there, and they live in term-time with an aunt and uncle who, although they don't seem to have children of their own, also fit the traditional pattern, for he is a doctor and she keeps house and does voluntary work. When these series started, India was still part of the Empire and a plausible place for parents to be. Biggles was born out there and only came home to attend public school, but of course that was much earlier. (British children were generally not kept with their parents in India because they were prone to suffer from fever in the climate; Biggles was told he would die if he did not leave the country.) America is also a popular place to send unwanted parents; in the first *Denehurst* book the girls are sent to boarding school for safety during the Blitz, but the second takes place in the summer holidays, and they have to stay with their cousin because their parents are going to America. Courtney does the same, for different reasons, with Mr Verney in *Stepmother* and the parents of the six *Girls of Friar's Rise*, though in those books domestic drama rather than a spy adventure is the result of the children being left alone. Julian, Dick and Anne's parents also go there on occasion.

Married couples

The mother of these three mostly appears briefly at the beginning of a book, and their father very little at all; much more integral to the *Famous Five* stories are George's parents, Fanny and Quentin. At first sight they are particularly strong stereotypes, since she is not only a housewife and a good one, she is gentle and lovable too, while he is not only a scientist (a distinctly "male" profession) but hot-tempered and dictatorial. The household revolves around his whims, although this is partly because he works at home and hates being disturbed by the children's noise. However, the fact that he is a scientist and therefore, naturally, absent-minded, means that actually Fanny sometimes behaves more like his mother than his wife, scolding him for forgetting to eat and for not doing tasks which are meant to be his province. For instance, in *Five Go to Smuggler's Top* a tree blows down on the cottage in a storm, because Quentin has neglected to have it seen to although he knew it was dangerous, and Fanny reproaches him and says she will see to things like that in future. This does make one wonder why she hadn't done so before; the boundary between male jobs and female jobs must be so strong for her that she only steps over it when it becomes absolutely necessary. There is a similar situation in *The Island of Adventure*, where Aunt Polly has to slave away running a large inconvenient house in the middle of nowhere, without electricity or running water, because her husband finds it a good place to write a book; he is as selfish and as impractical and forgetful as Quentin.

Most of the books present models of parents with a traditional relationship. In the *Lone Pine* books, Mr and Mrs Morton are among the most prominent adults. In the first book he is away at the war, but later he is out at work, while she is a housewife. She is portrayed as very understanding of how children's minds work; on their first day at Witchend, the house in Shropshire which is the focus of many of the stories, she tells the twins "Today you can start by going along to make friends with the Ingleses and getting the milk, and when you get back there'll be time to make the first trip into yonder impenetrable forest!" (*Mystery at Witchend*, 23). This is reminiscent of Mrs Walker in the Ransome books, who waits patiently for Roger to "tack" across a field (pretending to be a sailing boat) so she can give him a message, and immediately becomes Man Friday when she visits the island and finds Titty alone being Robinson Crusoe. She is known to the children as "the best of all natives", natives being their word for adults. Mothers in general are warm and sympathetic, and respond to children in danger with worry, while fathers are kind but strict, and sometimes get angry. And when fathers' work takes them abroad, even if it is the school holidays, mothers normally accompany them.

Elinor Brent-Dyer only really has parents in *Fardingales* of her thrillers, since in the other family-based adventure, *Chudleigh Hold*, the parents are dead. The Roseveares, with four children, live at Fardingales and are visited by the Anthonys, with three: the two wives are sisters. Mr Roseveare has inherited the house and estate on the death of a cousin, and he runs the estate while his wife manages the house. Mr Anthony is a bank manager and his wife "had all the housework and shopping on her shoulders" (2). Rather like Fanny in the *Famous Five*, she seems to feel that her husband could not possibly cope with basics like meals without her; when they are invited to stay with the Roseveares, Mr Anthony cannot get away from work immediately and plans to join them in a fortnight, suggesting that she go with the children, but she insists on taking the children and returning to look after him. "Who's going to look after you?" she asks, to which he replies "Myself, of course", but she will not accept this, saying "Well, you're not! I know what that means" (21). This finds an echo in many of Brent-Dyer's girls' books. For example, in *A Head Girl's Difficulties*, a kindergarten teacher tells an anecdote:

> "Betty Trevennor, who came this term, wanted to know why God made Adam first. Why not Eve? When I said because God wanted man to be there first, so that he could look after woman, she said, 'Yes, but wimmens looks after mens'" (174).

Gwendoline Courtney also offered an array of devoted wives. The mother of Elaine and Moira in the *Denehurst* books stays in London during the Blitz because her husband has a government job and has to be there, and in the sequel, as already related, she accompanies him to America. The girls' housemistress in the first book, by the second has married their cousin and given up teaching. In *The Grenville Garrison* Nigel's mother is with his father in Czaravia, where the latter is British Ambassador, and the parents of Nigel's cousins, the rest of the Grenvilles, are visiting them because the husband wants to study some ancient manuscripts there, but "things there are a little unsettled at the moment" (24), so the children must holiday in England without their parents. Wives go into danger with their husbands, but children do not join them. In her family books it is not a question of danger, but in *The Chiltons* Mrs Chilton is a vicar's wife, and that is essentially her role in life, though it means having to be pleasant and hospitable to unlikeable parishioners. In the same book Dr Leigh, a historian, is a widower, lonely and unsociable until his widowed sister comes to keep house for him, a kind of wife-substitute. In *Stepmother* Nan had, like her brother, been an actor but gave it up to keep house for him when he became famous. She then married an author and took on the job not only of running his house for him but also looking after his four daughters.

Most of the wives in these books appear to have no skills beyond the domestic. An exception is Mrs Walker, the mother of the Swallows. Not only does she join in the children's make-believe to a great extent, speaking to them in an imaginary language as a "native" visitor to their camp, for instance, but she herself is a good sailor and swimmer, and athletic enough to climb up the lookout rock in *Swallowdale*. This is the more striking because she would have been growing up in Edwardian times. She is Australian though, and in fiction at least, but probably also in reality, "Colonial" women tended to be tougher, more independent, and have a range of outdoor skills which their British counterparts lacked. She does not particularly use her skills as an adult, and in fact is a good Navy wife, staying at home in England and looking after the children while her husband is at sea, and moving house when he gets a job ashore.

There are many couples with minor roles in the books, often farmers and their wives, since many of these tales are set in the countryside. The Ingleses of Ingles' Farm in the *Lone Pine* books are a good example: she is garrulous and friendly and a good cook, and he is large and kindly with a booming voice. Both work hard. Only really in *Man with Three Fingers* do we get a little subtlety in their portrayal; their nephew Tom is unhappy at the assumption he will follow his uncle's footsteps and take over the farm, and Alf Ingles, who is well-meaning but a little overwhelming, finally manages to step back and recognise that Tom is no longer a child. Mrs Ingles' role is to stay calm and offer cups of tea when there is trouble.

Blyton frequently has her children staying on a farm, where the food is always excellent and in enormous quantities. In *The Mountain of Adventure* it is a Welsh farm, for instance, and in *Five Go Down to the Sea* a Cornish one. The wives provide high teas of home-cured ham, salad with home-made salad cream, cherry tart with the farm's own cream and huge fruit-cakes. The husbands come in for meals and otherwise are out and about working. Mr Penruthlan is given a comic tendency to say nothing but "Ah!", which his wife interprets as meaning anything from "Yes, I'd like a cup of tea" to "Let's call the new calf Buttercup". This subscribing to the popular idea of women as garrulous and men as taciturn is also found in Ransome: the Dixons who farm near the Walkers' holiday home in the Lake District, and who provide the milk for the Swallows when they are camping, are just such a couple, he being shy and limiting himself to a few words.

Like Blyton, Ransome has farms as havens of warmth and friendliness. Yes, everyone works hard, but they are cheerful and kindly and provide fresh milk, butter and eggs, and sometimes other services; in *Swallowdale* Mary Swainson from the farm mends Roger's knickerbockers practically on a daily basis, as he tears them sliding down a slope of scree for fun. Other working-class couples have a similar ethos of hard work and friendliness. In *Coot Club* the twins initially say they cannot go on the trip south with the D's and Tom, but then events allow them to do so, and they take several chapters to chase after the others, hitching a lift on a barge with a friend, then on a tug with someone the friend knows, and finally with a pair of total strangers, the Whittles, who live on a barge, and who help them from sheer good nature. The gender roles here are explicit: as Mrs Whittle says:

> "I like things to be what I call nice ... It ain't no life for a woman aboard a barge. Nothing to keep clean. Not even a doorstep you can take a pride in. They won't let you doing nothing on deck. Everything must be their way, no matter 'ow much better it might be done. But I 'ave things my way in here [in the cabin]" (293).

Maids and cooks

From the 1930s domestic appliances were beginning to spread, supposedly making life easier for the housewife, although Pugh (2008) suggests that in fact what happened was that standards rose, so that having a machine to help simply meant you were expected to keep your house cleaner than before, and therefore time and labour were not necessarily saved. Whether or not this is true, firstly even in the 1950s and '60s by no means every household had a refrigerator or washing machine, for example, and secondly it appears from these books that some housewives took a pride in *not* using modern appliances. In Atkinson's *The House on the Moor*, for instance, Mrs Fenner cleans the carpet with a small brush and dustpan although there is a carpet sweeper in the cupboard. Elinor Brent-Dyer certainly has this in her girls' books if not her thrillers; in the *Chalet School* series Joey's maid Anna refuses even to use a liquid blacklead Joey has bought to save her trouble, insisting on sticking to paste and brushes and "elbow grease". "Talk about conservatives! Anna's a conservative of conservatives! She hasn't the smallest use for modern gadgets" (*Joey Goes to the Oberland*, 29).

This Anna is a splendid example of the "faithful maid" stereotype. With the various couples like the bargees and the farmers, the wives are of course doing a lot of heavy housework, which realistically was very time-consuming if well-done—and in books for children, adults who are positive role models nearly always work hard and do a good job. However, most of the mothers and aunts in the books are middle-class and have at least one servant. Fanny in the *Famous Five* has Joanna (sometimes called Joan), who is jolly and, naturally, a wonderful cook. The Lyntons in the *R Mysteries* have "Cook". Mrs Walker, mother of the Swallows, has at the least a nurse to look after her youngest child, and the Amazons' mother has "Cook". The Roseveares in *Fardingales* have "old Edith, who's one of the family, having been with us so long" (44), and the Mortons at Witchend have Mrs Braid, soon known as Agnes, although when they later move back to London they don't seem to have any help. This should leave the mothers free for other things, but in practice they still seem to spend most of their time on domestic matters. It appears that the ideal household is one where the father earns enough to keep a non-working wife, a maid, and children at private school, while the wife, though avoiding heavy cleaning and laundry, nonetheless supervises every aspect of the housework and is always at home smiling and offering refreshments when her husband or children return.

Working women

There are other models offered, however. Sometimes a husband and wife work as a team, as with the pair who are joint heads of a co-educational boarding school in the *Lockett* series, the school which Fenella and her brothers attend. Mrs Fortune wears trousers and smokes Russian cigarettes, and she and her husband have a modern (positive) attitude to children, expecting them to be a little high-spirited, and looking at the reasons for rule-breaking before dealing out punishment. When Fenella has blackmailed Jane and Bill Lockett into abetting a little gypsy girl to abscond from school, Jane is afraid she will be expelled when the plot comes to light, but the Fortunes are more understanding than that (*Going Gangster*). In Blyton's *Secret* series are the Arnolds, who fly their own plane together to the wilder parts of the world; in the first book they disappear for a year, prompting the children to run away from their cruel uncle and aunt and hide on the *Secret Island*, and later they crash-land in Africa and the children go to look for them (*The Secret Mountain*). Although Mrs Arnold is "kind and wise" (*The Secret Island*), she is also "strong", and she does not just accompany her husband; she is also a pilot.

Saville gives his journalist, James Wilson, who works with the Lone Piners in several books, a fiancée Judith who is determined and competent. When her car gets a puncture Wilson says sorry, he is useless at anything mechanical, to which she promptly replies that luckily she is not, and changes the wheel. Like the younger girls, she insists on being part of the adventure; in fact she is a contrast to Jenny, who assumes Tom will blow up her bicycle tyres for her (*Neglected Mountain*). However, the twins find this highly amusing, and in an earlier book Peter gets a puncture and is about to set about repairing it when she realises she has lent her kit to someone who did not return it, so the overall message is that young women should be able to do things for themselves.

Women do work, but the older ones only in particular circumstances. One of these is if they are widowed. Jon Warrender's father was killed in the war, and his mother inherits from her uncle the inn *The Gay Dolphin* in Rye (scene of several *Lone Pine* adventures) and runs it to support herself and her son. She is not shown actually making beds or cleaning baths, however, and in fact has a (male) manager to help her, since she has no experience of running a hotel (he turns out to be a villain). In *Saucers Over the Moor* the young journalist Dan has a widowed mother who runs a cafe which she bought with her husband's savings when he died. Both these women are portrayed very positively, as being courageous and persevering in difficult circumstances, but the assumption is still that it is a man's place to be the breadwinner, and if a woman has to work it is a shame. In *The Secret of Grey Walls* the Lone Piners meet the mother of Alan Denton, a sheep farmer: she is also a widow, "her face was often sad" and "her hands ... were worn with work" (120). There is also a young woman in *Man With Three Fingers* who had to work even before she was widowed because her husband was "a failure" (80): her words. Saville's own wife of over fifty years was apparently a very strong character, perhaps the stronger of the two (O'Hanlon 2001), but he worked to support her and their four children while she managed the household. (During the war, this meant he lived in rooms while she and the three youngest moved for safety to Shropshire, the model for *Mystery at Witchend*.)

It is true that the *Lone Pine* girls all get jobs once they leave school: Peter in a local riding school, Jenny in a bookshop, while Penny goes to catering college; by the time the later books were being written in the 1960s and '70s the days of middle-class girls staying at home arranging flowers and going to tennis parties until marriage were over. However, Peter expects to live wherever David's job takes him, once they are married. In fact, he decides that once he has trained as a solicitor he will get work in Shropshire, her native county, where he knows she will be happy, but still this is his choice rather than hers. The last *Lone Pine* book has David and Peter getting officially engaged on her eighteenth birthday.

The characters in the *Marston Baines* books are that much older and do go beyond the "and they lived happily ever after" stage. In *Power of Three* Annabelle, the lively heroine of *The Purple Valley*, is newly married to Pierre, an artist, and they have opened a shop together selling his work and other things to tourists. Pierre is still struggling at the beginning of his career; he is a proud man who "resented the fact that he couldn't support his wife as he wished to do entirely by his own efforts" (52); Saville understands that a young woman might not be satisfied to sit back and let her husband support her anyway: "It was typical of Pierre not to appreciate that his wife also had her pride and that she was determined to make a success of the shop" (53). This clash of expectations colours their relationship despite the fact that they are very much in love, which is quite a realistic expression of that generation, caught between the past and the future.

In Blyton there is the widowed Mrs Mannering, the mother of Philip and Dinah in the *Adventure* series. In the first book Philip explains that he is proud of her, but also sad when he thinks how tired she seems, and he plans one day that "he'd be the clever one - earn the money, keep things going, and make things easy for his hard-working mother" (*Island*, 15). She actually runs an art gallery, which is reasonably genteel, but there seems to be an assumption that women get tireder than men when doing an actual job. Also, it is not their proper role; at the end of the book the children get a large reward for foiling a gang of counterfeiters, and Mrs Mannering can stop working. Jack remarks "She's just wasted as a business-woman ... She's a mother, and she ought to live like a mother, and have a nice home of her own and you and Dinah with her" (190). In later books she does seem to have a job again, but finally of course she and Bill the police detective get married, and she can relax and just "live like a mother". This does jar very much with the modern reader, especially if one knows anything about Blyton's own life; she certainly put her writing career ahead of both husband and children.

Unmarried women

In addition to wives and widows, there are also spinsters, usually aunts or great-aunts. Some of these are notably independent and interesting. I have already referred to Great Aunt Merrill in *Chudleigh Hold*, who is in her seventies, and is unmarried because her bridegroom was killed in a fall from a horse on their wedding day. She creates a sensation in the family by smoking, suggests her companion, a very prim little spinster, should wear trousers instead of her long skirts, sleeps with a loaded revolver under her pillow and presents her elder nieces with one apiece. Some of this is perhaps posturing, much as a teenager might drink or take drugs to impress friends, but she is also genuinely enterprising. She comes to stay at the Hold with a great deal of furniture and rides down in the furniture van to keep an eye on it. When some of the girls fall into a pit on the moor walking home one evening, she joins the rescue party, and although she is not actually one of those hauling on the rope which pulls them up, her maid Morse is, while Great Aunt is "capering up and down the line like a madwoman, cheering and shouting: 'Go to it! *He-eave!* Put your back into it, Morse! Good heavens, woman, with your bulk you ought to be able to haul the Taj Mahal over!'" (186-7). And of course, as already described, she insists on joining Hawk and Crumpet in venturing down the secret tunnel at night after the criminals. Less eccentric but equally feisty, in *Top Secret* there is Aunt Freda, in her eighties, who is really the only female character. She came to New Zealand as a teenager and started a fruit farm which is now hugely successful and the family business: "she made good on her own while our other two great-aunts only got married" (89), says one of the young men of the family. She also demonstrates remarkable courage, to be discussed in chapter seven.

Not all great-aunts are loved as well as respected: the Amazons' "G.A." is a terror in the land. However, loved or hated, these elderly women are likely to be seen more as figures of interest than role models by young readers. Blyton has no-one as flamboyant as Great Aunt Merrill or the G.A., but Miss Pepper in the *R Mysteries*, who is Mrs Lynton's former governess, is a crisp, strong-minded spinster who is intellectual rather than good at cooking and in *The Ragamuffin Mystery* beats Diana in a swimming race, but she is also elderly though not decrepit.

There are however some younger spinsters who do offer a genuine alternative to marriage as a career. The Locketts have both a writer aunt who is the "editor" of their books, and an artist Aunt Lavinia, with whom they spend some holidays, and who is forgetful and casual and lets them do as they please. She lives by herself and pretty much does as she likes. And of course there are Captain Johns' Worrals and Frecks. In the wartime books Worrals has a boyfriend, Bill Ashton, who generally turns up to pick the women up at the end of an adventure. He is not just a glorified taxi-driver, as this involves flying a plane into enemy territory, but nonetheless it is a subsidiary role. After the war he appears in only one book, *Worrals in the Wilds*, in which he proposes marriage and asks Worrals to go out with him to Africa, where he is joining his uncle, a gold prospector. She refuses and he goes without her, disappears, and she and Frecks buy a plane and go to look for him; after various adventures including a lion hunt, an arrest and a brush with a murderous witch doctor, they rescue Bill and help out his uncle at the same time. The book ends with the women promising to come back on a visit once the gold mine is up and running, but later books do not refer to Bill at all, and in *Worrals Down Under* she and Frecks are flying round the world looking for possible business opportunities. Had Worrals married Bill, the books could still conceivably have continued, with him playing much the same role as ever, but Johns evidently decided against this. Worrals gets perhaps more stridently anti-male in the later books, but the male characters respect her and admit she is right, whereas in real life they would probably have been more antagonistic, or else sneered at her.

The other young woman of note is Ransome's Missee Lee, already described. She is not only an intellectual who wanted to be a teacher, she is also a very good sailor; when the children are escaping from her island the alarm is given and they have to sail through a narrow channel to have any chance of beating the pursuit, but it is very dangerous. Missee Lee, who is by now on their side, takes the helm and gets them safely through. It is hard to know what to make of her: she is very intelligent but the children don't enjoy the lessons she makes them take; she is an excellent sailor but does not now sail out committing acts of piracy, having men to do that for her while she is essentially a ruler; she has power but it is not what she wanted out of life; she gave up her career to be a dutiful daughter, and this is seen as the right thing to do but it does not make her happy. In short, she is not a simple model, positive or negative, but more an exploration of the real dilemmas facing an educated woman. Filial piety is of course a major element in Confucianism, which may seem to have no relevance to Western readers, but giving up one's own career to look after a parent was certainly a familiar tale to females. Brent-Dyer has one of her two great heroines in the *Chalet School* series, Mary-Lou, who goes to university and plans to be an archaeologist, saying she will give up her career to be with her mother now her stepfather has died and her mother is alone, two decades after *Missee Lee* was published.

Men to the rescue?

If it is a wife's job to keep house, it is a husband's not only to put food on the table but also to protect his family. Many of the adult males in these books, fathers and also uncles and friends, exemplify this, but there are others who buck the stereotype. Mr Morton in the *Lone Pine* series more than once turns up to rescue the children once he has realised they are in danger, as for example in *The Gay Dolphin Adventure* when they are caught by a tidal surge. Alf Ingles, Tom's uncle, with his big voice, is large and reassuring, and joins search parties and rescue parties when any of the children are lost. Even a less obviously virile character such as Harriet Sparrow's precise little grandfather comes charging to the rescue when the twins are caught spying on recurring villain Slinky Grandon (*Lone Pine London*). Some of Blyton's farmers turn up in the showdown with the villains, as in *Five Get into a Fix*, when Morgan Jones, another character with a huge voice and in this case a pack of large dogs, sees off the bad guys by calling his seven dogs down to where he and the children are being held prisoner.

Blyton's police officers are always burly and convey a sense of security. Her archetypal uncle figure is Bill Cunningham, the police detective whose cases the children always end up solving in the *Adventure* series, and who in the end marries Philip and Dinah's mother. However, although he is another burly, cheerful character whom the children like and trust, in practice it is they who rescue him rather than vice versa. In *The Sea of Adventure* he is captured by gun-runners and the children save him, literally under fire, while in *The Circus of Adventure* he and his wife are lured out of the house and held prisoner so that the little prince, known as Gussy, can be kidnapped; it is Jack, out looking for owls and therefore not with the others in the house, who manages to stow away in the car boot and later save the day. Blyton manages to give Bill the desired characteristics by what the children say, at the same time as giving the latter the starring roles, which actually leaves Bill looking somewhat ineffectual to an objective eye.

Bill is not the only man who gets this sort of treatment. In Courtney's *Well Done, Denehurst!* the four children are supposed to be helping Elaine and Moira's Intelligence Officer cousin Deryk keep watch on three men, one of whom is a spy, but before too long he has been rendered hors de combat by someone dropping a large stone on him from a great height, and the children first get him to hospital and then take over the investigation. Captain Flint in the Ransome books is supposedly in charge of the children, but in *Peter Duck* he goes looking for them and nearly gets captured by Black Jake, having to be rescued by John and Nancy as already recounted in chapter three, and in *Missee Lee* only the children's importunities to her save him from execution. This is made poignant because the children several times express the expectation that he will save the day. "Captain Flint'll know what to do", as Titty says (112).

Not all of Saville's fathers fit the protective model either. Peter's (Petronella's) father looks after a reservoir in rural Shropshire, which in the first book is a useful plot device as the adventure is about sabotage of

Britain's water supply, but in later books it is stated he has been given this job as a sinecure in retirement, and he is referred to as an old man, more like a grandfather than a father of a teenager. From the beginning he is a little unusual in that he is very precise and tidy, and cannot bear mess; while he likes the Mortons, he is always on edge when they visit in case they make a mess, and only relaxes when the washing up is done and everything tidied away. In *Strangers at Witchend* (1970), one of the last books, he is disturbed at the description of one of the "strangers", and the children, recognising this though not understanding why, conspire to protect him by not telling him things. It turns out that a few years before, the man Jones had been fleeing the scene of a robbery and Mr Sterling had tried to stop him and been knocked down and hurt, and had had to give evidence at the trial. He had found the whole experience deeply upsetting and kept it secret until now. David says "none of us likes the idea of Mr Sterling staying here alone until this business has sorted itself out" (112). Not only the children but also Alf and Betty Ingles act protectively towards him. He is a gentle, shy, unworldly man who has to be sheltered from life's harsher realities; in earlier books Peter has trusted and obeyed him even when he wanted her to do something she was not happy about, but here the pair seem to have the reverse of a traditional father-daughter relationship.

In a somewhat similar vein, in *Worrals Goes East* she rescues an archaeologist who has been held prisoner for three years in a cave with his two adult daughters; Worrals gives the guns she has captured to the two young women, and when they take up a defensive position he just sits there while they defend him. This is presented without comment.

In *Sea Witch Comes Home* the Mortons go to stay with Paul and Rose Channing, whose father is mysteriously absent. Mr Channing is a charming, reckless character who is less than a perfect father; not only does he leave his motherless children alone (Paul is seventeen, Rose twelve) while he goes off on little trips, he has foolishly trusted someone he should not have and carried stolen paintings out of the country in his boat, *Sea Witch*. Paul suspects he may have got involved in something shady although Rose is fiercely loyal; in the end he resolves to be more careful in future, but although he does prove honest he is not exactly reliable, and one is not sure how long this resolve will last.

M.E. Atkinson's Locketts meet a number of solid and trustworthy adults but also some who are less so. There is Anna and Robin's landlady in the Scilly Isles, who when Anna gets ill hides her away for fear of scarlet fever, which her own son has and which she has not reported as she needs the money from her lodgers. Robin, only seven, is left mystified and afraid and finally telegraphs the Locketts who come to help. In *Mystery Manor* there is Mr Hugh, the sole remaining member of the family which used to own the manor, now living nearby in a small cottage, and a very odd character. He has a tendency to groan aloud when writing his memoirs, and is generally very emotional and possibly a little weak in the head. He is so obsessed with the manor that he breaks in at night to write his memoirs in situ, so to speak, giving rise to suspicions that the place is haunted. The local grocer, who used to be his family's butler, helps him because he feels sorry for him, and the children begin by imagining him a villain and end by also feeling pity.

Although the parent-child relationships in most of these books are quite modern in terms of when the books were published, with the children being given freedom to develop and meeting friendship and sympathy more than rules and discipline, and certainly not corporal punishment, the husband-wife relationships are much more traditional. Most of the wives live purely domestic lives. There are a number of eccentric spinsters but these are largely elderly; however, some younger women do offer alternative models as independent and self-supporting, although the jobs they have are usually ones which would have been acceptable for "ladies" a generation earlier, namely writer, artist or teacher. Fathers and uncles are usually big, strong, reliable and protective, but there are some exceptions, even sometimes with the father of a central character like Peter Sterling.

CHAPTER SIX

BORN LEADERS AND BENEVOLENT TYRANTS
LEADERSHIP, AUTHORITY AND POWER

Reynolds has suggested that power is more important than biological sex: "ultimately gender is a system based on unequal power relations associated with the relations between men and women but not exclusive to them" (Reynolds 2002, 100). Most societies are and have been controlled by men; throughout history female rulers have been worthy of remark simply by being female, and female war leaders have been more legendary than factual (e.g. the Amazons). Elizabeth I's famous speech on the eve of the Armada "Though I have the body of a weak and feeble woman, I have the heart and stomach of a king, and a king of England too", indicates how this political power derives ultimately from the simple fact of greater physical strength in the days when Might was Right and the king was the greatest warrior. This assumption that a greater ability to kill others with primitive weapons somehow confers the right to power in all areas of life, and that because the one is natural, the other must be also, and therefore cannot be contested, is at the root of millennia of male domination of the female.

This domination of course involves the spiritual as well as the temporal, and the individual as well as the collective. Since men have the power, they must be more intelligent and spiritually advanced, mustn't they? Therefore spiritual authority has also largely rested with the male sex; the Church of England was still debating whether to permit women to become bishops in the twenty-first century and the Roman church is still a complete patriarchy. Although in earlier days some abbesses such as Hilda of Whitby ruled over both monks and nuns, this was soon quashed, and nuns owed obedience to priests. In much the same way, wives owed it to husbands: their property became their husband's, if they worked their wages belonged to him, and he had rights over their bodies. As mentioned in chapter two, it was not until 1937 that marital rape became a possible grounds for divorce in the UK, and not until 1993 that a *Declaration* by the UN High Commissioner for Human Rights made consent to marital sex a basic human right, although that is still not incorporated into law in all UN countries.

Given these deeply-rooted inequalities in society, it would not be surprising to see power largely in male hands in any twentieth-century literature. If it merely reflected the status quo, this is what we would expect, but one function of literature is to point the way to possibilities and thereby question the status quo. This chapter will look at representations of leadership and authority in the books, and examine the power relationships between boys and girls, and between women and men. Clearly power also enters into the child-adult relationships, but that is outside the focus of this study.

Captains and First Mates

When fictional teams or groups have adventures, there is usually a leader. I am distinguishing this from a random group of people who happen to be involved in an adventure, as for instance in the typical disaster movie or book. Sometimes in this case one person does develop into a leader; an example would be John Christopher's *Death of Grass*, where one ordinary twentieth-century man, through his role as husband and father, takes on the role of protector, then primitive war leader of a small group including his family, as the total social disruption caused by the death of all cereal crops drives people to defend food stores and territory, and each little group has to fight to survive. In many adventure stories, whether book or film, the protagonists are not random; a small team sets out on some venture, and in this case, there is usually a leader, and this leader is almost invariably male. An interesting example is the *Star Trek* TV series: in the first, the Captain was a white male and the women were a glorified telephone operator and a nurse; in the second, the Chief Medical Officer was female but the Captain and First and Second Officers were still white men; in the third (*Deep Space Nine*) the Captain was a black man, and a woman had made it to First Officer; only in the fourth set, *Voyager*, was there finally a female Captain and Chief Engineer. This would suggest racial inequalities were more pressing than gender ones to many Americans, and this may be reasonable in light of America's history. However, *Voyager* aired in the 1990s and still stands out as a great rarity: shows with female commanders, like books with female commanders, are less likely to sell. It is still the case that a female leader is seen by many as a ball-breaker, a threat.

Ransome very specifically has naval ranks among his Swallows and Amazons, and they follow orders as if these ranks were real. Thus John

Walker is the captain, Susan the mate, Titty an able-seaman and Roger the ship's boy, (promoted in later books to able-seaman). The *Amazon* has a crew of two, Nancy the captain and Peggy the mate. This means that when the two crews work together there is room for individual personality: "'Belay that,' growled Captain Nancy. Captain John was really commodore, but in some things Captain Nancy could not help taking the lead" (*Swallows and Amazons,* 302). Nancy is a vital, dominating character who never gives up and who is always full of ideas. In *Great Northern?* we are told that "Nancy's plans always did work" (232): the others quickly come to rely on her to come up with a plan when one is needed, and she naturally then gives the orders. When she and John are being decoys a few pages later, she is telling him what to do. Sometimes it is explicit between them: when they meet Missee Lee, Nancy says "Look here, John. She's a she-pirate. Let me do the talking" (166), and he agrees.

Saville's Lone Pine Club has rules and an official captain, David Morton (Peter his girlfriend is the vice-captain and cook). However, in practice mostly it runs as a democracy. In the original lineup, David was the eldest, but Jon Warrender, who first appears in the third book, is actually older and has a mind of his own, the girls go off and do things when the mood takes them, and the young twins in particular frequently do exactly as they choose. David is portrayed as steady and sensible rather than dynamic and dominating. There are occasions when "David made his decision" (*Lone Pine Five*, 120), when he is recognised as "boss", or when in a moment of crisis he is the one who shouts what to do and the others obey, but there are many more situations when there is a group discussion and consensus. David has no authority over the other teenagers except what they give him, but he is expected by his parents to look after his twin siblings, who are six years his junior, and as I have remarked, the twins often go off by themselves, sometimes against his explicit orders. Saville seems to have kept changing his mind as to which of the twins was dominant, as each is described as the leader at one point or another, and often they simply act in concert by a kind of telepathy, but on balance it is Mary who is the stronger character; for instance, in *Seven White Gates* we read that "This was one of the times when Dickie accepted her leadership without question" (124).

Some of the other groups, while not pretending to be a military organisation or a club with rules, nonetheless have an explicitly acknowledged leader. With the Locketts it is Oliver, although Jane is the eldest: "[t]he Locketts are noted for sticking together, and Oliver for taking the part of leader in all their main activities" (*Widgeon Weir*, 180). Oliver thinks things out beforehand, while Jane is the one who thinks quickly in an emergency, so her intelligence is recognised. In the rival family, Fenella dominates over her brothers by force of personality, and indeed in *Going Gangster*, which does not feature Oliver, Jane is given a stronger role: "[h]itherto there had been little love lost between herself and Fenella. Both were born leaders. Both wanted to lead. Up in the Border country the two wills had clashed" (20). This somewhat contradicts the statement above about Oliver.

Most of Courtney's books do not feature a hierarchy, indeed often one of the younger characters is the strongest and very much goes her own way (this is generally a girl), but in *The Grenville Garrison* Edward, the oldest, is acknowledged leader. Perhaps this is because of the semi-military nature of the situation, with the family besieged on an island by armed villains intent on kidnapping the prince. In Brent-Dyer's *Fardingales*, it is Anstace who is determined to investigate the villains, to "find out what their game is—put a stop to it" (63) and Humphrey agrees to join her on condition he is made "captain". Anstace accepts this, but insists that this does not mean the girls won't share the adventure: "No hogging it all to yourself just because we're girls!" (64), to which he agrees. His captaincy seems to be a sort of nod to the conventions, and in practice they do share the adventure; because he is injured she looks after him when they are captured, and they are rescued by a third party, the fisher boy Tom.

The groups of children in Blyton's books do mostly have a leader of sorts, but not necessarily labelled as "captain", and not always with authority unquestioned by the others. Normally it is the oldest boy: Julian in the *Famous Five*, Barney in the *R Mysteries*, Jack in the *Secret* series (and these latter two are interesting because Barney and Jack are the working-class additions to a middle-class family group), though in the *Adventure* series Jack and Philip take equal responsibility over the girls. Sometimes this authority is wielded quite explicitly and heavily. For instance, in *Five Have Plenty of Fun*, Julian says to Berta "You haven't any brothers to keep you in your place ... Well from now on, while you're here, Dick and I are your brothers, and you've got to toe the line, just like Anne, see?" (57). It is hard to imagine any real girl in 1955 swallowing that without a protest.

As already commented, in each of Blyton's series the eldest is a boy, giving these characters a double advantage of age and gender. Barney the fairground worker and (*Secret*) Jack the farm boy also have skills which the other children lack, and a greater knowledge of the world. In *The Secret of Spiggy Holes* Nora is ashamed of doing something silly and declares herself happy to accept Jack as captain and will always do what he says. I have already referred to Barney "not letting" Diana come on a midnight adventure in *The Ring O'Bells Mystery*, and in a later book, *The Rat-A-Tat Mystery*, Roger the next oldest is joined with him in authority, when the children are going to stay in Rat-A-Tat House with only a housekeeper, which slightly worries the adults. Snubby points out that Barney is very sensible, and Mrs Lynton, mother of Roger and Diana, says: "I hope Roger will see to that, as well. He's quite old enough to take charge, with Barney" (21). Similarly, Julian is given authority both by his peers: "They all looked at Julian. He nodded" (*Five Have a Mystery to Solve*, 93); "Julian always sounded so very grown-up when he gave them a plan of campaign. [Anne] felt very proud of him" (*ibid* 142); and by the adults: "I'd bank on Julian any time to keep the others in order and see they were all safe and sound", says Uncle Quentin in *Five Get Into Trouble* (12). Nonetheless there are occasions when Snubby, the youngest in the *R Mysteries*, goes off and does things on his own in defiance of the others, just as George does in the *Famous Five* books.

It seems that there is usually some sort of hierarchy, which may be explicit, and the leader is usually male but also the eldest. Skills are also relevant: Barney and Jack have skills such as climbing ability and knowledge of how to build a campfire which give them authority; and personality also enters into it: Nancy Blackett's age and nautical skills make her captain of the *Amazon*, but she is more dominant than John Walker of the *Swallow* because of her vivid personality. Captain Johns also combines the factors of age and personality, where gender is not applicable. Biggles and Worrals are unquestionably the leaders of their respective teams, and each is slightly older than his or her lieutenant, Algy and Frecks, but also a stronger personality. Both Algy and Frecks are portrayed as rather light-hearted, often making jokes, and willing to follow, though each is quite capable of initiative when the leader is captured or otherwise unavailable.

Initially, Biggles and Worrals have military rank which gives them authority, but their dominance continues after the war (the First for the men, the Second for the women) when they are no longer in the forces. Biggles then acquires a teenage protégé, Ginger, through whose eyes the reader sees much of the action, so that age (and experience) continues to be a factor when the difference between Biggles and Algy has been lessened by time (the difference between seventeen and eighteen is much greater than between, say, thirty and thirty-one), but the force of Biggles' personality is frequently brought to our attention. In *Biggles Goes to War*, when he meets the princess "His intense personality was drawing her secrets from her" (44), and in the Second War he is given a squadron of difficult characters, with "a disinclination to submit to discipline ... Nevertheless, by example, by the force of his own personality, and by a queer sort of discipline which appeared to be lax, but was, in fact, rigid, Biggles had moulded them into a team ..." (*Biggles in the Orient*, 11).

The situation with Worrals is a little more complex. She not only leads her team of two, herself and Frecks, she also gives orders to various men in the course of the books. During the war she commands characters such as the various men she meets in France in *Worrals Carries On* (soldiers who had missed the boats at Dunkirk), and Corporal Timms, who had been shot down and stranded on a Pacific island and whom she rescues and makes part of her team (*Worrals of the Islands*; she was an officer and as such outranked him, but I am not sure if in practice WAAF officers normally gave orders to RAF men, particularly since in reality WAAFs did not fly; it was the ATA who ferried planes, but Johns presumably realised there was more scope for adventure in the air). She also gives orders to the French resistance fighters, Lucien and Raoul; in their first adventure together there is a certain amount of discussion, although Worrals is the one to come up with the plans, but by the next book she is definitely in charge. After the war she gives orders to both villains and male civilians on occasion. In *Worrals in the Wasteland* she goes to the wilds of Canada to pick up a female Nazi war criminal who is believed to be hiding out there; one of the Germans has been left for dead by this woman, and Worrals looks after him but also makes him obey her, and when she meets some elderly trappers they address her as "miss" and "ma'am" and although she phrases her ideas as suggestions rather than orders, they quickly agree to her plans. In *Worrals Goes Afoot*, when she is sent to Egypt to find some gun-runners who are making trouble, there is a British secret agent who has been assigned to help her to whom she says things like "I shall need two vehicles", assuming he will dutifully provide them, and also a retired Askari sergeant and his son who agree to work for her.

Worrals' authority is essentially the same as that of Biggles, a combination of personality and rank, set within a hierarchical system which is masculine in nature, whatever the gender of the individual characters. Missee Lee, a "Twenty-two gong Taicoon" takes precedence over the Taicoons of Tiger and Turtle Islands, who only merit ten gongs apiece, although her power is shown to be precarious when she breaks her father's rule of keeping no English prisoners. A ruler's authority is also found with the princesses in *Biggles*, although in *Biggles Goes to War* this is threatened with a coup, possibly because a young woman is seen as easier to overthrow than a man capable of military action. Agnes Morvyn in Courtney's *Mermaid House* has authority over the local people because her family are the traditional squires of the area, even though she herself is only a schoolgirl. And while Worrals may give orders to lower ranks, she also has to accept them from her senior officers, even if she does not always respect them.

Maternal authority

The strand of feminism which focuses on gender equality might delight in having female characters with power and authority, but this does not take us away from traditional power hierarchies, it merely substitutes some of the actors. An alternative is to celebrate female attributes. There is an interesting result of assigning the domestic activities to Susan Walker in Ransome's books, in that she becomes invested with a kind of maternal authority. She controls the bedtime of her younger brother and sister, for example, and this is confirmed by the adults. In *Missee Lee*, for instance, Captain Flint says Titty and Roger can stay up till the first yawn: "That all right, Susan?" (19), and in *Secret Water*, little Bridget's permission to go with her elder siblings depends on Susan: "'Ask Susan if she'll have you,' said Daddy" (24). Bridget takes Susan's authority very seriously, and when she, Titty and Roger are trapped on the mudflats by the rising tide, and Titty proposes to swim Bridget ashore (she cannot swim alone), the child asks "Would Susan let me?" (308). In theory, John is the captain, but Susan is the arbiter of certain things.

However, this is not merely confined to bedtime and looking after small children. In *Peter Duck* there is the question whether they should go after the treasure and try to reach it before Black Jake, and "it was Susan who, in the end, gave the deciding vote", and in *Missee Lee*, when the boom has been lowered across the river and they realise their only escape route lies through a very dangerous gorge, Captain Flint asks Susan for the go ahead, and everyone else waits for her answer. No explanation is offered as to why her opinion is decisive. One thing which is stressed in several of the books is her skill with building a fire and keeping it going, which obviously goes with the cooking, but is perhaps more than that. Control of fire touches the primeval; is there an element of the earth mother in the otherwise prosaic Susan?

Other feminine girls are imbued with a similar maternal authority, if less powerfully. Anne in the *Famous Five* starts off as a "little girl", small and weak, explicitly less able and less knowledgeable than her brothers. As time goes by she takes on the role of cook and stores-manager whenever they are camping, and although sometimes she is taken for granted: "Come on, Anne - get us some food, there's a dear" (*Five Have Plenty of Fun*, 127), it is also an area where she has control, and she loves it. "Put the heather outside the cave, please George ... I'll make the beds inside when I'm ready" (*Five Run Away Together*, 109); "She decided that the room above, under the thatch, should be for the three boys" (*Five Have a Mystery to Solve*, 40). Peggy in *The Secret Island* does the cooking and mending, takes charge of the boys' wet clothes and sends her younger sister Nora off on errands. Mostly she herself takes orders from Jack; the children are living rough on the island and he is the one with the knowledge of the countryside which enables them to survive. When he twists his ankle, however, she binds it up and tells him "You mustn't use it for a while", and when he is going to the mainland for stores, he asks her "Peggy, could you let me have some food to take with me?"

The powers that be

In all the books, the adult authority figures are usually male. There is Air Commodore Raymond in both the *Biggles* and *Worrals* series, who gives them many of their missions, and in the wartime *Worrals* books the irascible Squadron Leader McNavish who has charge of the airfield where she is based. Blyton generally has a group of "burly" policemen who arrive when the villains need rounding up. Saville has Marston Baines, of course, and Baines' boss in England is also male, likewise various colleagues and contacts, such as the chief of police at Marseille on whom he calls for help in *The Purple Valley*. The Lone Piners require police help in many of their adventures, and not only are the senior officers all male, but the odd WPC is really there just to be sympathetic. This does reflect the social reality of the 1950s and '60s; it would have been improbable had Saville introduced a female Chief Inspector, say, but an ambitious detective sergeant would certainly have been possible.

Courtney's *Wild Lorings* books and the first *Denehurst* one are all set in girls' boarding schools, so the authorities are naturally the female staff. The headmistress in *The Denehurst Secret Service,* typically of headmistresses in fiction, has "keen eyes" and is graceful and dignified, but plays very little part in the book; it is Elaine's house-mistress, Miss Lockwood, who is more involved in day-to-day discipline, and who is young and attractive as well as strong-willed and sensible, and therefore has little trouble managing the girls. This is all part of the tradition of the girls' school story. However, Elaine and Moira's cousin Deryk is in the offing, with a whole campful of British soldiers, and it is they who come in and take over when the girls have identified the spy. Similarly in *The*

Grenville Garrison the children are eventually saved by an official force of men sent to deal with the armed villains.

Mr Loring arrives towards the end of *The Wild Lorings at School* more to explain a mystery than to take charge, though he does try to do that, but then he is a rather unconventional father with a very relaxed attitude to parental discipline. Other fathers in Courtney's books are perhaps more traditional. In *The Denehurst Secret Service* it is specifically the girls' father who gives permission for them to be involved in Deryk's mission, not both parents. In *The Chiltons*, one of her family books, the vicar's wife runs things on a daily basis, but when "something really big crops up" she "relies completely" on her husband (62); this is compared to her two eldest children, Kit and Fiona, where similarly Fiona is constantly referred to as a managing type, but in a crisis she would rely on the more relaxed Kit. *Swallows and Amazons* begins with a telegram from the absent Commander Walker, who although abroad with his ship, has to be consulted as to whether the children may camp unsupervised on an island in the lake. His wife, left in England in charge of their five children, is apparently not to be trusted to make that decision herself.

I have already mentioned (chapter three) how the two fathers in Brent-Dyer's *Fardingales* send their wives to make a meal while they go looking for their missing children, and in *Condor Crags Adventure* take it upon themselves to keep Humphrey's danger from the women. Here the men are not merely the final arbiters for the children, but treat their wives in a sense as children also. This comes out very clearly in her girls' books, where decisions of importance, such as taking a girl from one school or sending her to another because of her bad behaviour, tend to be made by her father or guardian with little or no consultation, and where husbands, even those who are portrayed as having a loving and teasing relationship with a strong-willed wife, nonetheless give her orders on occasion. Sometimes this comes in the guise of doctor's orders, as with Jack and Joey Maynard in the *Chalet School* series, where he seems to give her a sleeping draught and send her to bed after every adventure, but even Julian Lucy, who is a lawyer not a doctor, "ordained that [his wife] should go to bed early that night" (*Janie of La Rochelle*, 143). In Courtney's *Long Barrow*, a family adventure, the mother is a widow (another widow who struggles to work, this time as a teacher) who finally admits she cannot manage and turns to her brother, who takes charge of her and gives her and her four children a home. From then on, major decisions are for him to make, and in particular he takes on the job of disciplining her lazy son.

Strong women, good and bad

Men have the power to give or withhold permission because they are men. Yet women may also have power thanks to their personalities. I have already discussed Fenella in the *Lockett* books and Nancy in Ransome. In *The Wild Lorings at School* there is a female villain, who disguises herself as a new Sixth former to gain access to the building but is in fact a grown woman, the widow of the crook who stole the Loring family treasures and hid them in the house. She is working with her brother, and "[a]pparently the war left him frightfully highly strung, and he's always been deadly scared about the whole business—Pamela was the master mind behind it" (223). Rather more humorous is Dolly, a local woman in the village in *Mermaid House*, whose brother Joe is afraid of her, perhaps with reason as she at one point hides his clothes to prevent him leaving the house. Dolly used to be Agnes' nanny, and there is a good tradition of fearsome nannies, presumably a genuine phenomenon in middle-class lives in the early twentieth century. The archetype is probably Nanny in *Chudleigh Hold*. She is the same age as Great Aunt Merrill and has been nanny to two generations, but she still rules the household with a kind of benevolent tyranny. The eldest children are of age, yet they feel they must consult her about everything, such as whether or not to invite an unknown cousin to stay.

This Nanny although technically a servant is really an example of the older spinsters described in the previous chapter, as is Edith in *Fardingales*, "the household tyrant, and beloved Nanny for all of them" (138). They all tend to be strong personalities whom others respect and obey. Great Aunt Merrill demands that the family gather in her room of an evening, and they all dutifully do so; it never occurs to them to say they have other things to do. However, they are all very fond of her, and the reader is won to sympathy by the tale of her tragic love affair, melodramatic though it may sound today. The Great Aunt in *Swallowdale* and *The Picts and the Martyrs* is not at all loved, but she constrains everyone to obey her, including "Captain Flint", her nephew, and a variety of local men including a colonel and a sergeant of police. When she stays with her niece, the Amazons' mother, she insists that the girls behave as children had been expected to in her day, and is horrified at the freedom they are normally allowed. When they come in late for meals, as they naturally do from time to time since their timekeeping partly depends on the wind as they sail home down the lake, she forbids them to go out at all the next day, and when their mother leaves them alone one holiday because her doctor has ordered her to go on a cruise for her health, "the G.A." invites herself to the house to look after Nancy and Peggy and has them doing ladylike activities, playing the piano and learning poetry and, most improbably, mowing the lawn in white frocks. The girls accept her orders because they know she will make their mother miserable if they do not, but Captain Flint also obeys her and shuts up the houseboat where he normally lives and goes to stay with his sister for the duration of the G.A.'s visit (*Swallowdale*). When she disappears overnight in *The Picts and the Martyrs*, and Nancy calls the police and has the local firefighters searching the land around the lake, the G.A. is furious at all the fuss and speaks scathingly to the men, who admire her for her spirit and go away with their tails metaphorically between their legs.

There is a similar Great Aunt in *Mermaid House*, whom the children go to stay with, over seventy and "quite as dragon-like as her name [Miss Pendragon] suggested, with firm features, piercing dark eyes, and a deep, masculine voice" (16). She had previously cast off the children's mother for not marrying a Cornishman, and generally expects instant obedience from everyone. Enid Blyton has Old Ma in *The Rilloby Fair Mystery*, who is the only person the villain is afraid of; by her sobriquet not a spinster, yet she is also an old woman with a powerful personality, an echo of the witches of medieval times. Saville has a number of powerful women to be considered below, but occasionally they are neither good nor evil: in *The Purple Valley* there is Mme Chastel, wife of the hotel-keeper, who does not really play much of a role in the narrative, yet Charles remarks "I'm terrified of that woman" (p83).

The Amazons' "G.A." is unlovable, strict, a proponent of an outmoded way of bringing up children, but she is not evil and the reader is even made to feel a sneaking admiration for her at the end. There are other women in the books in this study who are criminals, and in some cases outright evil. Lamb and Brown (2006) have a section in their chapter on movies and television entitled "Powerful Disney women are evil and ugly" (69). They cite examples such as Cruella DeVille in *101 Dalmatians* and the Queen of Hearts in *Alice* as well as the standard fairytale wicked stepmothers and queens. The White Witch in the Narnia books would be another example, though she is evil and beautiful rather than ugly. In real life, powerful women have often been demonised; Elizabeth I was a great queen to the English but an evil heretic to the Spanish, and the still-persistent tale of Catherine the Great and the horses was a way of diminishing a ruler of considerable talent in the eyes of the world. Lamb and Brown suggest that "[g]irls and boys alike are led to believe that girls who want power must also want to control them" (ibid, 79). Powerful females who are also corrupt and destructive may reinforce traditional gender stereotypes rather than challenge them.

Some of the characters in this study fall into this category. In the *Marston Baines* adventure *Power of Three,* the "Three" are a trio of master criminals, one of whom is a woman, "The Signora", of whom he writes "If it were possible to classify evil, this woman would be at the top of the list" (68). She is described as handsome, but she does have a suspicion of a moustache and a deep voice, and she dabbles in black magic as well as ordinary crime. "She had resource, patience, an implacable will and a fanatical hatred for ordinary decency and ordinary people" (196). Although this all sounds negative, the reader may be intended to find her ruthlessness in some sense admirable; there is a tradition in adventure stories that a strong ruthless villain is more worthy of respect than a merely conniving one. In the first *Baines* adventure Rosina identifies Signora Salvatore, the wife of the sinister doctor, as actually the mastermind in the plot, and she escapes at the end; my inference is that this is the same woman. In that book, there is no question of admiring her: Rosina says "now I feel dirty because I've been in the same house with her. I didn't know people were so wicked and there was so much hate" (218).

Other writers have female Nazis, who naturally lend themselves to being portrayed as evil. In *Worrals in the Wastelands* one Anna Shultz, "The She-Devil of the Stenberg Internment Camp", is believed to be hiding out in northern Canada, and Air Commodore Raymond dare not send a man after her because she is golden-haired, blue-eyed and very alluring. Worrals is happy to go because "[a] lump comes into my throat and nearly chokes me every time I think of those poor helpless victims she tortured to death" (11). Shultz is not in fact merely hiding, she has a boyfriend who discovered gold in Canada before the war and they are out to take as much as they can before moving on; the young man is besotted and has no idea she is already married and would have killed him once he had revealed the location of the gold if it were not that he had the means to fly her out. Shultz is a different archetype: not evil and ugly, but evil and beautiful, like the Snow Queen. For centuries Western philosophers from the Greeks to the Christian Fathers demonised female sexuality; fear of a woman whose beauty gives her power turns such women into monsters.

In *Well Done, Denehurst!* the children eventually identify the vicar (actually an impostor, the vicar's half-German half-brother) as the spy among their three suspects; he is aided by his housekeeper "Miss Trent", a verbose and silly woman they have completely discounted, who turns out to be a very clever actress whose real name is Minna and who is at one point described as a "tigress" (182). When she is first revealed as an enemy, "a grim light shone in the pale blue eyes that before had been so expressionless" (144). She, however, is not irredeemably evil. She advises the vicar to accept Avice's parole, and in the end the children are not to be killed but taken as prisoners to German territory in a submarine. This rather less black-and-white approach is also found in *The Wild Lorings at School*, where the female criminal, Pamela, knocks out one of the juniors, prompting the head girl to exclaim "She must be a fiend!" (222), but in fact she has no interest in hurting people, she simply wants to get the loot and make her own escape.

Just as Saville's *Lone Pine* girls have more agency than the young women in his Young Adults books, especially Rosina, his female criminals in the younger series are also less caricatures of evil and more like real people. The chief of these is Miss Ballinger, who appears in several books (having sometimes served time in prison since we last saw her, although the Lone Piners have hardly aged), and whom he made a point of including in the final book of the series. She is fat and "waddles", and extremely short-sighted so she often fails to recognise their faces even though she is wearing glasses, but in *The Gay Dolphin Adventure* when Jon and Penny first meet her on the train to Rye, she is charming and friendly and they trust her enough to read out portions of a letter which unfortunately tells her they have a clue to some treasure she is seeking. She later locks up Penny and the twins in her bungalow at Winchelsea just as the sea is about to break its floodbanks, having failed to browbeat them into telling her anything useful. Working for her is "Slinky" Grandon, and her niece Valerie, who is young and attractive and whom both Jon and David find disturbingly attractive. In *Lone Pine London* she is running a big gang of art forgers, but in *Treasure at Amory's* she seems diminished by prison, and in the final book the reader almost feels sorry for her; she and Val are involved in counterfeiting currency but she is no longer in control, being given orders by "Tom Seymour", who has a hold over her. When she hears the twins' voices in a market one day, she has such a shock that a kindly local woman is moved to look after her. At the end, when Peter has come to rescue David from the cottage where the counterfeiters are based, she finds that the men have fled but left "the Ballinger", sitting helpless without her glasses, which they have taken from her. Peter is moved to tears, and David thinks "Ballinger may be an old villain ... but she's going out with courage" (187).

In these books leaders are usually male (and usually the eldest), and their position is sometimes formalised by ranks or by being acknowledged captain. This is often reinforced by adult approval. However, gender may be overridden by rank (Missee Lee), or by a combination of personality and rank (Worrals, Nancy Blackett). Girls may also be imbued with authority by virtue of their domestic role (Susan Walker, Anne in the *Famous Five*). Among adults, power, especially the power to bring safety after danger, is normally vested in males, and the women who challenge that power are often elderly and unmarried (great aunts, nannies). Some women achieve or seek power for evil purposes, and they may be archetypal fairytale witch-figures, but sometimes are more natural criminals, with strengths and weaknesses and more interest in the loot than in power for its own sake.

CHAPTER SEVEN

STIFF UPPER LIPS AND CRY BABIES
COURAGE AND SENSITIVITY

Today we think of courage as a quality expected of males throughout the ages. Certainly many cultures have had (and some still do have) rites of passage for males which involve some kind of test of their courage as well perhaps as their physical prowess and / or endurance. Exactly what qualified a man as honourable has varied considerably, however. In the West, jousting and knight-errantry probably spring to mind as examples par excellence of the noble male, defending his own honour and that of the weak and helpless. In actual fact of course the knights of the twelfth and thirteenth centuries were more likely to abduct a woman than protect her out of mere disinterest; if they protected her, it was probably because she was an heiress and they wanted to take control of her lands. Richard the Lionheart on more than one occasion carried off a woman he fancied because her father or brother was unable to stop him. Yet when it came to fighting, it was by no means always "to the death"; the ransoming of prisoners taken in battle was quite normal, and the only people likely to be killed intentionally, at least, were those who were not worth much financially.

In any case, all this applies really to the aristocracy, a very small proportion of society. In Georgian times it was common for the nobility to fight duels of honour, and a gentleman would lose all credit in society if he refused a challenge, yet books for children at that time were emphasising prudence over courage, because they were aimed at the middle classes who did not subscribe to the same code. Gradually through the nineteenth century "pluck" came to be related to manliness, especially of course in adventure yarns such as those of Henty and Ballantyne. This was picked up by boys' school stories and when girls' school stories also became popular, they often applied the same standards, although the girls were not normally going into battle or expecting to do so, and pluck was more usually about standing up to difficulties and "playing the game" than boxing one's foes behind the fives' court. The First War naturally gave impetus to the importance of courage; if ordinary people had valued prudence above courage, the whole conflict would have been rather different. One impact of this very different kind of warfare, which saw numerous cases of shell shock (essentially what we would call post-traumatic stress disorder), was to make both males and females recognise that courage was not a simple virtue, and failure of nerve under fire did not necessarily mean one was a failure as a person. Nonetheless courage continued to be valued; medals are still given to civilians who save life at the risk of their own, even to animals who do so. Fiction continued to praise brave deeds even while recognising that overcoming fear is also a virtue.

Clearly in a primitive society where part of a man's role is to defend his family, clan or tribe, physical courage is important in a male. There is no very clear reason why it should continue to be so in a world where war is a matter for the state, the morality of war is anyway questioned by many, and laws protect the individual with reasonable effectiveness. A British young man today will only fight in a war if he chooses the armed services as a career, and is unlikely to have to fight on a personal level to defend himself or his home or family, again unless he opts for a certain lifestyle. The latter (personal defence) was also true in the 1930s to 1960s, but the Second War of course involved conscription, and after that came the Cold War, when many feared the country would be drawn into a further conflict. Therefore it is more understandable that books written in that period would emphasise the value of courage than recent works, though in fact many more recent works do continue to make the assumption that courage is praiseworthy and cowardice contemptible.

Male courage

In the adventure genre in particular, it is not surprising to find examples of physical courage. However, in few of the books I have studied was this completely unquestioned, even with regard to the male characters. Biggles constantly goes into dangerous situations, and there is a kind of understanding that after the war this is partly because he has become an adrenalin junkie, unable to settle to a normal job. Sometimes he is asked to undertake missions for the government, such as in *Biggles, Secret Agent*, when he has to ascertain whether an important scientist really has died abroad or has in fact defected or been abducted; often, however, he sets off out of pure love of adventure, as in *Biggles in the South Seas* when he is looking for pearls, or *The Cruise of the Condor* looking for the traditional lost city in South America. At no point do any of the heroes, Biggles, Algy, Ginger and later Bertie, falter or hesitate, let alone fail to act out of fear. However, they certainly experience dry lips and racing heart at moments of danger, or feel shaken after the event, as when Ginger escapes the Germans in a stolen car on a twisting mountain road (*Biggles "Fails to Return"*) and it goes over a cliff while he just manages to jump clear. Much more interesting is Henry Harcourt, a character in a First War story (later rewritten to fit the Second War in *Spitfire Parade*), who turns tail and flees when he first meets enemy fire. Naturally, in the end he finds courage and becomes a reliable member of the squadron. Johns must have known men who struggled to face fire in the war, but it is good that he chose to put one into his stories for boys. However, this is a small part of the whole Biggles oeuvre.

Brent-Dyer's male heroes very much fit the Henty tradition. In *Condor Crags Adventure*, Godfrey Chudleigh is held captive by a tribe of "Indians" in South America in an inaccessible mountain. He is threatened with being blinded and otherwise maimed if he does not organise the return of some jewels, originally belonging to this tribe, which had been taken to England by an ancestor of his. "Despite himself, the prisoner blenched slightly" at this threat (14), but he continues to shrug, speak calmly, and when he writes a letter to his brother manages to put in some "family code" and a clue to where he is. In *Top Secret* his brother Hawk, cast adrift in a lifeboat after a Japanese mine blows up his ship, keeps his cool and navigates to the best of his ability, also spending time looking after a teenage boy who was injured in the blast. Later when the villains have caught up with him, they bastinado him to find out where the secret papers are; in fact, he has no real means of stopping this as they do not believe the truth, namely that the papers are no longer on the island, but he does not explain how they left, as that would put the pilot who took them in danger, and he does not scream with the pain, but only gasps or keeps silent. His feet are so badly damaged that it takes him eight months to recover and be fit for work.

Some of the other authors allow their male heroes a little more weakness. David and Jon in the *Lone Pine* series may be afraid when caught by villains, though they try not to show it (as for example in *Lone Pine London*, where in fact they are sixteen and facing only one man, albeit a large one, so one might have expected them to fight and even win). Lone Piner Tom is afraid of heights, and when he and Jenny have to climb a watchtower in *Wings Over Witchend,* again, he tries desperately to hide this; later when they need to descend to help the others, she offers to go first, saying "I don't mind heights" (179), and Tom is amazed that she had realised what he was feeling. The three older boys are portrayed as very ordinary and not particularly heroic, except perhaps in the eyes of their respective girlfriends; whenever one of the girls is in trouble, she always has faith that "her" boy will come to the rescue.

Blyton's boys also feel fear, although they overcome it. In *The Island of Adventure* when Jack has got separated from the others in the secret tunnels and is lost, he is described as "terrified" (159), and again in *The Castle of Adventure* when he is on his own in the castle overnight, and sees a flash of light from the tower, he has to screw up his courage to go and investigate. In the *R Mysteries,* Barney is always brave in investigating mysteries, but Roger sometimes joins him reluctantly (*Ring O'Bells Mystery*, 121) and Snubby often gets very scared. Snubby is the youngest, and it may be that allowance is made for age in this respect. In Ransome, John Walker tends to feel doubt rather than fear, doubt in his own ability, but his younger brother Roger is several times scared in the earlier books, as in *Swallows and Amazons* when they are sailing in the dark up a river and run into some water lilies which catch at the boat, and he is afraid they are octopuses: "In Roger's voice there were clear signs of panic" (224), and John has to pick a bloom to show him what they are.

Even the younger characters generally attempt to hide their fear; older boys in particular sometimes seem to be more concerned about what others think than what they actually feel. Tom's bravado on the tower, which he need not have climbed at all, is one example of this. Antonia Forest similarly has Peter Marlow afraid of heights and very unwilling to admit it; in fact, he deliberately does things to prove he is not scared. In *The Marlows and the Traitor* he and his sister Nick go walking along a cliff path in a storm even though he has been told it is dangerous, and in *Falconer's Lure* he joins their neighbour Patrick in visiting a peregrine's nest on a cliff (obviously in the days before these birds were a protected species) because he felt if Patrick could do it, he had to, and not "funk", and in fact he sticks, unable to move back or forward, spreadeagled against the cliff, and causes the others a lot of trouble. Forest does not seem to be advocating this kind of bravado so much as recognising that it is a part of many boys' makeup. John Walker of the Swallows' fear of looking a fool or incompetent is perhaps similar in that he is as much concerned with what other people will think. For instance in *Peter Duck* he is ordered to steer into the harbour, and he is worried in case he makes a mess of it, while Nancy is frankly envious of the opportunity.

Female courage

In many traditional stories, and in fact in many quite recent movies, it is much more acceptable for a girl or woman to show fear, scream, and panic. However, in general in these books the girls assume the same ethic as the boys: one should be brave, keep one's head in a crisis, if possible risk one's life for others, and above all not *show* that one is afraid. Peter's sister Nick in *Falconer's Lure* not only completely accepts his insistence on going on the cliff even though she knows how he feels, she has a moment herself when Patrick admits to being scared, but "When you were thirteen and a girl, you had to be more careful" (161). For much of human history men must have struggled with society's expectation that they would be physically brave; at this time the same was beginning to apply to women. In the real world, every time a man failed it would mean he as an individual was written off as a coward, which is bad enough, but every time a woman failed it is likely to have had an impact on attitudes to her sex as a whole: "Oh, she's only a woman, what can you expect?"

Some of the girls and women in these books behave like traditional heroes, acting bravely without doubts and fears. Nancy in the Ransome books is frequently described as "confident", and her somewhat reckless courage shows up clearly in the two metafictional books. In *Peter Duck*, when they are being shot at in the *Swallow*, Captain Flint tells the children to lie down, but "'Rot,' said Nancy. 'They can't see us now the light's gone. They've got nothing to shoot at. Keep still while I paddle her out'" (358). (This is also an example of how she tends to take charge; the other two people in the boat were her uncle and John Walker.) Again in *Missee Lee* when she and Peggy are on the junk which has picked them up after a shipwreck, the junk fires its cannon and Peggy sobs, but Nancy tells her off: "We're firing. You've got nothing to worry about. That's guns, not thunder!" (65). This sounds like an odd priority, but Peggy's fear of thunder comes into several books; this is apparently an acceptable fear, and Nancy treats it as just one of those things and does not try to jolly her out of it.

Saville's Peter Sterling (her surname being very fitting) is another girl whose physical courage is never in doubt, although unlike Nancy she has other weaknesses, being rather shy and uncomfortable in large groups. In *The Secret of the Gorge* she cuts her leg badly enough to need stitches escaping from an old cottage where the villains have locked her in, but nonetheless when one of the bad guys falls in the river she, as the best swimmer of the group, unhesitatingly dives in to rescue him. On another occasion she, David and Mary are in a cave hiding from a scientist who has been experimenting on dogs, and when Peter feels herself slipping over an edge she deliberately lets go of the others so David won't be pulled over with her, saying "Hold Mary". She breaks her ankle in the fall, but the other two are safe (*The Neglected Mountain*, 169).

Other examples include Maud in *The Wild Lorings*, who as previously related cheerfully climbs out of second-floor windows, but in fact in the second book, after the rescue in the lake when her sister swam into a dangerous current to save a foolish junior, the reader gets a glimpse of buried feelings: "'All right, Elspeth?' she demanded, without the faintest show of feeling in her voice, although her dark eyes looked suspiciously bright" (121). However, this reveals fear for her sister rather than herself. Worrals is also often described as "confident" and does not seem to be afraid or to shrink from quite daunting experiences: in *Worrals in the Wilds* she deliberately poisons the witch doctor who has been poisoning Bill, so that he will reveal the antidote, and in *Worrals Goes East* she hides in an occupied coffin to escape detection. Sometimes she is shaken, as in the first book when she has to fire at an enemy plane on a transport flight ("I've got to do it. This is war": 12); realistically she was unlikely to have been totally calm the first time she killed someone, and Johns has his male pilots undergo the same experience. In *Worrals Flies Again* she is also oddly shaken, feeling faint, when a German is killed by a crossbow bolt in front of her, although later in the same book when a German pilot crashes her plane and burns to death, she is quite cool about it. Possibly Johns felt he ought to portray a woman as being more sensitive than a man, but as he wrote more *Worrals* books she became essentially Biggles with another name. As I shall demonstrate in chapter eight, the language used about and by the two is very similar, and despite the occasional mention of lipsticks or nylons, and the comments from and about the male characters who struggle to accept female competence, what she actually says and does is very much what Biggles would have said or done.

Frecks, however, does quite often show fear or talk about being afraid, and this is perhaps a difference between the male and female characters in the books: more of the girls are scared, even if they act bravely, and their courage is more commented on by the other characters. In other words, it is still considered remarkable if a female displays physical courage. Frecks, for instance, is very upset by a snake which is found in Worrals' bed (not her own) in *Worrals Goes East*, and in *Worrals in the Wilds* she gets jumpy about all the wild animals which roam Africa. However, when the chips are down, she always keeps her head, and indeed in *Worrals Flies Again* when she thinks it is Worrals who has crashed and burned, she feels she ought to cry but cannot, and instead keeps thinking and planning. With the exception of Maud (above), most of Courtney's girls are more like this: they feel trepidation, especially when adventuring at night, but they pull themselves together and do what needs to be done. Maud's sister Elspeth, for instance, investigating what she thinks is a practical joker in the school one night, hears a moan from another prefect who has been attacked by a burglar, and is extremely scared but makes herself go down and investigate. Afterwards everyone is very admiring, saying they would not have had the nerve, and Rose is of course grateful as otherwise she would have been left lying concussed all night. In *Well Done, Denehurst!*, Avice is keeping watch in the dark when she sees a mysterious stranger and "knew that if she funked investigating at once she would never be able to face the others—particularly Bob, who would be very scornful of anything in the way of cowardice" (95-6). Again, it is partly fear of *looking* afraid which motivates her.

Because Saville has several girls in the Lone Pine Club, he is able to show different types of courage. Penny Warrender is lively and excitable.

> "Penny loved danger. She was impulsive, moody, quick to love and quick to hate, but she liked excitement and adventure. Peter's courage was of a different sort and not quite as spectacular, perhaps, but she never lost her head once she had made up her mind" (*Secret of Grey Walls*, 239).

These two are contrasted with Jenny, who is scared of many things including the mountain she calls "Neglected", which is reputed to be haunted locally. When they first meet her David comments to Peter "I don't think she'd be much use in what Dickie would call a 'crissis', but she's good fun" (*Seven White Gates*, 111). He admires Peter's physical prowess and courage. However, Jenny conquers her fears when others depend on her; in *The Secret of Grey Walls*, for instance, she goes off on her own at night to fetch help because her beloved Tom is in danger. She also follows a villain in *Man With Three Fingers* to try to help Tom. Harriet Sparrow, who is nearer the twins in age (twelve), likewise follows the villain Slinky Grandon when he visits her grandfather's shop (*Lone Pine London*); she is scared and excited and lost, but she doesn't want to let her new friends (the Lone Piners) down.

Saville also has the twins, who are much the youngest of the Lone Piners, feeling fear on many occasions. In the first book they are only nine, and when captured by the spies Mary is near to tears with fear, but when one of them slaps Dickie she immediately loses her fear in anger. In *Seven White Gates* they are following Uncle Micah at night, and when he heads for the stone called the Devil's Chair, which has a spooky reputation, Dickie doesn't want to follow, but Mary insists. In most of the books there are moments when one or both of them is afraid, but they are nonetheless frequently described by the others as brave, they do often stand up to the villains, and sometimes in fact behave quite recklessly, walking into the lion's den, so to speak.

I have already mentioned Anna in the Lockett series, who similarly forces herself to do things she does not excel at in order to help her friends, although mostly these are simply things like cricket and swimming rather than anything dangerous, and her fear is of failure and letting people down. This fear is stronger than pain; she is hit by a cricket ball, which really hurts, but carries on. This looks superficially like John Walker's fear of failure, but in his case it is about losing face, whereas Anna is concerned about her friends. In need, however, she does also have physical courage. When their caravan is threatened by a moorland fire in the first adventure, she is the one who keeps her head and drives the horse out of danger (she is good with animals). And when the children are attacked by some local louts she joins in the fight with a cudgel, even though it is against her gentle nature, because one of those threatened is her little brother Robin, aged five. Interestingly, Jane Lockett who is in general quite a tomboy, with short hair and similar skills to her brothers as regards swimming, climbing, cricket and so on, is often scared. In the first book she and Oliver together frighten themselves hearing noises in a possibly haunted mansion, but in other books she is afraid of the dark (although she still takes her share of midnight vigils, she ends up shivering in terror) and of cows. Presumably she was meant to appeal to the average reader as someone they could relate to; her rival Fenella is more like Nancy of the Amazons, fearless and reckless.

Blyton generally seems to equate tomboys with physical courage, while more feminine girls are often afraid but brave at need. George in the *Famous Five* is fearless and determined, but this is constantly remarked upon rather than taken for granted as Amazon Nancy's courage is. In *Five Have Plenty of Fun* George is kidnapped by mistake for Berta, and the others are sure she will not reveal the mistake to the villains as this would put Berta in danger: "'George is brave all right,' said Dick. 'As brave as any boy could be when she's in a fix!'" (119). There is even more praise of the feminine girls when they are brave, particularly Lucy-Ann in the *Adventure* series. At one point when they think Philip is being attacked by wolves (it is actually a pack of alsatian dogs) she picks up a stick and rushes to help: "valiant little Lucy-Ann" (*Mountain*, 78), and later when he has been selected to test some experimental wings, which involves jumping out of a helicopter to probable death, she steps forward with her knees knocking and offers to go in his stead (ibid, 153). The constant praise for Lucy-Ann used to annoy me as a child, while Dinah's courage is taken for granted ("She wasn't afraid, and if she had been she wouldn't have shown it": *Circus*, 136), yet her fear of her brother Philip's insects and animals is made light of. In every book he makes a pet of a wild animal, often things like mice or snakes, which Dinah finds abhorrent, but she is unsympathetically told to put up with it if she wants to be part of the group.

Blyton also has a particular feature in several of her books which might be termed "wild children". There is an element of this in her *St Clare's* school stories with the little circus girl, Carlotta, who submits badly to school discipline but is brave and a skilled gymnast. Barney in the *R Mysteries* has self-discipline, but lives a free life, going from fair to fair taking casual jobs, and again is both brave and skilful. In the *Famous Five* there is the gypsy girl Jo, naughty and disobedient but who often comes to the rescue of the Five, and in *The Castle of Adventure* there is the little Tassie, apparently about eight, who lives with her mother in a hut on the mountainside, and attaches herself to Philip in particular. When the children are taken prisoner in the castle, she reaches them by following Philip's tamed fox cub through a tunnel in the earth where a stream flows into the castle courtyard, a terrifying experience as she has no idea if it will be wide enough for her. This is perhaps part of Blyton's romanticisation of the countryside; her gypsies and other "wild" characters, children and adults, (e.g. Tammylan in *The Children of Willow Farm*) are not amenable to normal social rules, confident in their own area but shy with people, very knowledgeable about natural history and always to be relied upon in a crisis.

Elinor Brent-Dyer is the only author in this study who really has both adults and children taking part in the adventures. (In fact, the oldest boys in some of Courtney's books are of an age with Biggles and Worrals in the first stories about those two, but the former are perceived as children because they are still at school.) I have already discussed Brent-Dyer's great aunts, Merrill in *Chudleigh Hold* and Freda in *Top Secret*. After the villains have beaten the flesh off Hawk's feet, they threaten to blind Aunt Freda if he does not talk. This is not merely words; they begin to heat up a steel rod over an oil stove. Hawk is helpless because he has already told them the truth and they didn't believe it. Freda "was mustering all her courage to meet what threatened without giving this brute the satisfaction of knowing that she was afraid" (168). Luckily for her, Hawk hears sound of their rescuers outside and draws their tormentor's fire by taunting him into a loss of control; he beats Hawk about the face wildly, and by the time this is over, the rescue party is set to burst in. Nonetheless, this is quite a powerful threat. Where the protagonists are children there is rarely much physical violence as they are usually overpowered quite easily. In Saville's *Treasure at Amory's*, Penny Warrender is kidnapped by Miss Ballinger's niece Valerie and her boyfriend and taken to the nearby pub where they

are staying. Here her three captors, two of them women, shout and fire
questions at her, and threaten to write a note to her friends saying she has
had an accident to send them all off on a wild goose chase, but although
she has been rather manhandled, nobody even hits her, and the worst they
plan to do is tie her up. Nonetheless she was "desperately afraid now, and
knew that she would probably weaken if they threatened Jon" (159).

Fear for others

Aside from fear of spiders etc., girls more often than boys are portrayed
as being afraid for someone else. I have already referred to Anna's defence
of her little brother Robin in the Locketts. In *The Rockingdown Mystery*
Diana is "pale with fright" when Barney is climbing up a rope and the bars
to which it is secured break. In Courtney's *Mermaid House*, when the
children discover a hole in the clifftop which leads down to a cave, Giles
climbs down first and his sister Fay is scared on his behalf, not for herself.
Is this a kind of rehearsal for the days when they will be mothers worrying
about their offspring? There are several examples of worried mothers,
although the Locketts and most of Blyton's children are generally off
doing something independent which their parents only find out about
afterwards. Mrs Mannering in the *Adventure* books is usually removed by
being ill or having to go and care for a sick relative, but in between times
does manage to worry about the children, and in *The Mountain of
Adventure* she is so concerned about the fact that they always seem to end
up battling criminals that she insists on accompanying them on holiday to
Wales (only to have a door bang shut on her hand so she cannot join them
on a donkey trip, which of course is the point where they head into
danger). Whereas Bill's role is often to join the children, and either rescue
them or be rescued by them, she mostly sits at home anxiously waiting for
them to return.

There is something similar if not as pronounced in the *Lone Pine*
stories, where Mrs Morton is left at home to worry while her husband
more than once sets off to pick the children up from wherever their
adventures have left them. In *Wings Over Witchend* the twins have
disappeared and their dog turns up without them, hurt; she goes very white
and has to sit down suddenly. In *Lone Pine London* after Jon and David
have disappeared, the others go looking for them with James Wilson, the
friendly journalist, and his fiancée Judith. Mr Morton and Harriet's
grandfather Mr Sparrow drive after them and join the chase. When they
locate the villains' headquarters, the three men accompany the police raid,
while the children and Judith are ordered to stay put (of course, they

ignore this order). Mrs Morton is presumably sitting at home wondering when if ever she will see any of her family again.

Lone Piner Jon's mother likewise stays at home and worries through several adventures, as does Ransome's Mrs Walker, mother of the Swallows. Despite the fact that she herself was rather a tomboy, she several times comes to check up on them as they are camping, disguising this as a visit from a "friendly native". In *Swallowdale* the children have actually sunk their boat (due to John trying to emulate or outdo Nancy) and although Captain Flint and John have both assured her everyone is safe, she cannot be happy until she has seen them for herself. This is somewhat of a contrast to the tone of her husband's telegram in the first book, giving permission for the children to camp on the island: "BETTER DROWNED THAN DUFFERS IF NOT DUFFERS WONT DROWN" (15). In real life of course parents do worry, and have to strike a balance between encouraging their children to develop independence and protecting them from harm, but in these books the worrying seems largely to be done by the mothers.

One interesting incident occurs in Saville's *Where's My Girl?*, when Peter and Jenny have been held prisoner and are rescued partly by David and Tom and partly by their own efforts; Tom's uncle and Peter's father come to collect them, and Jenny's stepmother accompanies them. Previously Jenny's relationship with her stepmother has not been good, and Jenny is surprised that she should have come rather than her father, but someone had to stay and look after their shop, and as Mrs Harman says: "...I thought maybe you'd rather have a woman around. I didn't know what had happened to you" (170). This is the only mention I have found, amid a great many imprisonings and abductions, of any possibility of girls being subjected to sexual attack. When they are creeping around at night following strangers they sometimes worry about "tramps", but that is usually the limit. Most girls in the twenty-first century would certainly think about the possibility and this would add an extra level to the courage needed to face armed villains, but children's authors at this time were either more concerned to protect the innocence of their readers, or simply believed that their heroines would not have felt such fears at that time.

Empathy and tears

Fears for others may be an aspect of a generally greater sensitivity accorded to females in much fiction (and by many people in real life). There are many examples in these books of female empathy. When Jon and David decide to go off hiking together without consulting Penny, who with Jon is staying at the Mortons' London home, she is deeply upset and Mrs Morton is the one who understands how she feels. Mary Morton is often shown to be sensitive, as for instance in *Seven White Gates*, where Peter's Uncle Micah is a real odd-ball, and nine-year-old Mary says "Charles [his son] has broken his heart, Peter" (104). Again in *The Elusive Grasshopper* the twins meet a widow who is sad at having to sell up her home and Mary at once takes charge and makes her a cup of tea (in her own kitchen). In *Five Have Plenty of Fun* when Berta is coming to stay because her father has received kidnap threats about her, George's reaction is to sulk because Berta will have to sleep in her room, but both Anne and Aunt Fanny feel sorry for the child (Anne hugs Fanny).

Often this empathy extends to the criminals. A rather extreme example of this which struck me very much the first time I read it comes in Dorita Fairlie Bruce's *The School on the Moor*, when Toby the heroine hears a prisoner has escaped from Dartmoor and not only feels sorry for the man being hunted, but actually when she meets him helps him to hide and brings him food. He turns out to be the brother of one of her teachers, who had been wrongly convicted, but she did not know that at the time. An escaped prisoner also features in the *Lockett* story *The House on the Moor*; he steals Aunt Lavinia's car, leaving her and the children stranded, but "while Bill ranged himself alongside the pursuers, the sympathies of his sister were all with the fugitive" (16). Similarly in *The Valley of Adventure*, when the children are hiding in a cave watching the men searching for them by a large waterfall, it is quite on the cards that the searchers will be swept away by the water: "Dinah and the boys watched in glee" (73) but Lucy-Ann looked away, shuddering. This tenderness applies even in wartime: in *The Denehurst Secret Service* when the girls hear that the U-boat has been "got" by a destroyer, Elaine is upset about the fate of the crew and relieved to learn they were all (improbably) taken prisoner. Nor is this a peculiarity of female writers, as the same thing occurs in Saville: when Miss Ballinger is arrested in *The Elusive Grasshopper*, Penny suddenly feels sick, and in this case her feelings are shared by Jon, "I know how you're feeling. I hate it too" (154).

The desirability of a "stiff upper lip" was a creation of the late nineteenth century, alongside "pluck" becoming a key feature of "manliness". Men today still struggle with the legacy of this, with much social pressure to conceal or overcome emotions rather than display them. However much talk there may be about the "new man", in practice most people still find male tears, for instance, embarrassing, yet Henry VIII was known to break down in tears in his Council meetings, and no-one would call him a wimp. Like other aspects of gender-related behaviour, this is culturally determined and far from fixed. As girls and women in fiction began to be given slightly more active and exciting roles, they also came under pressure to "grin and bear it". They had always been expected to suffer adversity cheerfully, but this was now extended to match the models in boys' school and adventure stories. It is interesting therefore to look at examples of tears in these adventure books, and also at demonstrations of affection, which come under the same taboo.

Blyton never has any of her male protagonists crying, but occasionally one of the other boys does, such as Gussy, the boy who turns out to be a prince in *The Circus of Adventure*, who cannot cope with being teased, and Martin in *Five on Kirrin Island Again*, who though older is more justifiably miserable because his guardian forces him to be involved in criminal activity. It is far from unusual for her feminine girls to cry: Anne cries in the same book because George has run off and may be hurt, Nora cries when she does something stupid and is told off by captain Jack, and Lucy-Ann has tears in her eyes when her brother plans to take a risk. As with her attitude to girls taking a share of the action, Blyton seems to be largely stuck in an earlier world, with sweet emotional girls who have to be protected, and tough adventurous boys who look after them, but occasionally there are flashes of something less stereotyped. None of the *Five* laugh at Martin, and although Julian is at first exasperated with him, when they hear the reason for his tears they all "felt sorry" for him (165).

M.E. Atkinson seems to have similar views about male tears, although her girls do not cry either. In *Smuggler's Gap* the Locketts catch Maurice, the son of Anna's landlady (this is the book where Anna has mysteriously disappeared) in an ambush and his response is to sob, which makes the boys uncomfortable but arouses Jane's motherly instincts. Bill, who is about the same age as eleven-year-old Maurice, eventually gets impatient and orders him to stop crying "tired of this display of the water-works and feeling that they were treating the prisoner much too gently...After all - Maurice wasn't a girl." Gwendoline Courtney made explicit that even girls shouldn't cry, although most of her girls are older than Maurice: in *Well Done Denehurst*, when the children hear that Deryk is going to be all right after his accident, "Avice disgraced herself for ever in her own eyes by sitting down abruptly and bursting into tears" (73). Although they worry, mothers too generally subscribe to the "stiff upper lip" ethos; Mrs Walker makes rather a joke of counting how many of the children are still alive to make sure none has been drowned (*Swallowdale*), and in Brent-Dyer's *Fardingales*, when the two oldest children are missing, Humphrey's mother thinks "All the same, having hysterics about it would help nobody"

(87), while her sister "looked paler than usual, and her mouth was set in a grim line".

Ransome generally follows the stiff upper lip line, even to the extent that when their beloved ship *Wild Cat* sinks in *Missee Lee* "John, Susan and Roger heard Titty's gasping sob and hoped it had not been noticed by the others" (37). However, in *Peter Duck* the boy Bill who has joined their crew is captured by the pirates, and left tied up, injured and gagged with soap; he bears this stoically but then "blubbers" when he starts thinking about the other children, who have been good to him, and what might happen to them if Black Jake catches them. Interestingly, the other male writers tend to break the mould rather more than the women do. In the focus books of this study Biggles is generally cool under pressure, but in some of the early stories less so: in *The Decoy*, for instance, when a fellow pilot dies in his arms, he looks down at him "through a mist of tears", and there is the sound of another man "sobbing in the distance" (*Pioneer Air Fighter*, 55). In *Biggles in the South Seas*, the Marquesans Full Moon and Shell Breaker are "weeping unrestrainedly" when Biggles and friends leave at the end of the adventure, and Ginger's eyes are "misty with tears" (158); this is a much slighter cause than over the death of a comrade.

Saville has most of his boys reveal their emotions at times. In *Mystery at Witchend*, the first *Lone Pine* book, David is near tears when the twins have got lost and he is looking for them: "He knew it was babyish but he couldn't help it" (130), and when he finds them he hugs and kisses Mary. (The Swallows and Amazons tend to limit their physical contact to the occasional handshake.) Similarly when the dog Mackie disappears (*The Neglected Mountain*), Dickie cries, though he turns his back on the others, and David hands him a handkerchief. In *Not Scarlet But Gold*, David is buried in the earth by a landslide, and Mary cries, but "Dickie had no tears. He would have felt better if he had. His little world was crumbling about him" (231). And in *Where's My Girl?,* the penultimate book, when Jenny is talking about their friendship lasting forever (a major theme in Saville is loyalty and friendship), "David's hand closed over Jenny's" (96); although she is Tom's girl, David can be demonstrative with her. It is rather unexpected that Blyton's boys also seem comfortable with physical demonstrations of affection: for instance in *Five Run Away Together*, when the Five rescue a small girl who has been kidnapped, at one point Dick puts his arm round her to comfort her (168), and on another she slips her hand into Julian's (170).

Although there are many examples of physical courage in these books, moral courage is less in evidence; not that it is necessarily lacking, but the opportunity for it arises less. In the typical school story there is often a case of someone either being tempted to do something they know they shouldn't, or being falsely accused of something and having to stand firm when everyone is despising them. Dorita Fairlie Bruce seemed to specialise in this in her girls' schools stories, but it is found in many boys' books too, such as Talbot Baines Reed's classic *The Fifth Form at Saint Dominic's* in 1887 with an accusation of having cheated on an exam; several of the *Billy Bunter* books for instance involve false accusations and subsequent vindication. The one clear example in this study of someone standing by their principles is in *The Grenville Garrison*, when Edward is accused of cowardice by the prince but refuses to be pressurised into changing his mind and leaving the island undefended instead of, as he knows is right, staying there and letting Helen go to rescue Roy. This is very different from John Walker or Peter Marlow worrying about what people will think, but then Edward is older than either (seventeen).

Unsurprisingly, courage is a major theme in many of these books. Sometimes it is dealt with quite simplistically (Enid Blyton), sometimes it is just taken for granted or not really remarked upon (Johns), but the other writers have more variations and different types of courage. Girls' courage is more likely to be remarked upon, but boys may also be shown to be afraid. Both genders may be partly motivated by public opinion, not wanting to be seen to be afraid, but boys are more likely to be goaded into taking foolish risks. Girls are more likely than boys to be afraid for others, brothers or boyfriends, which may be an aspect of their generally more empathetic natures, or may be a kind of foreshadowing of mothers worrying about their children. Both genders not only hold firm under threats and keep calm in a crisis, they also risk their lives for others, especially the other members of their team or family. Biggles' enemy Von Stalhein knows that when he catches one of the airmen, the others will inevitably try to rescue him. Saville's great theme is friendship and loyalty. The other writers perhaps stress it less but let actions speak for themselves. The two episodes which stand out for me are Peter deliberately letting go of David's hand so he would not fall over the cliff with her, and Lucy-Ann offering to take Philip's place in jumping out of the helicopter: these are the most striking instances of cold-blooded self-sacrifice, very much highlighted by the author in each case, and they are both by girls.

There is in all the books definitely an ethos of "stiff upper lip", but some of the authors allow their males as well as their females to show weakness and emotion. The basic recklessness of investigating mysteries is never questioned, but then, the books would have been rather short if the protagonists had favoured discretion over valour.

CHAPTER EIGHT

PRETTY GIRLS AND NICE MEN
GENDER AND LANGUAGE IN THE TEXTS

There have been many studies of the interplay of gender and language in the past few decades. Early linguists, including the highly-influential and respected Otto Jespersen, tended to make sweeping statements about women's use of language, based entirely on their own prejudiced expectations, but linguistics has moved beyond that, thankfully. Technology has aided the search for data as evidence, and research has covered, to name but a few things, turn-taking and interruptions, use of "bad" language, frequency and types of compliments offered, and collocation of specific words or expressions with a particular gender in a range of text types and media. At a theoretical level, philosopher Judith Butler's enormously influential *Gender Trouble* (1990) suggested (put simplistically) that gender is not something one either has or is, but something one does. Language use is part of the performance of gender. As Jennifer Coates wrote in *Women, Men and Language* (1993, 144):

> "[I]n becoming linguistically competent, the child learns to be a fully fledged male or female member of the speech community; conversely, when children adopt linguistic behaviour considered appropriate to their gender they perpetuate the social order which creates gender distinctions".

The relationship between language and gender in a literary text has perhaps even more complexities than in other types of written and spoken text. Some of the language is in the narrative voice, and some is purportedly conversation, but conversation as imagined by the author, rather than as actually used by a range of individuals. All texts however, literary or verbatim from life, may be seen as merely an arrangement of vocabulary and grammar, with only potential meaning until interpreted by a listener or reader, who is in turn embedded in a social context. Critical discourse analysis would not attempt to interpret a text without a context. I believe we now have a reasonable picture of the context of these texts; I should like to examine the texts themselves for linguistic data, and then attempt some tentative interpretations.

In my initial examination of the texts, I noted linguistic features which seemed to me significant or interesting, but I later came to realise that more analysis was needed. The first section below outlines some of the findings from the initial study, and later sections introduce a more in-depth analysis of selected texts.

Descriptions and collocations

A study as recent as 2017 found that literature aimed at teenage girls, while featuring active, dynamic protagonists, nonetheless had an emphasis on physical attraction including frequent descriptions of the characters (Suico, 2017). Most of the main characters were beautiful and this was important. If this is still true in the twenty-first century, it would not be surprising to find something similar in the mid-twentieth. In particular, one would look for this in the books featuring teenagers or adults rather than eleven or twelve-year-olds, that is in Saville, Brent-Dyer, Courtney and Johns rather than Blyton, Atkinson and Ransome. To some extent, this proved to be the case.

Suico's findings are actually supported by data from a wide range of texts. Modern dictionaries no longer depend on the whims and prejudices of their compilers, but are solidly based on actual usage as represented in corpora such as the COBUILD (Collins Birmingham University International Language Database) one. The Bank of English (COBUILD corpus), developed in the late twentieth century and containing over 200 million words of spoken and written texts in a range of genres, provides linguists with data for an enormous variety of studies. One published by Herriman in 1998 found that words for physical attractiveness collocated most frequently with "woman", while those describing height, abilities and personality most frequently with men (Goddard and Patterson 2000, 31). This finding is not particularly surprising, but the development of corpus linguistics has provided evidence to support, or sometimes refute, what in many cases were previously merely native-speaker intuitions.

Some of the authors in this study fit Herriman's pattern. Malcolm Saville's girls are all pretty, and are all described, so that the reader is in no doubt as to their build and colouring. This applies equally to his Young Adult books and his children's books. In *Power of Three*, for instance, he refers to Annabelle's "beautiful dark eyes in her exquisite heart-shaped face" (9), and in the *Lone Pine* series, Mary, Jenny and Penny all have curls (which in girls' books the pretty heroines generally do, as indeed in adult romantic fiction), and the latter two's red hair is frequently mentioned. Others often judge them as "pretty", "attractive" or "beautiful", sometimes heads literally turn when they pass, and of course they are also slim. They also receive a range of adjectives which emphasise their femininity: "enchanting"; "gamin-like"; "sweet". By contrast, *Lone Pine* captain David is described as "friendly and nice" (*The Neglected Mountain*), Jon is identified as clever and untidy, and Tom's appearance is so unimportant that in one book he has fair hair and in another black; Saville had clearly forgotten his previous description.

Brent-Dyer has a great deal of physical description of characters in her girls' books, and almost all the girls and mistresses are pretty, with however the interesting exceptions of her main characters: Jo Bettany (later Maynard), younger sister of Madge who begins the Chalet School, is thin and bony rather than slim, and has a pale pointed face and very straight ("lank") black hair, and not even her best friends would call her pretty, but all agree that she has a strong personality, with a great gift for getting on with others, which in later books as she grows up develops into an ability to help all sorts of troubled teens; Mary-Lou, also in the *Chalet School* series, and Janie Lucy in the (linking) *La Rochelle* series are likewise not pretty (Janie is "quaint" and "puckish") but vivid, charming, and widely-beloved. However, in later books Jo has "delicate, mobile" features, and Mary-Lou actually undergoes a major physical transformation after an accident, growing tall and slim instead of sturdy, and acquiring curls! The message is somewhat mixed.

The five thrillers Brent-Dyer wrote are by no means as uniform in this respect as her other output. The first two, *Chudleigh Hold* and *Fardingales*, have quite a few "family" moments surrounding the central adventure, and in both cases there is a large family with a range of girls, mostly pretty, rather like her girls' books but with the addition of male characters. *Condor Crags Adventure* and *Top Secret*, however, have far less description, although Hawk Chudleigh is definitely tall, lean, dark and adventurous, like the hero of many a romance. Like Saville, Brent-Dyer generally lets us know the colouring (hair and eye; everyone is white) of her female characters, but unlike Saville, also that of most of the males.

Most of the other authors, however, give the reader very little in the way of physical description of characters at all. Johns tells us that Biggles has fair hair in perhaps three or four books out of ninety-six, and changes his mind about his eye colour. None of his heroes is described as handsome, but then neither are Worrals and Frecks pretty. In the first book we learn that Worrals is dark and Frecks fair, and like Ginger in *Biggles,* Frecks' nickname tells the reader one of her physical characteristics, but otherwise there is little information. The few women who do appear in the Biggles books, however, *are* always beautiful, and given quite long descriptions. I shall return to this later.

Ransome never gives any information about the looks of his children. The few descriptions he does give of people are of minor adult roles, often middle-aged farmers or boat-builders or the like. We do not know the colouring of any of his protagonists, let alone whether they are pretty or good-looking. In fact, we also do not know much about their characters from any narrative description; this knowledge comes from their words and actions. M.E. Atkinson gives the reader a little more, but not a great deal, and Blyton is rather idiosyncratic, since she describes George of the *Famous Five*, Barney and Snubby in the *R Mysteries*, and all four children in the *Adventure* series, in almost every book, yet we never find out the colour of Julian's hair, for instance, or indeed whether Anne, Peggy or Lucy-Ann, the "girly" girls, are pretty. This is definitely different from her girls' school stories, where the heroines are pretty and the reader knows what every girl looks like.

Gwendoline Courtney actually uses, not so much the "pretty" range but the "feminine" range of descriptors to a particular effect, namely to contrast how some of her girls look with what they are actually like. For instance, Fay in *Mermaid House* is "that dainty little piece of gossamer" (83), so that others doubt if she is tough enough for the action, but of course she is really fit, strong, an excellent swimmer and very brave. The lively Audrey in *Grenville Garrison* is "ethereal-looking" (179), and in *The Wild Lorings at School* the girls are told how the Loring girls "aren't really civilised", go off on their own tracking wild animals and birds, fall out of trees and tear their clothes, etc., then they actually meet Elspeth Loring, who is a "small, slight girl" with "a neat, dainty figure, and a face with a wild rose complexion" (26), which is not at all what they had expected. In the sequel, someone tells Elspeth she is "a particularly frail bit of Dresden china" (54), which gets "a hoot of derision" from a classmate. "Frail! She's got wrists like steel!" to which the reply is that the frailty is of looks only.

Courtney also plays with the reader's expectations by more than once using the word "slender" of a male, once of Nick Loring, and once of an adult in Mermaid House. Other gender-related collocations include grin, smile and giggle. Most readers would probably anticipate that boys would tend to grin and girls to smile, and not only is that generally true in these books, but Saville actually makes it explicit at one point, writing of the twins that "the girl was smiling and the boy was grinning" (*The Elusive Grasshopper,* 81). The same occurs with Bill and Jane Lockett in

Atkinson. None of the authors have the adult males giggle, and certainly many of the girls do, but Atkinson also uses this verb for Bill, who is quite young (ten and then eleven) but quite traditionally masculine, noisy and aggressive and active. With Captain Johns, it is reporting verbs which stand out: in addition to "said", "gasped", "muttered", "queried" and "asserted", which are probably gender neutral and depend on the context, he also has "grated", "yelled", "grunted" and "growled" being used by Worrals and Frecks. These verbs and the adverbs which often collocate with "said" like "curtly", "grimly" are a feature of his style in *Biggles* and his other boys' books which has been parodied; there seems to be no difference in this respect between his boys' and girls' books. Even the names he chose for his heroines echo those of the males: short forms of a surname or a nickname based on a physical characteristic.

Girls—or at least, "young ladies"—were long expected to speak differently from boys, and this included not using slang, or at least not "vulgar" slang, and of course not swearing. By the twentieth century, books for girls did tend to use quite a lot of slang as part of a more lively style; often this would involve abbreviations and a range of terms of approval and disapprobation ("top-hole", "jolly", "rotten"), which some critics did object to as being "empty" words, but there were boundaries of the acceptable. "Lousy", for instance, if used by a girl would normally be condemned by another character. Brent-Dyer stands out here because in her girls' books she made a great deal of fuss about "slang" as being inappropriate for girls, to the extent that her Chalet School had a rule against it with a list of forbidden terms and a fine for their use, the money going to charity. The thrillers sometimes follow this line, as when Crumpet in *Chudleigh Hold* is told off for saying "I'll bet" and "I nearly bust", but her elder sister at another point tells her siblings "Don't scoff the lot!" (41), and Anstace in *Fardingales* thinks "the blighted pigs" when she's in a rage with the villains. I feel Brent-Dyer was making a conscious effort, particularly in the last two books, to have her male characters speak colloquially, using expressions such as "pronto", "get cracking", "get it in the neck"; there is nothing here that would not appear in her girls' books, but it is not questioned or commented on when the men do it. The one feature which is distinctive to the thrillers is the use of "ain't" by some of the men, as used by fictional upper-class males such as Billy Bunter or Peter Wimsey: "seeing I ain't even engaged" says Godfrey in *Condor Crags Adventure* (14).

Atkinson, Blyton and Courtney all have their girls and boys using slang, with no clear distinctions by gender, and none of the girls being reprimanded for it. Ransome uses a particular type of colloquial language as part of his depiction of Nancy Blackett, the Amazon captain. It is definitely language for which Brent-Dyer would fine a Chalet girl ("you chump-headed galoot"; "stir your stumps"; "my throat's as rough as the inside of a seaboot"), but it is also heavily nautical ("shiver my timbers"; "splice the mainbrace"). All the children use nautical language to some extent, and are frequently referred to as "the able-seaman", "the mate" and so on as an alternative to their names. However, Nancy is the most consistent in her usage, and the others sometimes quote her ("as Nancy would say"). The others come in and out of their assumed roles, but Nancy maintains hers firmly. One is reminded of Jo March in *Little Women* clinging determinedly to tomboyish ways rather than grow up and become a young lady. Nancy is possibly the oldest of the six, certainly not younger than John, and in *Missee Lee* the pirates mistake her and Peggy for Captain Flint's "wives", suggesting they are well into their teens; we know they are physically well-grown from the first book. Perhaps she persists in her roleplaying as an acceptable means of establishing an identity which is at odds with the social norm.

Folklinguistics (i.e. popular belief about linguistic matters) suggests that women do not swear as much as men. It is likely that in the period of this study there was some truth in that, in that swearing by and in the presence of women was taboo for some British people, in particular the middle classes. We do not have sufficient data on how effective this taboo was, but modern studies of the British National Corpus of Spoken English indicate that, while in practice nowadays British women of all classes do use "bad language", the distribution of such terms varies according to gender, with males preferring some terms over others, females preferring different terms, and generally using fewer of those which are categorised as "strong" or "very strong" (McEnery 2006).

In children's literature the additional taboo against using "bad language" in front of children is likely to come into play, especially in this period. In general, this is what I found. Where the protagonists are adult males, as in Saville's *Marston Baines* books and Johns' *Biggles*, it is probable that in real life these characters would swear in moments of tension, but they do not. *Biggles* characters use expressions like "My sainted aunt", "Great Scott" and "By Jove". Interestingly, in Brent-Dyer, although the men generally likewise use euphemisms like "By Jove" and "By Jupiter", in *Condor Crags Adventure* Godfrey exclaims "Damn!" on one occasion, and on another says "It's been—well—hell" (180). This book seems very much modelled on boys' adventure yarns, but the same is not true of *Chudleigh Hold*, where nonetheless Charles at one point says "I told him damn all" (41), speaking in front of his sisters.

The *Girl's Own Paper* was aimed at females between twelve and twenty-five. Among the non-parallel treatment identified in Miller and Swift's (1995) *Handbook of Non-Sexist Writing* was the custom of referring to women as "girls" but males of an equivalent age as "men". I have certainly observed this in a variety of adult literature both pre- and post- Second World War. Agatha Christie sometimes used "girl" to describe a woman well into her thirties. Nor did it necessarily depend on her marital status. In the *Marston Baines* books, the girl-man dichotomy is clear; here the characters are in their early twenties, and mostly unmarried. It is quite probable that at the time, Saville would have believed he was being courteous; women were often coy about their ages, and many well-meaning men have perpetuated (and still perpetuate) patronising behaviours under the illusion that they are being gentlemanly. Saville also frequently has males carrying bags for females, and even pushing their bicycles for them. Less acceptable probably is Mr Roseveare addressing his wife and her sister as "girls" in Brent-Dyer's *Fardingales*: they are old enough to have children aged sixteen to seventeen.

Bill Ashton in the *Worrals* books goes further, and routinely addresses Worrals and Frecks as "kids" or "kid". Each time they "flare" or "snap" at him not to do so. (In the first book he is less than twenty and Worrals is eighteen.) Bill apparently does it as a joke, but it clearly annoys the women; it is entirely plausible that, in view of the role he is given, kept out of the main action and having to see the woman he loves taking command of dangerous missions, he feels the need to assert his male superiority in some small way. On the opposite side, in *Worrals Flies Again*, while the French Resistance operatives Lucien and Raoul are described in the narrative as "young men", Worrals in talking to Frecks calls them "the boys" (156). In the days before "guy" became common usage in Britain, it could be difficult to know how to refer to males around the age of twenty; I found this myself at university in the 1980s. However, I suspect this choice of Worrals' reflects her attitude to males generally; she is constantly questioning whether they are as wonderful and superior as they themselves believe. In *Worrals Goes Afoot* she addresses their liaison officer, who has come to rescue them (unnecessarily in her view): "Thanks, and all that, for what you've done, but you chug-chug along home like a good boy" (97).

A minor but interesting feature which presumably derives from the lack, or perceived lack, of any equivalent female-specific term, is the use of expressions like "good chap" to refer to a female character as a term of approbation. This occurs in *Fardingales*, where Humphrey reflects of his cousin Anstace that she is a "decent chap. She rarely *said* sympathetic things in the way that Jill and Lettice did; but she could always be relied upon to *do* them" (87). This is occasioned by her volunteering to read to his little brother, who is an invalid, on the face of it a good traditional feminine occupation. In *Condor Crags Adventure*, where she has a very minor role, he twice refers to her as "a jolly good chap". Somewhat similarly in Courtney's *The Denehurst Secret Service* Deryk says to his cousin Elaine "Good girl! You've been a brick over all this!" (210). The expression "brick" is used in girls' school stories too, admittedly. Possibly these terms were felt particularly appropriate from a cousin or brother rather than a potential boyfriend or husband? Praise is given in terms which would be used to or of a male friend, thereby conferring some kind of (comradely) equality. Peter in the *Lone Pine* series is, like Anstace, competent and athletic, also loyal and reliable, and therefore a good candidate for being termed a "good chap", but this does not occur; however she writes David a letter about Penny and Jon suggesting they could join the Lone Pine Club because "they sound like good chaps" (*Gay Dolphin Adventure*, 54). The opposite of this, in a way, is the use of "just like a girl" and similar to express contempt. Mike (a rather dominant friend of the Locketts) says this of Jane in *Mystery Manor*, and is immediately shouted down by her brothers: "No, she isn't!" (293). Nobody, including Jane, questions that being "just like a girl" is an insult, they merely refute the idea that it applies to her. I found several examples like this in Atkinson, Brent-Dyer and Blyton.

Modification of female and male characters

The above points emerged from my initial study of the primary texts. After completing this, I felt more was needed, and decided to select one book, or in some cases two, by each author and scan them for all modifiers relating to the male and female characters. The books selected should not be the first by that author (first books are not always typical of an author's developed style), and if possible should be of similar date. They were as follows:

Captain Johns	*Biggles "Fails To Return"* (1943) and *Worrals on the Warpath* (1943)
Enid Blyton	*Five Go Adventuring Again* (1943)
M.E. Atkinson	*The Monster of Widgeon Weir* (1943)
Malcolm Saville	*The Gay Dolphin Adventure* (1945; the book from 1943 is the first in the series)
Arthur Ransome	*Swallowdale* (1931; this is earlier than any of the others selected, but the nearest, in 1942, does not have the Walker family in so is not typical. This just features the Swallows and

	Amazons, and is not one of the metafictions, so it seemed the most suitable)
Gwendoline Courtney	*Well Done, Denehurst!* (1941) and *Sally's Family* (1946) Courtney, being less prolific than Johns or Brent-Dyer, did not produce a "family" and an "adventure" book in the same year; these two are as typical of her two genres as possible, though the boundary with her is a little unclear.
Elinor Brent-Dyer	*Top Secret* (1955) and *The Chalet School Does It Again* (1955) Brent-Dyer's thrillers were all published in the 1950s, later than Ransome or Atkinson, but luckily there is a school story from the same year for comparison.

With each of these books, I originally planned simply to identify modifiers of males and females and compare them, but it soon became clear that it would be more profitable to identify them for each of the main characters and some minor ones individually. I defined "modifier" quite loosely as adjectives and adjectival phrases, longer expressions, and also adverbs of manner. Once listed, it was possible to group them into categories referring to particular traits which were frequently, but not always, loaded, i.e. carrying positive or negative connotations. I have not included all the data in this book, but as an example those for Blyton can be found in Appendix B.

In the 1970s Sandra Bem developed her sex-role inventory (BSRI), which required a subject to answer questions on a Likert scale (later also simplified as a version children could complete). In the full inventory, 200 characteristics valued as male or female, and 200 valued as neutral, of which half were positive and half negative, were presented, and the subject had to identify on a seven-point scale the extent to which s/he believed s/he possessed that characteristic. This was a tool of gender schema theory, to which I will return briefly in chapter nine. The BSRI gave a very good picture of gender stereotypes in white middle-class America in the 1970s; this does not mean it is valid in all cultures or all times, and indeed although a retest in 1998 suggested it was still fairly accurate for its original context, African-American or Latino-American cultures fit less well, and in 1997 Wilcox and Francis had found it did not really represent the views of British teenage girls. However, I feel it is relevant to the period of my study, so when I speak of "stereotypical" characteristics, they are generally taken from here. Table 8-1 lists some of the key characteristics from the BSRI.

What first leaps to the eye with the Blyton book is that the girls are described a great deal more than the boys, and there is in fact nothing in the modification of the boys which is not also at some point applied to the girls; in other words, the boys are the unmarked gender. Anne's negative points seem to be that she is often afraid, cries easily and cannot keep a secret, while on the plus side she is happy and eager to please, and loyal to the group. These would seem to conform to stereotypical "feminine" attributes. She is also, as the youngest, weak and small, inviting a protective attitude from her brothers. George is almost a complete contrast: positively she is brave and truthful, but these characteristics are heavily outweighed, numerically, by references to her quick temper, sulks, disobedience and aggression. One masculine stereotype in boys' literature is of the boy who is bad-tempered and disobedient but nonetheless to be relied upon in a crisis; Vernon Smith, the "Bounder", in *Billy Bunter* springs to mind. Yet George is also a "little girl", who sometimes "squeals" with excitement, and the high proportion of references to her negative features suggests that the reader is intended to view her ambivalently. George, the girl who wants to be a boy, is an anomaly.

Table 8-1: Key characteristics from the Bem Sex-Role Inventory (adapted from behavenet, n.d.)

masculine	feminine	neutral
self-reliant	yielding	helpful
independent	cheerful	conscientious
athletic	shy	happy
assertive	affectionate	reliable
strong personality	loyal	truthful
forceful	sympathetic	sincere
analytical	sensitive to others' needs	solemn
leadership ability	understanding	friendly
willing to take risks	compassionate	
makes decisions easily	eager to soothe hurt feelings	unsystematic
self-sufficient	soft spoken	inefficient
dominant	warm	conceited
willing to take a stand	tender	secretive
aggressive	gullible	jealous
individualistic	childlike	unpredictable
competitive	loves children	theatrical
ambitious	gentle	moody

Swallowdale in general presents an enormous contrast. The book has over 420 pages and is approximately 2.5 times as long as *Five Go Adventuring Again*, but contains very few adjectives or adverbs of manner. Modification comes mostly in phrases or sentences, such as "No-one was as good at lighting a fire as Mate Susan" (26). Of the two boys, we learn very little about John, the elder. He is honourable, and reticent, especially about problems, worries and fears. Roger, the youngest, is noisy, quick and lively, and usually hungry. Between them they embody a number of traditionally masculine attributes, but they are far more individual than Blyton's Dick and Julian, who are essentially very similar to Roger in her *R Mysteries*, Jack and Mike in the *Secret* series and Philip and Jack (except for the animal skills) in the *Adventure* series. All of these are basically brave, loyal, polite to adults, obstinate on occasion, and protective of their sisters.

There are four girls in *Swallowdale*, and of these the reader learns least about Peggy. The other three are all clearly distinct: Susan is competent, sensible, and pragmatic rather than imaginative; Titty expresses her emotions, is imaginative and empathetic, yet dogged and determined when things get difficult; and Nancy is, like Susan, admired for her competence (though as already discussed in chapter four, their skills are rather different), cheerful and noisy. This last is interesting in that it is a trait neutrally or even positively described: "[her] voice alone was stronger than the rippling of the stream" (52), her laugh is loud and cheerful; yet a female being markedly noisy might have been perceived as disruptive and inappropriate. Elinor Brent-Dyer's third *Chalet School* book (*Princess*) features a disliked matron whose voice is loud and harsh, and the girls, to get back at her for her unfair treatment, begin to deliberately imitate her tones, causing great dismay to the headmistress, who makes them write out punishment lines from *King Lear*, referring to Cordelia: "Her voice was ever gentle, sweet and low, An excellent thing in woman". No-one in Ransome is embarrassed or irritated by Nancy; both the other children and various adults admire her (with the exception of the formidable Great Aunt), and her loudness is merely an expression of a justifiable self-confidence and her generally cheerful nature. Ransome seems to equate confidence with cheerfulness, whereas the BSRI has "cheerful" a feminine characteristic (though personally I am not clear what the difference is between that and "happy", which is neutral). The loudness, on the other hand, would fit with "forceful" and "assertive" which are masculine on the BSRI.

M.E. Atkinson, like Ransome, has a range of distinct characters, but at the same time among them the males demonstrate typically masculine traits, the females typically feminine, except Fenella. Oliver is old for his age, wise, calm, and thinks things through, all of which make him a good leader, although the negative side of this is that he can be "superior and Public Schoolish" (58). Bill is confident, honest, enthusiastic and bold (positive), but also quick-tempered, impatient, and lacking in staying-power. We have not only descriptions like "impetuous", "in high spirits" and "in no mind to hang back", but also verbs such as "burst in", "burst out". These are very different characters, but yet recognisable masculine types. On the BSRI, Oliver would score highly on "analytical" and "leadership ability", Bill on "athletic", "aggressive", "competitive" and "willing to take risks". Similarly with the girls: Jane is modest, tactful, tidy, sympathetic and sensible, while Anna is humble and shy, with little self-belief, but both are extremely loyal and to be relied upon. It might be noted, however, that while the modifiers used of the boys are both negative and positive, of Jane they are all essentially positive, including her key characteristic of being quick-thinking, which is not a traditional "feminine" one. Anna could also be seen as entirely positive provided one regarded modesty and self-effacement as positive; the Victorians certainly would have done so, in a female.

There are in this book also Fenella and her sister Podge, and Brenda and Evelyn, who are all different but again, all essentially positive. Brenda is slim and elegant but also very competent in a boat; little Evelyn is enthusiastic, brave and loyal; Podge is placid and comfortable. There are several references to her plump appearance, but these are given a positive spin: "her fat laugh", "comfortably-built Podge". Even Fenella, who could be the villain of the piece, is sparkling and fiery and dynamic, physically striking, clever and (justifiably) self-confident. This is a notable contrast with Blyton's George; there are no really negative descriptions of Fenella. She clearly fits a "masculine" stereotype on the BSRI (almost every masculine adjective on the list in table 8-1 could apply to her), but she is not "trying to be a boy", and no-one suggests that she is like one. There are more girls than boys in this book, and so overall there are more modifiers of females, but the males are not, as in Blyton, under-described.

Saville, like Blyton, gives us much more information about his girls than his boys. In this book we learn that Jon is untidy physically, intelligent, cautious and patient and reliable, but David is just "a very nice boy". Of Penny, however, we have a whole range of descriptors: some relate to her red-haired temper (and again, this is not portrayed negatively like George in Blyton; we have words like "flamed", "stormed", which are dramatic and beautiful, rather than George's "fierce", "frown", "difficult" "scowl" and so on); others show her as impulsive and quick, another supposed attribute of red hair ("breathless", "impetuous", "brightly", "excitedly"); she is also charming and courageous. There is a marked degree of repetition, both within this book and across the series, of particular words or phrases associated with particular people, especially Penny. Although the characters are individual, they do often conform to stereotypes: redheads are quick-tempered and impulsive, foreigners are "slinky" and unnaturally elegant of dress. Miss Ballinger's male sidekick actually gets nicknamed "Slinky" by the children, and is described as "slimy", "slinky" and "sulky", while on occasion he flashes his teeth and bows gracefully, something no Englishman would do!

However, Saville does rise above this with some of his characters. Miss Ballinger, his serial villain, is initially "friendly and interesting" and succeeds in charming the cousins Penny and Jon. In most of the books in which she appears we see a degree of complexity in her makeup; at the same time, she is physically ugly to match her unpleasant character (she "waddles" four times in this book, and has an "ugly, bespectacled face": 185). The verbs used to describe her actions are often ones more associated with masculine behaviour, strong and aggressive: "roared", "boomed" and "snarled", for example; while she also speaks "curtly" and "with malevolent triumph". Her niece Valerie, by contrast, is pretty and feminine, with "an attractive voice"; this is necessary as both Jon and David find her sexually attractive and are confused and upset by the experience. Once revealed as one of the villains she also sneers, drawls and is "too clever".

Mrs Warrender, Jon's mother, also has a reasonably large role in this book. All her descriptors are positive: "very understanding", "brave smile", "happy", "brightly". She is kind and sympathetic (though can be firm in insisting on good behaviour), warm, and courageous in facing her widowhood. In all but the last of these she is very similar to Aunt Fanny in the *Famous Five*, who is also warm and smiling and affectionate. Quentin, Fanny's husband, is clever but stern and often angry. Most of his modifiers are negative: "frownier", "irritably". Although he is two-dimensional, he is at least different from most of Blyton's fathers and uncles who are generally strict but jolly and kind. In Ransome, Mrs Walker, like Fanny and Mrs Warrender, laughs and smiles, and is described by the children as "the best of all natives": again, entirely positive. Captain Flint, the Amazons' uncle Jim, mostly receives only physical description (he is fat), but is also "very sporting". He bears some resemblance to Bill Cunningham in Blyton's *Adventure* series: Bill is bald rather than fat, but also jolly, able to join in the children's activities, approving of their skills and adventurous spirit, viewed by them as utterly reliable yet paradoxically having to be rescued by them on occasion.

I shall turn now to the three authors for whom I analysed two books for purposes of comparison. Broadly speaking, two of these, Courtney and Johns, proved to have a largely consistent style across genres, whereas Brent-Dyer revealed more contrast. To begin with Courtney, in both her family and adventure genres she includes a degree of physical description, but this is not enormously detailed and is frequently related to character, as for example "there was something very reliable in the blue-grey eyes and firm chin" (*Sally's Family*, 68). Her girls are not necessarily pretty: Lucy, for instance, in *Sally's Family*, is "at the ugly duckling stage" (68), while Sally herself merely has a "slim, vigorous figure" (38); in the *Denehurst* books, Avice admittedly has golden-brown curls, but none of the girls is "pretty" or "beautiful". Most of the modification is in fact about character. In *Sally's Family* the two boys and four girls of the family are all quite distinct, the boys being more standard types than the girls. Robin reminds one of M.E. Atkinson's Bill, being noisy, enthusiastic and sometimes belligerent, while Guy is reliable, responsible and good-natured as befits an older brother. The girls show more variation: Sally is frank, cheerful and determined under difficulties, Kitty is a spoilt sulky beauty who learns the meaning of hard work and unselfishness through the book (both of these are also fairly standard "types" from girls' books), while Lucy is a bookworm, extremely clever, and Jane the youngest is solemn, serious and prim, thanks to having been evacuated to an elderly professor and his sister during the war. There is more description of the girls than the boys, although the contrast is not so sharp as in Blyton, for instance, and they all have mostly positive but some negative characteristics (Lucy forgets her household tasks when she is lost in a book, Robin is tactless), except Kitty who is largely negative until her reformation.

Well Done, Denehurst! has proportionately less description, which makes sense as this book is about the action rather than the character development. All the four children are essentially positive, and the contrast is not between the boy and the girls but between the older two girls, who behave "thoughtfully" or "reflectively", and the younger pair, Moira and Bob, who are cheerful and confident and reckless. Indeed, Moira is four times described as confident, and like Nancy Blackett, her confidence is presented as simply part of her character, not in any way an annoying or inappropriate characteristic.

Captain Johns frequently uses the same or very similar language of and by Biggles and Worrals. They both speak "calmly", "evenly" or "imperturbably", keeping their head in a crisis. They both demonstrate authority by speaking "bitingly", "crisply", "tersely" or "in a brittle voice". Worrals in this book has "an astute brain", a term also applied elsewhere to Biggles. In the same way, Algy and Frecks both speak "sarcastically" or "sneer", not in contempt as those words out of context might suggest, but as a means of joking and lightening the mood. Frecks, however, also speaks "anxiously", "nervously" (three times) and "apprehensively"; as mentioned in chapter seven, it appears more acceptable to have a female character show fear, though as second-lead she also overcomes it. In *Biggles* there are four heroes not two as in *Worrals*. Ginger in this book in particular is quite emotional: he "snarled", "glared", "shouted ... triumphantly" and was "white with passion". Probably this, like Frecks' fears, is intended to help the reader identify with him, which could be difficult with the confident and overwhelmingly capable leaders. Bertie verges on being a figure of fun in some of the books, being rather effeminate and a caricature of an aristocrat, though loyal ("we do not desert our friends").

One feature of Johns' work, which contrasts with all the other authors in this study, is the amount of physical description of landscape he often puts in. In the two books analysed here, we find this particularly in *Worrals on the Warpath*: there is a two-page author's note at the beginning plus eight solid paragraphs through the book, in addition to several separate sentences, describing the Cevennes and the Camargue in France, the scenes of the story. As remarked above, there is almost no physical description of the main characters, however, although many of the minor ones are given a phrase or sentence: "an old thick-set man" (58), "a tall, bearded man in the roughest of rough clothes" (53). In *Biggles* "*Fails To Return*", in fact, there is probably more description of people than usual because the four heroes are separated and have different encounters with various other characters: since they do not always know the names of these people, at least at first, it is necessary to have a clear description of each so that the reader will know that, for example, this man Algy has just seen is someone Bertie met in the previous chapter.

What does stand out in this particular *Biggles* book is the detailed physical descriptions of two women, Jeanette and the princess, who are each introduced with a long paragraph, which is followed at intervals by other mentions of their looks ("her olive cheeks", "a pale, oval face"). Both these women play important roles in the story, although their share of the action is much smaller than that of most of the men. There is no corresponding description of Lucien and Raoul, the French Resistance fighters, in the *Worrals* book: they may be young and handsome, but the reader is not told so, nor even the colour of their hair and eyes. This is actually quite interesting, in that traditionally romance plays little role in boys' adventure stories, yet often quite a major role in girls' books, while here we have the opposite. The boy readers are being presented with two different beautiful young women, one of whom, Jeanette, infatuates Ginger, the youngest of the heroes, with whom the readers are invited to identify (though it must be admitted that in this respect *Biggles "Fails To Return"* is not typical of the series); the girl readers, on the other hand, are shown two young women who are attractive to males (the British pilots attempt to flirt with them), but essentially unmoved by them. The only male character shown in any depth is the middle-aged Resistance fighter, Louis, whose relationship to Worrals is more loyal servant than anything else.

It was difficult to select which of Brent-Dyer's thrillers to analyse, since as already mentioned the earliest two bear a strong resemblance to her family stories, while the last two are strikingly different (*The Susannah Adventure* is probably more akin to the two former). I felt it would be most interesting to look at the last, *Top Secret*. Although like *Chudleigh Hold* and *Fardingales* there is a large family involved, they remain mostly in the background, only some of the males being involved in the actual adventure, except Aunt Freda. Overall, there are an enormous number of physical and character descriptions of both major and minor characters in *The Chalet School Does It Again*; in *Top Secret* there are considerably fewer, though still many more than in Ransome or Blyton, and they are more concerned with dividing the characters into "good guys" and "bad guys" than with presenting character in any kind of depth.

The school story has a large cast of characters (all female) and many of these receive a short description, such as "a thin girl possessed of a sharp, fair prettiness" (22), "neat-fingered and artistically inclined" (96). In some cases this description takes the place of a name; regular readers of the series would recognise the former, for example, as Emerence Hope, who is a minor character in many of the later books. Either the plethora of descriptions or the frequent mention of new names would probably be confusing to a new reader, but the majority, as fans, presumably liked to see old friends appearing, however briefly. The physical descriptions often but not always include colouring and hairstyle, and mostly explicitly or implicitly prettiness ("a charmingly pretty girl" (38), "a handsome girl" (41), "an oval face lit by a pair of very dark Irish-grey eyes": 31), although occasionally we do meet one who is plain but good-humoured. The personalities vary more, with both positive and negative traits mentioned in about equal numbers ("sweet-tempered", "common-sense", "outrageously spoilt", "very proud" and so on). The new girl in this book, as is often the case, is somewhat of a problem and has many negative descriptors before she finally redeems herself by diving into a lake to rescue someone who has fallen in. As with *Sally's Family* described above, the reforming of a difficult character is a staple of girls' stories.

In *Top Secret* there is considerably more on character than looks, and some of the physical descriptions focus on fighting ability: "all muscle and whipcord" (85), "trained to the last ounce" (98). Everything related to the main characters is positive, even Hawk's rage ("his black eyes were gleaming with a dull reddish glow that came when he was fully aroused": 92) being fully justified by the situation, and also kept under control, unlike that of the villain who lashes out when goaded by Hawk ("mad with rage": 169). Hawk's "cool impudence" (159), which in the Chalet School would be a defiance of legitimate authority, is here a bold defiance of the villains' demands. Aunt Freda, the only female, is "a lady", young for her age, strong-willed and energetic, intelligent, practical and brave, exciting the admiration of all the male characters. Perhaps these traits are those of the heroine of a girls' book rather than typical of the odd female sometimes thrown into a boys' adventure story for the male characters to protect?

One common factor with the Chalet School is that mischief is seen as essentially positive. A number of the girls at the school are described as "mischievous" or "naughty" in a context of semi-indulgence, a feature of girls' school stories of the twentieth century which distinguishes them from earlier girls' literature, and can be seen as an influence of the growing women's movement, innocent mischief (as opposed to serious rule-breaking) being linked with initiative and high spirits. In *Top Secret* this link is almost explicit, with fourteen-year-old Archie, an "impish-looking boy" (97) who has broken his arm riding a forbidden horse, being the one who saves the day by sneaking off unseen by the villains to fetch help.

Aside from this point, however, these two books seem to me to be not merely different genres, but aimed at different readerships. The *Chalet School* stories focus on females interacting, helping one another to develop in a supportive atmosphere, though with a strong hierarchy. The mistresses are heavy on discipline but also sympathetic when anyone is in trouble: "[Matron] is nippy ... but she's awfully understanding" (146); the headmistress "always tempers justice with mercy" (162). *Top Secret*, like *Condor Crags Adventure*, has a focus on action, on physical courage and endurance, which seems much more typical of the traditional boys' adventure tale. Words like "pluck" and "iron" (of will) are applied to the heroes, and Hawk tells himself "contemptuously to stop being a sissy" (79), while Walter says of the fact that he will probably bear a scar for life "I'm not a girl to make a fuss about that!" (67). This extends from the language to the actual content: in the school stories accidental death frequently threatens, but there is always a last-minute rescue, and a couple of kidnappings result in the girls being returned unharmed; in both *Condor Crags Adventure* and *Top Secret* serious torture (maiming and blinding) is threatened and in the latter actually occurs, some of the villains are blown up by a Japanese mine, and in the former book Godfrey, having accidentally killed a puma, kills her cubs rather than let them starve without their mother. Even in *Chudleigh Hold*, which still has many elements of a "family" book, the fake "Cousin Merrill" kills herself when she accidentally lets go of a grenade with which she has been threatening others. This is all much stronger meat than Brent-Dyer offers in her other genres.

A number of conclusions may be drawn from this analysis. Firstly, the authors vary considerably as regards the quantity and nature of modification of the characters. It cannot be said, overall, that either gender receives more positive or more negative modification, yet it is true that the boys in particular tend to conform to stereotypes: noisy, hungry and adventurous or strong determined leaders who suppress their emotions. Most of the authors have either more female than male major characters or at least enough females to present a range of personalities, with the result that there are a number of girls and women who are skilful, bold, full of initiative and admired for their strength of character. In most cases these are presented with little or no negativity; the exception is George in the *Famous Five* (and Blyton does something similar if less pronounced with Dinah in the *Adventure* series). However, some characteristics such as being small and weak, having a tendency to cry, being sensitive and imaginative, are clearly associated with one or more female characters, and here they are neutral; I think it likely they would be negative if attached to a male, but there are no examples of this in these particular books. I cannot find any significant distinction between male and female authors' use of modification, only individual differences, and except for Brent-Dyer an author writing in different genres or targeting only boys or only girls rather than both does not seem to vary greatly in this respect either.

Talking time

There have been a number of studies of how much males and females talk, particularly in mixed gatherings. Folklinguistics would have it that women talk (a lot) more than men, but this is not borne out by the evidence. For example, in a 1975 study by Swacker where participants had to describe three pictures, males averaged 13.0 minutes per picture as compared with 3.17 minutes for females. In a dialogue, this is at least partly about dominance (power); research in the same year by Zimmerman and West of twenty pairs of same-sex speakers, ten male and ten female, found the number of "overlaps" (i.e. slight anticipation by one speaker of their turn in the dialogue) far exceeded that of "interruptions" (violations of the turn-taking rules of conversation), being three times as many. In eleven mixed pairs, however, there were five times as many interruptions as overlaps, and 96% were by the male speaker. In other words, in the mixed pairs, the males were wresting control of the conversation from the females.

Other studies indicate that male children are brought up to dominate conversation with the (probably unconscious) complicity of mothers, sisters and teachers (Talbot 2010). Research in the US, Britain and Sweden looking at teacher-pupil interaction found boys got more of the teacher's attention (Sarah 1980; Spender 1982; Sadker and Sadker 1985). The GIST (Girls Into Science and Technology) project studied 2,000 children in ten comprehensives in Greater Manchester. Teachers actively tried to give as much attention to girls as to boys: 75% of female teachers managed this, though only 50% of male teachers did so. A male head of science who achieved 50-50 attention said afterwards he *felt* as though 90% of his attention had gone to the girls (Coates 1993). It seems probable that the myths about female garrulity are at least partly rooted in the belief, conscious or otherwise, that woman's role is to be silent, so any speech is too much.

Most of the studies cited are quite old, but still later than the period of the texts in this study; much sociolinguistic research did not really take off until the 1970s. It can reasonably be assumed that if linguists in the 1970s and '80s found such striking differences between the genders, this would have been even more the case, or certainly not less so, in the 1930s to '60s. In fact, a recent (2017) BBC2 documentary looking at a primary school class had similar findings, sadly.

I decided to look at two contrasting books from the above study of modifiers, namely *Five Go Adventuring Again* and *Swallowdale*. Both feature a group of children rather than adults, but one author is female, the other male; one has so far shown marked differences in her treatment of the two genders, the other far less so. I counted the number of short speeches (defined as less than three lines of text) and the number of long speeches (defined as three or more lines of text) by each of the children. (Interruptions and overlaps are far less frequent in literature generally than in real life dialogue, so I saw little point in looking at those.) Of course, the texts do not show how much actual children actually spoke, but how much the author wanted them to speak. If the author had absorbed popular wisdom about girls talking a lot, one could expect to see that reflected in the text. If, on the other hand, the author had absorbed the prevailing gender power structure, one would expect to see the boys dominating the speech turns, especially the longer ones. The former would likely be a conscious choice, the latter probably not.

Table 8-2 below shows the numbers from the Blyton book, and figure 8-1 represents the pattern of long and short speeches by the four children. Taking the short utterances, there is a marked distinction, not between boys and girls but between George and Julian on the one hand, and Anne and Dick on the other. Julian is the leader and George is rebellious and defiant, and so they have more to say. The pattern with longer utterances is rather different, however: here we see that Anne has very little to say, but while George and Julian still dominate, Dick's share has increased. Since George's chief characteristic is her desire to be a boy, and she is frequently described as succeeding in behaving like one, whatever that means, this would suggest that Blyton is giving "boys" the power of dominating the conversation.

Table 8-2: Total number of utterances by the four children in Blyton

	George	Anne	Julian	Dick
short	145	80	151	77
long	47	9	54	24

Figure 8-1: Pattern of long and short utterances by each child in Blyton

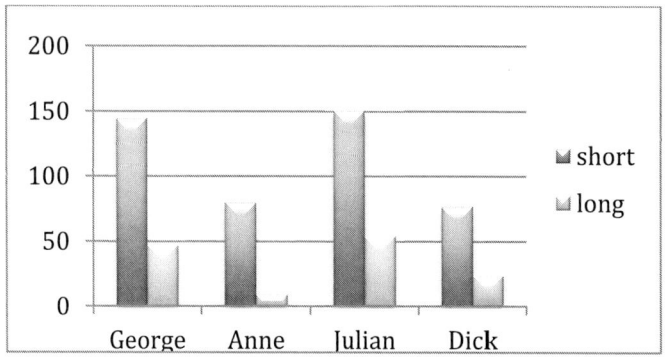

Ransome has a somewhat more complex picture. In this case, I not only counted total numbers of utterances, long and short, (see table 8-3), but also took into account that Nancy and Peggy only appear in seventeen of thirty-six chapters, the book being more about the Walkers, and there are other chapters which feature only Titty and Roger. Figure 8-2 shows the raw numbers, and figure 8-3 shows the normalised data, using the approximate method of dividing by the number of chapters in which each character appears and multiplying by thirty-six. (Of course, we cannot really know what share they would have had if they each appeared in every chapter, and this is a fairly rough approximation; had I been analysing recordings of actual speech it would have been necessary to be more precise.) There is also the point that there are two boys but four girls, in contrast to Blyton's two and two, so a direct comparison of the boys' total utterances with the girls' is also problematic. If one simply multiplies the boys' turns by two, the overall pattern would be that they had slightly more than 50% of the short utterances, but considerably less than half of the long ones. Figures 8-4 and 8-5 show respectively the proportion of long turns for the Walker family and then for the Swallows and Amazons together.

Table 8-3: Total utterances by the six children in Ransome.

	John	Susan	Titty	Roger	Nancy	Peggy
short	439	315	490	412	260	116
long	42	21	44	6	61	13

Figure 8-2: Pattern of utterances in Ransome, raw numbers.

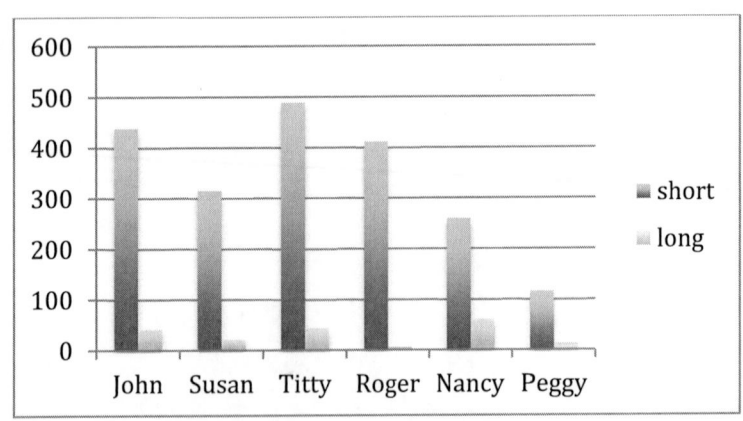

Figure 8-3: Pattern of utterances with normalised data.

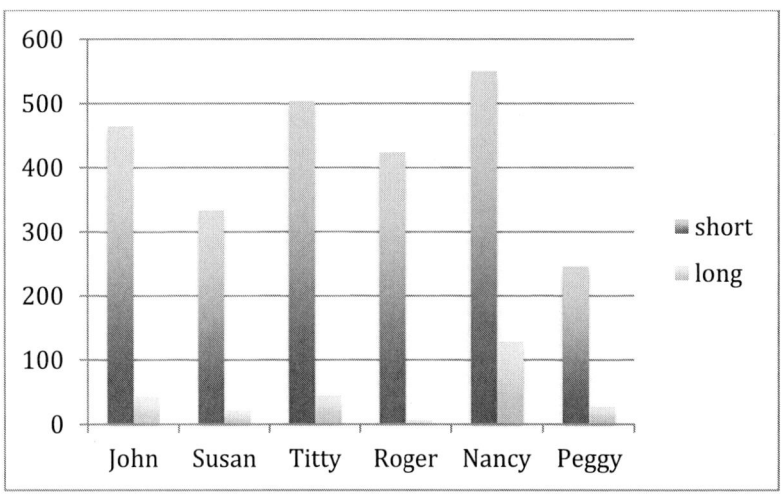

Figure 8-4: Long utterances by the Walker children, normalised

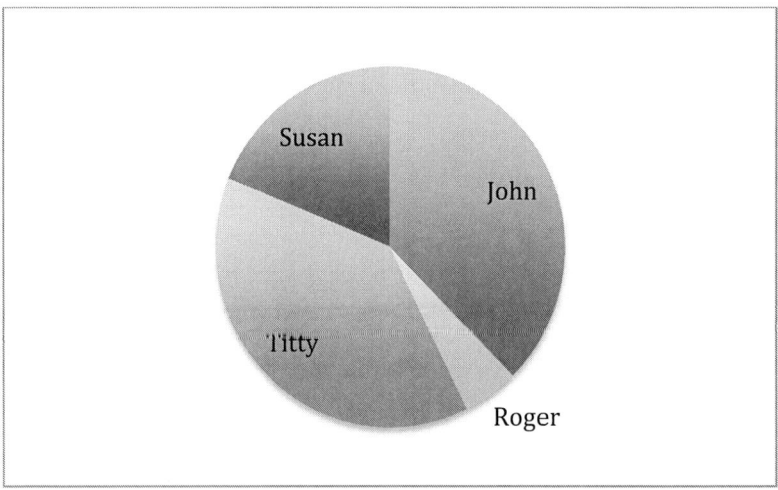

Figure 8-5: Long utterances by all six children, normalised.

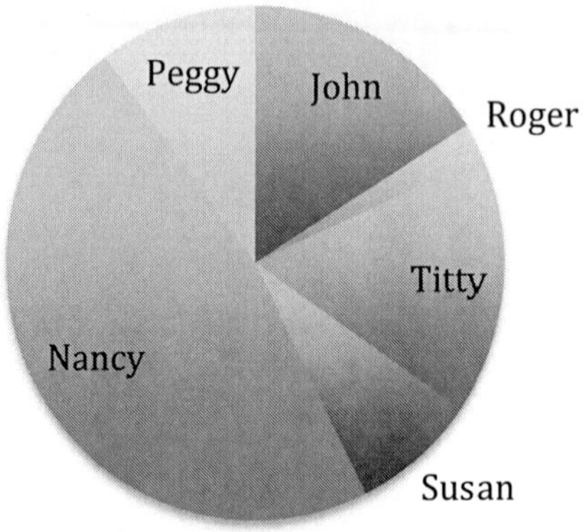

What is happening here? If we look first at the four Walker children, there is a marked difference between John and Titty on the one hand, and Susan and Roger on the other. Longer speeches tend to be associated with decision-making, as the decision is often accompanied by an explanation, or may involve different directions to different people. This explains why Julian in the *Famous Five* has 40% of the long speeches, and also why John Walker has a lot. Titty too takes the lead in several chapters where she and Roger go off alone, since she "outranks" him. However, some of her longer turns are expressions of her vivid imagination: in this book she makes the cave she and Roger find belong to the imaginary "Peter Duck", and constantly weaves this character into the narrative. Roger, as the least powerful of the four, speaks mostly in short comments (talking a similar amount to John and Titty), and has very few longer turns, while Susan is the least chatty but has more longer turns than Roger, mostly in connection with mealtime, bedtime and similar domestic details.

With the Amazons, a further factor comes into play, as they live in the Lake District, while the Walkers are summer visitors. In addition to Nancy exercising her leadership, therefore, we have both girls acting as experts, providing local information. Sometimes this also applies to George in the *Famous Five*, as the other three are staying in her house. A 1980 study of conversational dominance (Leet-Pellegrini, cited in Coates 1993, 113) found that gender and expertise were good predictors of dominance; a male speaker who was also well-informed was likely to dominate. Here we have only one of those variables.

Although a cursory glance at figure 8-5 would suggest girls are more talkative than boys in Ransome, figure 8-4 shows clearly that the picture is more complex than that. Numbers alone are insufficient for discourse analysis. In both Blyton and Ransome, it appears that power is the determining factor when it comes to share of the conversation, whether deriving from authority within the group or from a particular expertise. Where in the social context of the 1930s and '40s, however, both authority and expertise tended to lie with males, in Ransome Titty, to some extent Susan, and especially Nancy share the power and therefore the longer speech turns. The chief reason for George's large share in Blyton is not that she exercises power but that she defies it (vocally) in others. Thus although superficially figures 8-1 and 8-4 might suggest a similar dynamic in the two authors, with one girl and one boy dominating the talking time, in fact they are quite distinct. Blyton's males exercise authority through speech, while her anomalous girl defies it; with Ransome, both males and females have authority, though one cannot say there are no gender distinctions, since Susan's power, as explored in chapter six, derives largely from her quasi-maternal status, and many of Titty's utterances are expressions of her creative imagination and nothing to do with the power hierarchy.

CHAPTER NINE

IS IT A BOY OR A GIRL?
GENDER IDENTITY

Earlier I accepted the proposition that sex was biologically, gender culturally determined. This distinction is quite widely accepted among psychologists but has itself been questioned. Butler (1990) for example has suggested that even sex is a cultural construct. It is certainly true that, while most humans operate with a binary view of sex, even before developments in DNA profiling societies were aware of other options, commonly known as hermaphrodites (now more usually as "intersex"). An additional three sexes based on different forms of hermaphroditism have been suggested (Fausto-Sterling 1993, cited in Franklin 2012, 7). These conditions are typically "treated" with surgery, psychiatry, hormones or a combination thereof, on the assumption that they are abnormalities which need to be corrected. Some question this, however; they are only abnormal if we impose a binary view of sex on our species. Among the biologically "normal" it is also quite common to encounter gender dysphoria (discomfort with one's biological sex) and gender identity disorder (a persistent belief that one actually belongs to the opposite sex). Many grow out of these conditions, while some grow up and become transsexuals. To some extent these conditions may be exacerbated by society's expectations of how each gender should behave; if a little girl really wants to play with trucks and is constantly told, by adults and her peers, that that is not what girls do, it would hardly be surprising if she felt she should be a boy.

Over the past century or so a variety of theories has been proposed as to how our gender identities are constructed. Freud's concept of Oedipus and Electra complexes won both adherents and fierce opposition: many were not comfortable with the idea of child sexuality, and he focused moreover very much on the development of the heterosexual male. Erik Erikson, who built on Freud's ideas, was also criticised for seeing males as the unmarked gender (and females therefore as some kind of inadequate male, as in a sense in the bible with Adam and Eve), although he did try to address these criticisms, unlike Freud (Franklin 2012). However innovative, Freud was also a man of his time, and in his time males were dominant. Lawrence Kohlberg, influenced by Piaget, produced cognitive development theory, which proposes various stages of gender recognition and identity which arise as the child reaches an appropriate stage of general cognitive development. Once the child understands what male and female mean in its society, it will begin to model its behaviour on a same-sex role model. Social learning theory (later reformulated as social cognitive theory) takes the opposite view, that behaviour precedes understanding: gender appropriate behaviour in a child is rewarded (e.g. by approval) and inappropriate behaviour punished (e.g. by disapproval), and thus the child learns to behave appropriately as determined by society (Franklin 2012). All of these still have to explain how some people do not conform to a binary gender distinction: what about gays and lesbians? How do intersex children select a role model?

I have already outlined Bem's Sex-Role Inventory in chapter eight. This was a tool in her gender schema theory, the idea that we all operate with schemas, mental frameworks as to how things "work" in society, of which gender is one aspect. As we are socialised we absorb schemas which enable us to function in society, and to judge how appropriately others are functioning. Thus gender schemas are culturally specific. Social constructionism goes further: emerging in the 1960s out of ethnography and anthropology, it made central the cultural aspect of behaviour. Lev Vygotsky's *Thought and Language* (1986) was deeply influential, proposing that we learn about the world though interaction with it, and that conversations are socialised into children's internal thought processes. Rather than the child's cognitive development determining its socialisation, for Vygotsky all cognitive development is cultural.

In the face of a range of competing hypotheses, it is difficult for the layperson (I am not a developmental psychologist) to choose. Without swallowing any one theory hook, line and sinker, I am persuaded that there is strong evidence that the process of socialisation includes the development of gender identity, and that cultural concepts of "masculine" and "feminine" vary through time and space. It is therefore important to be clear that, whatever our twenty-first century perspectives, this study is focused on the mid-twentieth, on white British middle-class children. If what a child reads counts as dialogue, and dialogues are internalised by the child as part of its socialisation, how would these books contribute to the development of gender identity in their readers? As Rosemary Ross Johnston says (in Grenby and Reynolds 2011, 154) "books for children are rather like cultural mirrors that reflect what are widely held to be acceptable social positions." Pennell (2002, 55) claims that "[c]hildren's literature can make a significant contribution to whether or not child readers understand the patriarchal social order and oppositional gendered relationships to be immutable". While this may be true, it presupposes the authors themselves will recognise that this order and these relationships are not immutable; I am not sure it is reasonable to expect this of writers born in the nineteenth century, as most of those in this study were.

As Reynolds (2002) and others have pointed out, the traditional model of gender is polarised: "masculine" and "feminine" are opposite and complementary. Nowadays this is being questioned, but at the period of study it still held true. In the nineteenth century authors like Charlotte M. Yonge had expressed an explicit "feminine girls are good, unfeminine girls are bad" message, and what was meant by feminine was passive and self-sacrificing. This idea changed somewhat in the early twentieth century, as a more active type of female became acceptable (as in Angela Brazils' school stories). The tomboy is a feature of girls' literature from at least as early as *Little Women* (1868), and in many cases a feature of real life, but once in the mid-teens the tomboy has to make the transition to becoming a "young lady" or there will be negative consequences. Reynolds (1990) suggests that although at first sight tomboys and girl rebels in fiction look like positive role models, in fact they are used to perpetuate rather than challenge the traditional vision of acceptable womanhood. I shall look at the girls and women in these books to see how far that is true here.

While the tomboy is a recognised and indeed often positive character in literature, the "sissy" boy is far less acceptable. This is in line with real life, where a boy transgressing the gender code is more likely to earn strong disapproval than a girl. In the nineteenth century, "manliness" in both sex manuals and children's fiction was a blend of compassion, gentleness, strength, self-control and purity (Nelson 1991). However, from the 1870s the hearty-games-playing, stiff-upper-lip type of manliness was becoming prevalent. This reflected a gradual reclassification of attitudes and behaviour considered appropriate for males, influenced by several famous trials of transvestites and of homosexuals such as Oscar Wilde, which induced suspicion of any behaviour which might be regarded as "feminine". As women increasingly entered the male world in the twentieth century, for many there was a compensatory insistence on distinctive behaviours. Pennell (2002) suggests that even if a writer forefronts the female, or adds masculine attributes to female characters, they may still be reinforcing this binarism. In order to "degender" rather than "regender" it is necessary to offer a wide range of subjectivities, and in particular of masculine ones. Bonnie Smith (2013) remarks that for many "gender" means "women"; on the contrary, we need to look at the male roles in these books as well as the female ones, in order to understand what concepts of gender are being portrayed, and whether they are, as would be predictable, essentially binary and rigid.

The feminine

The girls and women in these books are, in general, portrayed as sensitive: sensitive to others' feelings, to beauty and, less positively, to offence, intended or otherwise. In chapter seven I described how Jane Lockett felt compassion for an escaped prisoner, Penny Warrender of the Lone Piners for Miss Ballinger when the latter was arrested, and Lucy-Ann twice shows similar feelings for their enemies. Even the tough Worrals sheds tears over the local man Oko when he is killed by the Japanese, and her Sikh companion tells her not to be ashamed: "I have seen warriors weep for less" (*Worrals of the Islands*, 92), though this is somewhat different as he is a friend. Blyton's Anne and Lucy-Ann are both deeply imaginative, especially the latter, as are Titty and Dorothea in the Ransome books. In *Swallowdale*, Titty makes a wax effigy of the Amazons' Great Aunt who is making their life miserable, accidentally drops it on the fire and destroys it, and spends several days suffering considerable distress thinking she may actually have killed the woman (whom she merely intended to make unwell enough to leave the girls alone). However much she dislikes someone, she is too compassionate to wish them dead.

Empathy with the unfortunate, criminals or otherwise, tends to be accompanied by a sensitivity to the natural world. In *Worrals Flies Again* she is affected by the desolation of the neglected chateau and its gardens; in *Five Go Down to the Sea* Anne shivers when she looks up at the cliffs which "frowned down at her" (41); and there are numerous examples of girls picking flowers, from Frecks, incongruously in the middle of a mission, to Atkinson's Jane Lockett and Anna. Dot in *The Picts and the Martyrs* even picks some to brighten up the hut she and Dick are camping in. In *The Valley of Adventure* the children find a cave full of stalactites, and both the girls remark upon its beauty, while the boys say things like "My word, what a sight!" and explain to the girls how stalactites are made. In the *Lone Pine* books, Peter is deeply devoted to her native Shropshire hills, and Jenny is terrified of the mountain she calls "Neglected". Saville's girls, however, also display a touchiness when their respective boyfriends fail them in some way, not writing a response to a letter in which they have poured out their hearts, or going off on some ploy without them. This is probably quite a realistic representation of teenagers' moods (even the admired and pragmatic Peter is not immune), but it is not a feature of the other authors here.

Is this sensitivity shown as a particularly female characteristic, or does it also apply to the males? Jane Lockett's brothers do not share her empathy with the prisoner, nor do the boys or Dinah share Lucy-Ann's. Jon Warrender does agree with Penny, however, and Captain Johns has numerous examples of beautiful or desolate landscapes arousing emotion in his male heroes as well as in Worrals. I cannot find any examples of males picking flowers, though. Nor, less trivially, are there any examples of males feeling upset, angry and hurt at others' behaviour; the closest is John Walker being deeply upset at Captain Flint calling him a liar (in the first book, when they were still strangers). This is a matter of "honour", a traditionally male problem, rather than a question of having one's feelings disregarded, as with the girls.

A society may consider it desirable for females to be sensitive (as this will enable them to be responsive to the needs of their husbands and children); for some of these authors it is, if not desirable, at least acceptable for them also to be weak in some respect. A physical example of this is seasickness: in *The Susannah Adventure* Anstace and Humphrey rescue a brother and sister, Kevin and Kennie, and Kennie is very ill with seasickness aboard the *Susannah*; Blyton's Lucy-Ann is seasick in *The Sea of Adventure*; in *Peter Duck*, when the Swallows and Amazons go to sea for the first time, Nancy and Titty are both overcome for a while; in Antonia Forest's *Marlows* books Nicola, the most important girl, likewise suffers. The treatment is not the same, as in Brent-Dyer there is, as always about any ailment, a great deal of fuss made, while in the others it is a problem to be overcome, and other people carefully do not comment. Nonetheless, it is notably the girls who suffer, not the boys. One exception to that is Gussy, the disguised (and rather sissy) prince in *The Circus of Adventure*, who gets carsick. This evokes no sympathy; Dinah tells him to go ahead and be sick, "But don't make a FUSS" (62). Part of the storyline of this book involves the little prince, who has been pampered all his life and cries when "normal" children tease him, learning to be tougher. However, this also demonstrates how Dinah fails to conform to the feminine stereotype; she does not like small children. I return to this below.

More psychological than physical are nightmares. In Brent-Dyer two different girls suffer from these, a minor character (younger sister) who has to be protected in *Fardingales*, and Crumpet, the heroine, in *Chudleigh Hold*. The latter is portrayed as courageously battling with a weakness; her oldest sister and Nanny are sympathetic, although another sister thinks she should "pull herself together", and her overall courage is not in doubt. She is a much stronger character than Kennie, who is not only seasick but also a mass of nerves as a result of bad experiences (essentially a kind of child abuse, with her brother being forced by their guardian to commit crimes). As we have seen, many of Brent-Dyer's girls are strong, bold characters (like Anstace), but at the same time she does not have any males succumbing to nerves or nightmares. A contrast there would be Dorita Fairlie Bruce, one of Brent-Dyer's contemporaries who also wrote girls' books; she introduces the man who marries one of her heroines as recovering from a nervous breakdown (*Dimsie Grows Up*, 1938), and he takes most of the book to be able to return to a normal life.

Saville gives his girls a strange kind of sensitivity which goes beyond the normal: in different books each of Peter, Penny, Jenny and Harriet has a dream which proves prophetic in some way. In *The Secret of Amorys* Penny dreams of the rites in a Mithraic temple, the ruins of which the children later discover. Peter in *The Secret of Grey Walls* dreams of herself and an unknown girl hurrying towards an unknown house with a moor fire behind them; when she meets Penny she recognises her from the dream, the rest of which also comes true. There are no other elements of the supernatural in the books; it seems that girls have some special powers? It is true that in real life poltergeists and other such manifestations are often associated with adolescents, though not necessarily girls. Did Saville see adolescent girls as having some sort of window on other realities?

Blyton does not go in for subtleties like nightmares and nerves, but her "girly" girls, Anne and Lucy-Ann, are often scared and are allowed to hold others' hands in moments of fear. These include not only reasonable fears when the villains are shooting at them, for instance, but Lucy-Ann also holds Bill's hand when crossing the couplings in a train (*Sea of Adventure*) because she's afraid it might come in two while they are going across. The other children are scornful, but Bill is sympathetic. He "liked all the children very much, but Lucy-Ann was his favourite" (53). She is admittedly the youngest, but only a year younger than Dinah.

Although Blyton often pairs the boys and girls separately, she does not explore female friendship particularly. Dinah tends to be rather contemptuous of Lucy-Ann and they have little in common; similarly with George and Anne in the *Five* books. However, whereas Suico (2017) found that modern texts aimed at teenagers tend to feature "friends" who are in many ways actually rivals, driven by spite and envy and competing for attention, there is very little of this in my texts. Saville's great theme is loyalty, and this applies to the sexes equally; Brent-Dyer in her school stories portrays deep female friendships (Auchmuty 1992), though there is less opportunity for this in her thrillers; Courtney's girls are good friends, though she does not lay particular emphasis on this, and Johns' Worrals and Frecks are very close, united against the world of men in which they operate. Possibly this is because these authors grew up in an era when close female friendships were normal and acceptable and unlikely to be construed as having lesbian overtones.

Doing gender is about many things, including what one wears, how one moves, what activities are acceptable or appropriate, and which are not. Sometimes this is addressed explicitly in these books. Ransome uses the "G.A." (Nancy and Peggy's Great Aunt) to attack old-fashioned ideas of how children should be brought up, which is about both the relative freedom and independence they should be allowed, and what behaviour is suitable for girls. When the pair are late for meals thanks to being involved in adventures with the Walker children, she forbids them to go off for the day on their own; the Walkers are horrified later to see them sitting primly, on one occasion in a carriage, on another in a boat, dressed in white frocks and gloves, being "young ladies" (*Swallowdale*). Their usual attire is "knickers" (shorts in later books) and red caps. Even Timothy, an adult friend, says "Of course it isn't her [i.e. Nancy's] fault" (82). In *The Picts and the Martyrs* she makes them practise the piano and learn poetry, as these are ladylike activities. Sailing, wearing shorts and turning up for meals when they feel like it are unacceptable. Even though at the end of the latter book the G.A. is revealed to have a slightly more positive side, the message is clearly one of disapproval for ideas which are out of date; the children are all upset that the G.A. makes Mrs Blackett cry with her criticisms, and Mrs Walker is so careful in her comments it is evident she dislikes the G.A. Children should be allowed freedom and independence, girls as much as boys.

This is an enormous contrast to George in the *Famous Five*, and to a lesser extent Dinah in the *Adventure* series. George refuses to answer to her real name, has her hair cut very short, and is delighted when strangers take her for a boy. She puts her hands in her pockets and tries to walk like Dick (*Five Go Down to the Sea*). She is very independent and this is partly about having the freedom to do as she wants, but also she is respected for her "masculine" qualities, courage and initiative. However, as we saw in the last chapter, although she is praised for these things, overall there is much more negative language about George than anyone else; she is moody and difficult and bad-tempered. Dinah does not actively want to be a boy, but she is also hot-tempered, having physical fights with her brother. She is portrayed as tough, unsympathetic to others, and her fear of the animals and insects her brother collects is belittled. Philip hits her, despite the code that boys should not hit girls, because she started it. Afterwards, she is the one to apologise; aggressive behaviour in a girl requires an apology. By contrast, Lucy-Ann is constantly praised for being "valiant" despite her fears, adults find her appealing, and even Philip, Dinah's brother, is delighted when she hugs him, which Dinah would never do. Like Anne but even more so, Lucy-Ann is the sweet feminine little girl whom everyone loves. Nancy Blackett is never compared to or with a boy, and although her talents and interests are traditionally "masculine" this is seen as entirely positive, with others including adults expressing admiration of her, and the Great Aunt's attempts to turn her into a young lady as negative.

While Nancy is the tomboy par excellence, the other girls in Ransome all join in the sailing, and all but Dorothea have short hair, although the Walker girls wear skirts in the illustrations. We do not have the sharp contrast between the tomboys and the feminine girls which Blyton provides. The other authors have a similar mix. Jane Lockett has bobbed hair and is very good at cricket and climbing trees, but not very interested in clothes, yet at the same time she picks flowers, does the cooking and is scared of the dark. Maud Loring and Moira in the Denehurst books are athletic and reckless, but they express no wish to be boys. Peter Sterling of the Lone Piners is likewise athletic and boyish, but also empathetic, bonding with Mary who needs a female role model.

Blyton's children never grow up, so we do not know what would have happened to George, but in some of the other series characters make or approach the transition to adulthood. Peter gets engaged to David in the last *Lone Pine* book, which is presented as the natural conclusion of their friendship. On the way to buy her engagement ring, he says "You must help me to be masterful" (139), a strange mixture of the assumption that it is a man's role to be masterful and the recognition that that is not quite how their relationship works. The main piece of actual action in that book consists of David heading off to try to resolve the question of what "the Ballinger" is up to before the day of the engagement party, getting caught, and having to be rescued by Peter.

In *Secret Water* the secret message from the Eels says "Father took two females round to our island". After Nancy has read it, she asks "But who are the two females? We haven't seen any grown-ups about at all." Titty points out it is she and Peggy who are meant, and she "turned suddenly red" (176) and was very indignant. Anstace is taken aback in *The Susannah Adventure* when Commander Treatt addresses her as "Miss Roseveare", and asks him to call her Anstace; her hair is "up" but she is not quite eighteen. (In all her girls' books, Brent-Dyer retains the Victorian custom of having girls put their hair up as a signal that they are grown up, while giving a nod to the fact that in real life many women had bobbed or shingled hair when she was writing.) From being quite a tomboy, strong-willed, athletic, good at sailing and taking an equal share in the adventure, Anstace is now moving into a woman's role; in the next book her job is to cook for the men who are going off to rescue Godfrey Chudleigh. Mrs Walker in Ransome is perhaps Anstace in ten years' time or so: she was clearly tomboyish as a girl, swimming and sailing and climbing, but now her role is defined as mother and wife, and her own past simply means she is more understanding as a mother. As adult heroines, Worrals and Frecks are, of course, much more active than this, but they are marked off as feminine by some behaviours, such as wearing makeup and skirts, and the fact that men flirt with them (and Frecks expresses interest in men, though it never leads anywhere). They are not merely grown-up tomboys; however, they come closest in these books to integrating the qualities of the tomboy, freedom and physical activity and skills, into an adult female life.

Saville and Johns both, as we have seen, give considerable agency to their female characters yet do make clear distinctions between male and female. Their view seems to be that men and women are different, but both equally capable. Feminine qualities may be equally valued, or in some cases more so. Saville's characters, male and female, talk of feminine intuition without questioning it as a concept. At the end of *The Dagger and the Flame* Francesca makes a long speech which is a plea for maternal feminism:

> "women think that the solutions to all these horrible problems are simpler than men make them. Women see more clearly that there is just not enough love in the world. There's plenty of hate, selfishness, greed, envy, violence and male stupidity and arrogance, but there just isn't enough love" (156).

And in *Worrals of the Islands* she expresses much the same idea, if less eloquently, in response to a man's remark that wars aren't for women:

> "If you said they shouldn't be I'd agree with you ... Who started the war anyway? Men. Take a look at the world and see what a nice mess men have made of it. No wonder they had to appeal to women to help them out" (19-20).

The masculine

In a patriarchal society males are privileged. There are some examples of male privilege in these books: in *The Secret of Spiggy Holes* the boys get to drive a motorboat which is a present from the king whose son the children have rescued; in *Five on a Hike Together* Julian comments that the girls don't get as much pocket money as the boys, which could be a school rule but this is not stated; in *Five Have Plenty of Fun* Dick and Julian have been abroad on holiday while Anne was at a camp. These all come from Blyton, but even in Ransome the boys learn Latin at school, while the girls do not (most schoolchildren would probably not regard that as a privilege, but it was a sign of a "good" school). Oliver Lockett goes to a public school while his sister attends a school in the nearby town, and in *Going Gangster* she takes a week off school to accompany Bill to the seaside after he has been ill, suggesting her education is less important than Oliver's; however, some of their friends and their rival Fenella are at a co-educational, very progressive boarding school. Apart from Blyton there is nothing really blatant in the other authors' work. In the 1930s when "good" schools had to be paid for, it was not uncommon in real life for families to invest more in their sons' education than that of their daughters.

There is occasionally an assumption that boys are more worldly-wise, which fits with Bem's designation of "gullible" as a female characteristic. For instance, in *Five Get Into Trouble* they meet a boy named Richard who tells tall tales, which fool the girls, who are horrified, while the boys listen with superior amusement. In Brent-Dyer it is the men who are somehow all-powerful and all-knowing; I have already remarked upon the fact that in her girls' books many of the fathers / husbands are doctors and imbued with the authority of professional expertise, but in *Fardingales* we have Mr Anthony, who is a bank manager, at one point going down the secret passage to look for the missing children armed with a revolver, and on another taking a single quick look at a notebook in code (and Russian) and immediately realising how serious the situation is and that he must take the notebook "to London". Did Brent-Dyer, who never married, perhaps retain a child's conviction that fathers were omnipotent?

Other characteristics which Bem signifies as masculine, such as "athletic", "independent", "assertive" and "willing to take risks" clearly, in these books, apply to girls as well as boys, though it may be true that they do not apply to all the girls but do to all the boys, even ones like Oliver Lockett and Dick in the Ransome books who are intellectual. (Jon Warrender, the clever one in Saville is not athletic–he once goes to a football match rather in the manner of an anthropologist attending some strange tribal ritual–but he is self-sufficient and a risk-taker.) There is a range of both masculine and feminine subjectivities in these books, but the masculine ones are, in general, more constrained by convention. Even though there is nothing comparable to the G.A.'s pressurising the Blackett girls to subdue their natures, in all the books the boys either feel obliged to be strong, brave and skilful, and ashamed if they fail in any way, or they actually are brave risk-takers and feel ashamed of any other boys who do not match up. In other words, they have absorbed their culture's stereotype of the successful male. There is an interesting feature in Saville where his otherwise quite unaggressive boys get physical when their girls are threatened, such as intellectual Jon hitting the villain in *Saucers over the Moor* when Penny has fallen and hurt her back in a tussle with him, and David threatening to hit someone who swears in front of Peter in *Not Scarlet But Gold*. This seems like a socially-conditioned reflex.

I have discussed in chapter seven how some of the boys feel fear but overcome or hide it. Bill Lockett is quite irritated when another boy his own age is in floods of tears (*Smuggler's Gap*). In *The House on the Moor* he is happy to meet Rickie, a "normal sort of chap–no piano-playing musical genius about him" (129), unlike Rickie's temperamental cousin Caspar, whom Bill disapproves of. Little Robin in the Lockett books admires and emulates Bill; in *Smuggler's Gap* he "felt manly and important–ready at any moment to knock people down and jump on their prostrate bodies" (244) (he is seven years old). John Walker is often portrayed worrying about failing in something; it is important for him not to be seen to make mistakes, because he is the captain. Bill Cunningham exhorts Jack and Philip to protect their sisters in the *Adventure* books, and Mr Morton tells David to look after his mother and siblings in *Mystery at Witchend*. The girls might be admired for courage and resourcefulness; it is expected of the boys, by others and themselves.

One exception to this is Bertie in the *Biggles* books and his attitude to women. He is the one who makes jokes to hide his embarrassment when Ginger falls for a young woman (*Biggles "Fails to Return"*), and when Algy explains Biggles' history with Marie Janis (*Biggles Looks Back*). In *Orchids for Biggles* we have just Biggles and Bertie in South America, and unusually there are two young women, neither of them a princess but both actually working class, one working at the hotel where the men are staying, the other a dancer in a local bar, and both rivals for the same man, which forms part of the plot. One is "a pretty but cheeky half-caste girl" (44) and the other is "crudely painted, heavily built, but attractive in a coarse sort of way" (59). The latter sits on Bertie's lap in the club and he pushes her off, which draws unfortunate attention. Later Biggles explains to her "He meant no offence. He is afraid of women" (85). While it is understandable that none of the heroes marries or even has a steady girlfriend, this being what editors believed boy readers preferred, it was not necessary for Johns to give Bertie this actual fear of women, which is not explained but which makes him a more interesting character, less of a caricature.

Just as women in the modern world may still face a "glass ceiling", men may face a "glass escalator", the pressure to be ambitious, to gain promotion, to have a successful career because that's what men do, who are traditionally the breadwinners. It is notable in these books that those who have a clear idea of what they want to do as a career are mostly the boys. John Walker is going in the Navy, Roger wants to be an engineer, and Dick will be an ornithologist, but his sister Dorothea, although she may become a writer, expects to live with him and effectively be his housekeeper. Nancy, for all her skills, never expresses any interest in a career, not even, as Nicola in the *Marlows* books does, to say she does not really want to become a Wren because they do not go to sea, and that's what she's interested in. Dot makes up stories, and their mother's old teacher, with whom they travel on the Broads in *Coot Club*, is an artist. Of the Locketts' various aunts, one is an artist and one a writer; although Brenda plans to study medicine, none of the women is a doctor or an engineer. Most of them in fact are defined as wives and mothers, and even Worrals and Frecks do not really have careers once the war is over. In Brent-Dyer's thrillers, the men have careers or at least manage an estate, while the women seem to wait around for a husband and then run a house; in her school books the females are more enterprising, especially by the 1950s, with most of the girls planning careers, although those who take up teaching (primarily so they can continue as characters in the series) generally stop work once they marry, and certainly once they have children.

Courtney is ambiguous on this point: in the Denehurst books the girls' housemistress marries their cousin Deryk and stops work, even though this is wartime and he is often away from home on secret missions, and she is young and able-bodied and could have been doing war work. Yet in one of her family books, *A Coronet for Cathie*, the heroine has to have a governess for a year due to her ill-health, and her aunt, who is a qualified teacher, says she cannot take on the job as she has just got a promotion and if she gave up work it would be hard to resume her career afterwards. In fact, in her family stories we have a curious range, from the sisters in *The Long Barrow* who plan to sacrifice their chances so their brother can train as a doctor, to Lucy in *Sally's Family* who wants to be a surgeon, and whose ambition is treated equally with that of her likewise clever brother. There is also in two different books (Courtney's *Mermaid House* and Johns' *Worrals Carries On*) a suggestion by a male character that a female one should become a barrister. In both cases this is a tribute to their ability to argue logically, and partly meant as a joke, but it is not presented as a ludicrous idea. While for the most part the girls seem to feel no pressure to have a career, and the women who do have one tend to be doing the kind of work which would have been acceptable to the previous generation for a "young lady", i.e. teaching or something creative, there is some acknowledgement that the world is changing, that there are other options and that a career may be important to a woman as well as a man.

Cross-dressing

Flanagan (2002; 2008) has claimed that while there is a rich history of cross-dressing in children's literature, there is a striking difference between male-female on the one hand, and female-male on the other. The former, such as for example Toad in *The Wind in the Willows*, is mostly for comic effect and the males concerned are uncomfortable and unconvincing; this is logical as the humour defuses a potential threat to masculinity. For girls and women, by contrast, it is about allowing them to "inhabit the male world and experience many of the liberties denied them in their female form" (Flanagan 2002, 79). She goes so far as to claim this is "invariably" the case (2008, 101); her argument is weakened for me by the fact that she does not explain in detail what texts and genres she has examined. She includes some tales by Perrault, and one or two other texts which predate modern feminism, but most of her examples are later than second-wave feminism, i.e. 1990s.

Henty's *A Soldier's Daughter*, one of his few books with a heroine rather than a hero, fits this scenario: Nita dresses as a British officer when the fort she is living in is under attack, and later when she and the real officer have been taken prisoner she escapes in native male attire. However, this is not just about freedom but also safety. She wants not only to be able to fight but to avoid being raped when the fort falls to the enemy, and when they have escaped she needs to be able to move around the countryside without attracting attention as she and her companion make their way back to British territory. This latter motivation is the one I have found most frequently in the books in this study.

There are a number of examples of cross-dressing in these books. (Flanagan (2008) points out that the word "transvestite" has an association with sexual gratification and a popular association with homosexuality in the case of male-female, and therefore uses the term "cross dressing"; I have followed her in this.) I am not really including George here, as her cross-dressing is overt and acknowledged by her family and friends, and is really an extreme example of the tomboy stereotype, although she certainly fits Flanagan's finding that female-male cross-dressing tends to focus on performance of gender, on learning how to act as a boy / man. George is constantly portrayed as striding, whistling, putting her hands in her pockets and generally behaving "like a boy". She also fits the pattern Flanagan noted whereby females in male guise outperform biological males: George can swim and row a boat if anything better than Julian and Dick, and often demonstrates courage and daring which arouse their admiration. (Likewise Nita in *A Soldier's Daughter* rescues her male companion, rather than the other way round, and demonstrates great initiative during their escape.)

However, most of the examples I found had a very different motivation. In *Five Have Plenty of Fun* the little girl Berta is dressed as a boy to protect her from potential kidnappers. In *The Circus of Adventure* the prince, Gussy, is dressed as a girl for similar reasons, to hide him from the wicked count who wishes to use him as a pawn against his uncle the king. In M.E. Atkinson's *Going Gangster* the Locketts help Patsy, a little gypsy girl, escape from school where she is unhappy, and disguise her as a boy, "John", to evade pursuit, while in *Smuggler's Gap* they disguise Robin as a girl so he will not be recognised when they try to take him to find his sister Anna. In *The House on the Moor* the escaped prisoner steals their car with their luggage in, and perforce has to use Aunt Lavinia's clothes to replace his prison outfit.

Johns has several cases: in addition to the rebel escaping in his wife's clothes already described (chapter three) in *Biggles Flies Again*, in *Worrals Flies Again* the Gestapo officer, Von Brandisch, comes to reconnoitre the chateau (which is, as he suspects, the headquarters of the local resistance) dressed as a nun; in *Worrals Goes East* their room is searched by a French "officer" who is actually a woman in disguise; and I selected *Biggles, Secret Agent* for this study because the young blonde "girl" who puzzles Biggles and Ginger for several chapters, eavesdropping on their conversations and sneaking round the hotel at night, turns out to be a dark-haired young man, son of the scientist they are themselves looking for. Finally, in *Mermaid House* there is a "Miss Cathcart" staying with the children's Great Aunt when they arrive who is actually a man named Robert, nephew of the missing Dr Morvyn. In all, in my 126 focus texts I found three cases of female-male and seven of male-female cross-dressing, by three female and one male writer.

Interestingly, it is the cases where the cross-dressers are children where discomfort is most felt. Berta is deeply upset at the idea of having her hair cut off, though in fact as her hair is straight she actually looks more like a boy than George, whose hair is curly, (to George's chagrin). She rejects suggested names Tom or Jim and selects Lesley, which is in fact her middle name. Gussy is "angry and humiliated" (148) at being turned into a girl (in his case, his hair is long for a boy, a royal tradition; it is tied up with ribbons). In the event, he acts convincingly as a shy little girl (giving him an excuse to hide his face), and earns the praise of the other children for his performance; it is only he himself who is not happy with the situation. In *Smuggler's Gap* Robin swaps clothes with a girl, and "All little girls like to wear boys' things. I always did", says Jane (135); Robin, however, "hated the thought" but decided it would be worth it if it enabled him to see Anna. Bill's reaction is to laugh at him.

Johns' characters seem to take cross-dressing in their stride. Von Brandisch and the "French officer" threaten Worrals' missions by spying on her, but their choice of disguise is not commented on as such. Gustav Beklinder in *Biggles, Secret Agent* is initially described as a good-looking girl, and on another occasion as "wide-eyed with alarm" (122), and when "she" is arrested "she" "screamed in English" (136), all suggesting the feminine, but once "she" is revealed as male he is accepted, again without comment. There is not even any explicit justification of his choice of disguise. Disguise is often a feature of adventure yarns, and the options available to a child are limited, but Beklinder could have grown a beard, dyed his hair, any of the more usual ploys. Robert Morvyn is even more striking, in that he is older (Gustav is about nineteen), and he lives in the same house as the four children without arousing their suspicions of his gender at all. He has a "rather husky voice" (17) and spends a lot of time resting in his room, which does help him to avoid the children to some extent, although it is actually because he is out every night trying to locate the villains.

Contrary to Flanagan's assertion above, there is no comedic effect in any of these male-female transformations. Occasionally other characters laugh at them, such as Bill in *Smuggler's Gap*, but the reader is not intended to find it amusing. The males here have the same motivation as the females: they are disguising themselves for safety, to protect themselves from an enemy. In some cases, such as Robin, and all the adult examples, their chief motive is to be able to spy on the enemy without being identified. Comedy would arise from an unconvincing impersonation of the opposite gender; Gustav Beklinder and Robert Morvyn both successfully maintain the deception at close quarters over a period of days.

Of course, the fact that males and females at this period tended to wear distinctively different clothes and have different hair and mannerisms to a greater extent than would perhaps be true today made these disguises easier than they would be in this generation. Yet those very distinctions made cross-dressing less acceptable. Homosexuality was still illegal and, as outlined in chapter two, British society was much less flexible than today. The existence of the tomboy would probably make girl-boy cross-dressing relatively unproblematic, but it is remarkable that here boy-girl and man-woman disguises are also completely acceptable.

Flanagan (2008) has suggested that in male-female narratives, the male not only fails to perform femininity effectively, he reaffirms his masculinity once the cross-dressing episode is over. As I have shown, in my texts the first of these claims is not borne out: the characters in Johns, Gussy in Blyton and Robert Morvyn in Courtney all give successful female performances. It is however true that Gussy ends by becoming "tougher", a more traditional boy, and symbolically insisting on having his hair cut short, while Robert Morvyn is revealed as a hero rather than the villain he had been suspected of being, and is largely instrumental in catching the criminals. Johns' character Beklinder, however, once revealed as male, loses all agency and becomes merely someone, like his father, for Biggles and Ginger to rescue. Possibly the difference in my texts is that the cross-dresser is never the protagonist. I do not feel that any of these texts used cross-dressing to challenge traditional gender stereotypes, as Flanagan suggests hers do, and in some of the examples, notably those involving children, they tended merely to reinscribe such stereotypes. Yet the adult examples in particular in my texts may have achieved the effect of interrogating patriarchal masculinity, without necessarily intending to do so.

For most of the period of this study, gender in Britain was conceived of as binary and polarised. There were in society considerable differences in the treatment of the two genders, and in expectations of their behaviour. In these books there are some examples of different treatment and expectations: there is some privileging of males, an acceptance of weakness in females, approval of sensitivity in girls and of strength and dependability in boys. Yet it is also the case that most of the girls go beyond the simple tomboy / feminine girl distinction, demonstrating a wide range of strengths and skills; this is however somewhat diluted by the adult female roles, which are often much more traditional. There is more pressure on the boys to conform, to be "real boys" and later "real men", yet there are also many examples of male sensitivity and there is a remarkable tolerance of transvestite disguises.

CONCLUSION

This book has tried to re-examine a period of children's literature which has often been dismissed by the critics as either second-rate or propagating reactionary values or both. It has focused on a small group of authors in depth rather than attempting to survey the whole output of the period, and it has tried to set those authors and their works into their sociocultural context, rather than judge them solely by today's standards. It has not been looking at their literary quality, since this is anyway a matter of opinion; instead it has focused on one of the criticisms, namely that popular writing of the period presented a stereotypical view of gender which reinforced the cultural norms and consequently slowed social change. The adventure genre had previously been aimed at boys though read by girls; in this period it was explicitly aimed at both, with protagonists both male and female (and often younger than before). As adventure stories offer opportunities for action which would traditionally be assigned to males, I felt it would be valuable to explore how these two genders were treated in popular examples of this genre.

In the 1970s there were several studies of, in particular, American children's literature which highlighted the then unequal treatment of gender. Much-cited is that by Lenore Weizman and others in 1972 looking at picture books for pre-school age. Clark and Higonnet (1999) have rightly pointed out that while at that point the concern was chiefly equality, theoretical feminism has moved on and now focuses more on revaluing "female" virtues and ambivalent gender identities. They claim that, nonetheless, the paradigm established by Weizman and others has had dominance in the field of children's literature criticism and advocate opening this up to the influence of cultural and multicultural feminism, which indeed has begun to happen in the twenty-first century. However, in looking back at this period before second-wave feminism, I feel it would be anachronistic to apply modern theories in too wholesale a manner, and my intent was to set the texts within the sociocultural context of their authors' lives. One criticism of studies in the 1970s is that they tended to focus on gender without much reference to other variables such as race, class and age. The fact that for most of this period (1930-1970) British authors concentrated on white middle-class protagonists, assuming white middle-class readers, means that for this study the criticism loses some of its force; it was possible to largely isolate gender as a factor.

Most of the selected authors produced series with the same group of characters, sometimes over quite long periods (*Biggles* ran from 1932 to 1967, the *Famous Five* from 1942 to 1963, and the *Lone Pine* books from 1943 to 1978), but although other aspects changed, with Saville's teenagers gradually starting to wear jeans and carry transistor radios, for instance, and Johns' plotlines becoming more predictable, the gender roles did not seem to do so. Indeed, in Saville's case, his later *Marston Baines* series seems rather a step backwards than forwards in this respect, even though written in the 1960s and '70s when Women's Liberation was making an impact. In the case of authors writing in more than one genre, however, there were sometimes distinctions: Brent-Dyer's girls' school stories give much more action to girls, but at the same time dwell on the interplay of personality and stress the importance of looks, while her last two thrillers at least focus more tightly on the action, give technical details of boats and aeroplanes, but sideline the female roles; Courtney, by contrast, while having some quite strong female personalities in her family books nonetheless includes in them many domesticated and self-sacrificing women and girls, while her adventure stories forefront female initiative and daring.

In chapter three I looked at the extent to which females shared in the action, and whether or not their involvement was opposed by the males: in the Worrals books there are frequent comments by various male characters to the effect that danger is not a suitable arena for women, but the heroines always challenge this both explicitly in what they say, and implicitly in succeeding in their missions, often where men have failed; in Blyton, by contrast, the girls are often left behind out of danger, and this is approved by adults and sometimes, though not always, accepted by the girls themselves. Ransome is the only author who never has his characters question whether females should enjoy a full share of the action, but the other two male writers both answer the question in the affirmative, though there is a marked difference between the *Biggles* and *Worrals* books in this respect. Two of the women writers, Courtney and Atkinson, throw in the occasional objection but essentially give full roles to their female characters. Brent-Dyer is very prone to label certain activities and types of behaviour as suitable for one or the other gender, and grudgingly allows women some share of the action, especially elderly spinsters. As remarked above, this is a contrast to her girls' books, where the heroines frequently engage in exciting rescues. If anything, then, the male writers are the more willing to recognise female action; I am moved to wonder if this is because women writers felt more pressure to conform in order to be published and accepted. If in a society with strong gender discrimination a woman writes a book with a strong female character dashing off climbing trees, discovering secret passages and rescuing boys who have got into difficulties, that is an "inferior" being claiming equality for her sex, whereas if a man writes exactly the same story, that is a "superior" being generously giving equality to the other sex. Reactions will not be the same.

There is in general, in the West at least, more resistance to males taking on "feminine" roles than the reverse. This perhaps explains why, although most of these authors have their girls or young women able to perform many traditionally masculine activities (climbing, throwing, sailing, repairing machinery), they still tend to confine the domestic chores to the females. Boys may help with tasks that require strength, such as carrying water, but they do not do the cooking except in all-male environments such as boats, or missions in the *Biggles* books. We still see this half a century later in our society: a woman with a job or career generally has to take on most of the domestic responsibility too, even if her husband or partner "helps". It is true that Britain is much more accepting of males caring for children and doing housework than it was two generations back, but it is still something noteworthy. Unless or until gender is not remarked upon, it will still be an issue.

In the mid-twentieth century some women were actively seeking a share in the public life of work and government which had largely been denied them, but there was also considerable pressure from the authorities, the media, and from many men to confine them to the home and encourage them to have children. It is not therefore surprising to find in these books many models of "ideal" parents, with domesticated mothers and protective fathers. Chapter five pointed out that these models were fairly pervasive, but there are nonetheless some alternatives given: some young women have careers, some old women are feisty and dominant, some fathers are feckless, or sensitive and in need of protection themselves. Yet overall the message is mixed: the lively intelligent girls with the physical skills and the bright courage have nowhere really to go, except to become strong kindly supportive wives and mothers, or eccentric spinsters, the staple characters of girls' books for a century before.

Our society has been hierarchical in one way or another for centuries, if not millennia, and these books often feature an explicit power hierarchy, with authority often but not always invested in the males. They do offer a number of powerful females, ranging from the child Nancy Blackett to Great Aunts in their eighties; their power derives largely from personality, sometimes also from skills and abilities, and is acknowledged by the male characters. It may suggest merely a different hierarchy, as with the rank of "Captain" Nancy and of Worrals, and this would accord with the goals of the Women's Libbers who sought to gain women an equal share of the world's power and opportunities. Yet there are also other kinds of power, such as the maternal authority of Susan Walker and the determination and strength of will of such disparate characters as Moira in the *Denehurst* books, who goes her own way and stands up to anyone who opposes her, and Aunt Freda making her living as an immigrant, and facing torture with dignity. These, together with the value explicitly given by Johns and Saville to the female viewpoint, tend more towards "maternal" feminism, a rejection of masculine values.

Courage is highly valued in all these books, but it is not the unthinking courage of the hearty rugby-playing type. While fears and tears seem to be more acceptable in the female characters, they overcome them, and the most striking examples of cold-blooded courage come from girls. The males in most of the books are allowed to be afraid, sometimes equally with the females, and there are examples of sensitivity, empathy and tears from them, but it is also true that the characters most likely to act out of bravado are male. Female sensitivity tends to be assumed by most though not all of the writers, and sometimes it emerges as weakness, especially in minor characters, but it is also sometimes represented as a strength, enabling imagination, empathy with the unfortunate, and, ultimately, the "love" which the world has "not enough" of.

These aspects of the books are, or ought to be, representative of conscious choices by the authors. While a writer is presumably sensitive to language, gender-bias in language was not something which had been much investigated at the time they were writing, and I would expect their unconscious gender constructs to emerge perhaps more in their language than elsewhere. We do find considerable correlation with stereotypes here, but going beyond the use of "men" but "girl", and the emphasis on girls being pretty, some of the writers at least had more positive description of females than males overall, and Ransome seemed to be using conversational turns to reflect the different kinds of power he presents, which derive from age, personality and expertise more than gender. The great exception to much of the above is Blyton, probably the best-known and most widely-read, and the one with the most stereotyping. The ultimate negativity of her tomboy roles is particularly disappointing. Why did Blyton, who had rejected her own mother's pressure to make her a nice domestic type, and who relentlessly pursued her career to the detriment of her children and first husband, choose to fill her books with such conservative gender roles? Was it perhaps, even unconsciously, her attempt to compensate for what society might view as her own deficiencies?

Do these books simply provide "cultural mirrors"? If so, then the culture they mirrored was more complex than we might imagine. Some of the women writers are more conservative than the men, overall, but really they are all individuals, with individual viewpoints. I am not of course suggesting that any of them was a consistent advocate of gender equality or of alternate gender identities. Each has absorbed some aspects of the culture in which they lived, but not always the same aspects, and most of them do also consciously challenge traditional binary, polarised gender identities in some way, at some point.

REFERENCES:
PRIMARY TEXTS

Allan, Mabel Esther (1954) *Adventure Royal* London: Blackie and Son

Atkinson, Mary Evelyn
August Adventure (1936) London: Bodley Head
Mystery Manor (1937) London: The Children's Book Club
The Compass Points North (1938) Oxford: Bodley Head
Smugglers' Gap (1939) London: John Lane Bodley Head
Going Gangster (1940) London: John Lane Bodley Head
The Monster of Widgeon Weir (1943) London: John Lane Bodley Head
Chimney Cottage (1947) London: John Lane Bodley Head
The House on the Moor (1948) London: John Lane Bodley Head

Blyton, Enid
Five Run Away Together (1967) Leicester: Knight Books
(Brockhampton Press)
Five Go To Smuggler's Top (1967) Leicester: Knight Books
Five On Kirrin Island Again (1967) Leicester: Knight Books
Five Get Into Trouble (1968) Leicester: Knight Books
Five On A Hike Together (1968) Leicester: Knight Books
Five Go Down To The Sea (1969) Leicester: Knight Books
Five Have Plenty Of Fun (1969) Leicester: Knight Books
Five Get Into A Fix (1970) Leicester: Knight Books
Five Have A Mystery To Solve (1971) Leicester: Knight Books
Five Are Together Again (1971) Leicester: Knight Books
The Island of Adventure (1967) London: William Collins Sons and Co
The Castle of Adventure (1968) London: William Collins Sons and Co
The Valley of Adventure (1968) London: William Collins Sons and Co
The Sea of Adventure (1969) London: May Fair Books
The Mountain of Adventure (1975) London: Piccolo Pan Books
(Macmillan)
The Ship of Adventure (1969) London: May Fair Books
The Circus of Adventure (1966) London: May Fair Books
The River of Adventure (1994) London: Macmillan's Children's Books

The Secret Island (1965) London: May Fair Books
The Secret of Spiggy Holes (1965) London: May Fair Books
The Secret Mountain (1965) London: May Fair Books
The Rockingdown Mystery (1949) London: Collins
The Rilloby Fair Mystery (1967) London: May Fair Books
The Ring O'Bells Mystery (1967) London: May Fair Books
The Rat-a-Tat Mystery (1970) London: May Fair Books
The Ragamuffin Mystery (1959) London: Collins

Brent-Dyer, Elinor M.
Fardingales (2015) Coleford: Girls Gone By Publishers
The Susannah Adventure (2016) Coleford: Girls Gone By Publishers
Chudleigh Hold (2007) Coleford: Girls Gone By Publishers
Condor Crags Adventure (1954) London: Chambers
Top Secret (1955) London: Chambers
The Chalet School Goes to It (1962) Edingburgh: W & R Chambers
The Princess of the Chalet School (1968) London: Fontana Paperbacks
Trials for the Chalet School (1983) London: Fontana Paperbacks
The Head Girl of the Chalet School (1988) Edinburgh: W & R Chambers Ltd.
Joey Goes to the Oberland (1995) London: Harper Collins
The Chalet School Does It Again (2002) Coleford: Girls Gone By Publishers
Janie of La Rochelle (2003) Coleford: Girls Gone By Publishers
A Head Girl's Difficulties (2008) Coleford: Girls Gone By Publishers

Courtney, Gwendoline
Stepmother (1948) London: Oxford University Press
A Coronet for Cathie (2003) Coleford: Girls Gone By Publishers
The Girls of Friar's Rise (2004) Coleford: Girls Gone By Publishers
The Denehurst Secret Service (2005) Coleford: Girls Gone By Publishers
Well Done, Denehurst! (2005) Coleford: Girls Gone By Publishers
The Chiltons (2006) Coleford: Girls Gone By Publishers
The Wild Lorings at School (2009) Coleford: Girls Gone By Publishers
The Wild Lorings - Detectives! (2010) Coleford: Girls Gone By Publishers
Mermaid House (2011) Coleford: Girls Gone By Publishers
Sally's Family (2012) Coleford: Girls Gone By Publishers
Long Barrow (2015) Coleford: Girls Gone By Publishers

Fairlie Bruce, Dorita
Dimsie Grows Up in *The New Dimsie Omnibus* (1941) London: Oxford University Press
Dimsie Carries On (1950) London: Oxford University Press
The School on the Moor (2006) Coleford: Girls Gone By Publishers

Forest, Antonia
The Thuggery Affair (1965) London: Faber and Faber
The Marlows and the Traitor (2003: First published 1953) Coleford: Girls Gone By Publishers
Falconer's Lure (2003: First published 1957) Coleford: Girls Gone By Publishers

Johns, William Earl
Worrals of the W.A.A.F. (1942) in *Girl's Own Annual 1942*, volume 62 London: Lutterworth Periodicals Ltd
Worrals Carries On (1942) London: Lutterworth Press
Worrals Flies Again (1942) London: Hodder and Stoughton
Worrals on the Warpath (1943) London: Hodder and Stoughton
Worrals Goes East (1944) London: Hodder and Stoughton
Worrals of the Islands (1945) London: Hodder and Stoughton
Worrals in the Wilds (1947) London: Hodder and Stoughton
Worrals Down Under (1950) London: Lutterworth Press
Worrals in the Wastelands (1949) London: Lutterworth Press
Worrals Goes Afoot (1949) London: Lutterworth Press
Worrals Investigates (1950) London: Lutterworth Press
Biggles - Secret Agent (1940) Oxford: Oxford University Press
Biggles in the Orient (1944) London: Hodder and Stoughton
Biggles Takes a Holiday (1949) London: Hodder and Stoughton
Biggles "Fails To Return" (1950) London: Hodder and Stoughton
Biggles Goes to School (1952) London: Hodder and Stoughton
Biggles and the Pirate Treasure (1954) Leicester: Brockhampton Press
Biggles and Co. (1962) London: May Fair Books
Biggles Goes to War (1962) London: William Collins Sons and Co
Biggles in the South Seas (1965) London: May Fair Books
Biggles Looks Back (1965) London: Hodder and Stoughton
Biggles and the Rescue Flight (1965) London: Wm Collins Sons and Co
Biggles Sorts It Out (1970) London: Hodder and Stoughton
Orchids for Biggles (1975) London: Hodder and Stoughton

The Camels are Coming (2003) London: Red Fox (Random House Children's Books)
Biggles Flies East (2003) London: Red Fox (Random House Children's Books
Biggles, Pioneer Air Fighter (n.d.) London: The Thames Publishing Co.
Biggles Flies Again (n.d.) London: The Thames Publishing Co.

Marsh, Eileen (n.d.) *Lorna - Air Pilot* London: Sampson Low, Marston and Co

Ransome, Arthur
Swallows and Amazons (1962) London: Penguin Books Ltd
Swallowdale (1968) London: Penguin Books
Peter Duck (1968) London: Penguin Books
Coot Club (1993) London: Red Fox (Random House)
Secret Water (1969) London: Penguin Books
*Missee Lee (*1971) London: Penguin Books
The Picts and the Martyrs: or Not Welcome At All (1971) London: Penguin Books
Great Northern? (1971) London: Penguin Books

Saville, Malcolm
Mystery at Witchend (1971) London: Wm Collins Sons and Co
Seven White Gates (1970) London: May Fair Books
The Gay Dolphin Adventure (1945) London: George Newnes Ltd
The Secret of Grey Walls (1947) London: George Newnes Ltd
Lone Pine Five (1968) Feltham: Hamlyn Publishing Group
The Neglected Mountain (1969) London: May Fair Books
Saucers Over The Moor (1967) London: Paul Hamlyn Ltd
Wings Over Witchend (1964) London: May Fair Books
Lone Pine London (1965) London: May Fair Books
The Secret of the Gorge (1968) Feltham: Hamlyn Publishing Group
Mystery Mine (1959) London: George Newnes Ltd
Sea Witch Comes Home (1968) Feltham: Hamlyn Publishing Group
Not Scarlet But Gold (2012) Coleford: Girls Gone By Publishers
Treasure at Amorys (1978) London: Fontana Paperbacks
Man With Three Fingers (1969) London: Wm Collins Sons and Co
Strangers at Witchend (2014) Coleford: Girls Gone By Publishers
Where's My Girl? (2005) Coleford: Girls Gone By Publishers
Home To Witchend (2015) Coleford: Girls Gone By Publisher

Three Towers in Tuscany (2016) Coleford: Girls Gone By Publishers
The Purple Valley (1964) London: Heinemann
Power of Three (1968) London: The Children's Book Club
The Dagger and the Flame (1970) London: Heinemann
Shaw, Jane
Susan Pulls the Strings (1953) London: The Children's Press
Susan Interferes (1968) London: Harper Collins

BIBLIOGRAPHY

Auchmuty, Rosemary. (1992) *A World of Girls*. London: The Women's Press Ltd.
—. (1999) *A World of Women*. London: The Women's Press Ltd.
Avery, Gillian. (1975) *Childhood's Pattern*. Leicester: Hodder and Stoughton
behavenet. (n.d.) Bem Sex-Role Inventory http://www.behavenet.com/capsules/disorders/genderiddis.htm
Berresford Ellis, Peter and Williams, Piers. (1985) *By Jove, Biggles! The Life of Captain W.E. Johns*. London: W.H. Allen and Co.
Bristow, Joseph. (1991) *Empire Boys: Adventures in a Man's World*. London: Harper Collins Academic
Bruley, Sue. (1999) *Women in Britain since 1900*. Basingstoke: Palgrave Macmillan
Butler, Judith. (1990) *Gender Trouble: Feminism and the Subversion of Identity*. London: Routledge
Butts, Dennis. (2010) *Children's Literature and Social Change*. Cambridge: Lutterworth Press
Cadogan, Mary and Craig, Patricia. (1976) *You're a Brick Angela*! London, Victor Gollancz Ltd
Cadogan, Mary and Craig, Patricia. (1978) *Women and Children First. The Fiction of Two World Wars*. London: Victor Gollancz Ltd.
Cadogan, Mary. (1992) *Women with Wings*. London: Macmillan
Clark, Beverley L. and Higonnet, Margaret R., eds (2000) *Girls, Boys, Books, Toys: Gender in Children's Literature and Culture*. Baltimore, Maryland: Johns Hopkins University Press
Coates, Jennifer. (1993) *Women, Men and Language 2nd ed*. London: Longman
Coates, Jennifer and Pichler, Pia, eds. (2011) *Language and Gender, 2nd ed*. Chichester: Wiley-Blackwell
Cridland, Clarissa and Mackie-Hunter, Ann. (2004) Introduction to *The Denehurst Secret Service*. Coleford: Girls Gone By Publishers
Crouch, Marcus. (1962) *Treasure Seekers and Borrowers. Children's Books in Britain 1900-1960*. London: The Library Association

Cunningham, Hugh. (2005) *Children and Childhood in Western Society Since 1500, 2nd ed.* London: Longman

Eyre, Frank. (1971) *British Children's books in the Twentieth Century* London: Longman

Fine, Cordelia. (2011) *Delusions of Gender: The Real Science Behind Sex Differences.* London: Icon Books Ltd.

Fisher, Margery. (1986) *The Bright Face of Danger.* London: Hodder and Stoughton

Flanagan, Victoria. (2002) "Reframing Masculinity: Female-to-Male Cross-Dressing." In *Ways of Being Male: Representing Masculinity in Children's Literature and Film,* edited by John Stephens, 78-95. New York and London: Routledge

—. (2008) *Into the Closet: Cross-Dressing and the Gendered Body in Children's Literature and Film.* Abingdon: Routledge

Forest, Antonia. (2002) Foreword to *The Marlows and the Traitor.* Coleford: Girls Gone By Publishers

Foster, Shirley and Simons, Judy. (1995) *What Katy Read: Feminist Re-readings of 'Classic' Stories for Girls.* Basingstoke: Macmillan

Franklin, Leanne. (2012) *Gender.* Basingstoke: Palgrave Macmillan

Fry, Stephen. (1997) *Moab is my Washpot.* London: Arrow Books

Goddard, Angela and Meân Patterson, Lyn (2000) *Language and Gender.* London: Routledge

Grenby, Matthew O. and Reynolds, Kimberley, eds (2011) *Children's Literature Studies: A Research Handbook.* Basingstoke: Palgrave Macmillan

Haddon, Celia. (1977) *Great Days and Jolly Days The Story of Girls' School Songs.* London, Hodder and Stoughton

Harvey Darton, Frederick J. (2011) *Children's books in England: five centuries of social life.* London: CUP

Hendrick, Harry. (1997) *Children, childhood and English society 1880-1990.* Cambridge: CUP

Heywood, Colin. (2001) *A History of Childhood: Children and Childhood in the West from Medieval to Modern Times.* London: Polity

Hourihan, Margery. (1997) *Deconstructing the Hero: Literary Theory and Children's Literature* London: Routledge

Hunt, Peter, ed (1992) *Literature for Children: Contemporary Criticism.* London: Routledge

Hunt, Peter, ed (1999) *Understanding Children's Literature.* New York, Routledge

Hunt, Peter. (2009) "The Same but Different: Conservatism and Revolution." In *Children's Literature: Approaches and Territories,* edited by Janet Maybin and Nicola J. Watson, 70-84. Basingstoke: Palgrave Macmillan.

Johnston, Ingrid and Mangat, Jyoti. (2002) "Making the Invisible Visible: Stereotypes of Masculinity in Canonized School Literature." In *Ways of Being Male: Representing Masculinity in Children's Literature and Film,* edited by John Stephens, 133-149. New York and London: Routledge

Lamb, Sharon and Mikel Brown, Lyn. (2006) *Packaging Girlhood. Rescuing Our Daughters from Marketers' Schemes.* New York: St Martin's Press

LeGates, Marlene. (2001) *In Their Time: A History of Feminism in Western Society.* London: Routledge

Lehr, Susan S., ed (2001) *Beauty, Brains and Brawn: The Construction of Gender in Children's Literature.* Heinemann Education

Lesnik-Oberstein, Karin. (1994) *Children's Literature: Criticism and the Fictional Child.* Oxford: Clarendon Press

Lesnik-Oberstein, Karin., ed (1998) *Children in Culture: Approaches to Childhood.* Basingstoke: Macmillan

McClelland, Helen. (1981) *Behind the Chalet School.* Bogner Regis: New Horizon

McEnery, Tony. (2006) *Swearing in English.* Abingdon: Routledge

Marr, Andrew. (2008) *A History of Modern Britain.* London: Pan Books

Marr, Andrew. (2009) *The Making of Modern Britain.* London: Macmillan

Marwick, Arthur. (2003) *British Society since 1945, 4th ed.* London: Penguin Books

Maybin, Janet and Watson, Nicola J., eds (2009) *Children's Literature: Approaches and Territories.* Basingstoke: Palgrave Macmillan

Miller, Casey and Swift, Kate. (1995) *Handbook of Non-Sexist Writing, 3rd ed.* London: The Women's Press

Montogmery, Heather and Watson, Nicola J., eds (2009) *Children's Literature: Classic Texts and Contemporary Trends.* Basingstoke: Palgrave Macmillan

Nelson, Claudia. (1991) *Boys Will Be Girls: The Feminine Ethic and British Children's Fiction 1857-1917.* New York and London: Rutgers University Press

Nodelman, Perry. (2002) "Making Boys Appear: The Masculinity of Children's Fiction." In *Ways of Being Male: Representing Masculinity in Children's Literature and Film,* edited by John Stephens, 1-14. New York and London: Routledge

O'Hanlon, Mark. (2001) *Beyond the Lone Pine; A Biography of Malcolm Saville.* Mark O'Hanlon

Pennell, Beverley. (2002) "Redeeming Masculinity at the End of the Second Millennium." In *Ways of Being Male: Representing Masculinity in Children's Literature and Film,* edited by John Stephens, 55-77. New York and London: Routledge

Pugh, Martin. (2008) *We Danced All Night: A Social History of Britain Between the Wars.* London: Vintage Books

Ransome, Arthur, edited by Rupert Hart-Davis. (1976) *The Autobiography of Arthur Ransome.* Jonathan Cape Ltd.

Ray, Sheila. (1972) *Children's Fiction - A Handbook for Librarians.* Leicester: Brockhampton Press

—. (1982) *The Blyton Phenomenon.* London: Andre Deutsch Ltd.

Reynolds, Kimberley. (1990) *Girls Only? Gender and Popular Children's Fiction in Britain, 1880-1910.* Hemel Hempstead: Harvester-Wheatsheaf

—. (2002) "Come Lads and Ladettes: Gendering Bodies and Gendering Behaviors." In *Ways of Being Male: Representing Masculinity in Children's Literature and Film,* edited by John Stephens, 96-115. New York and London: Routledge

—. (2016) *Left Out: The forgotten tradition of radical publishing for children in Britain 1910-1949.* Oxford: OUP

Rose, Jacqueline. (1984) *The Case of Peter Pan, or the Impossibility of Children's Fiction.* Basingstoke: Macmillan

Rowe Townsend, John. (1990) *Written for Children.* London, Bodley Head

Rudd, David. (2009) "In Defence of the Indefensible? Some Grounds for Enid Blyton's Appeal." In *Children's Literature: Approaches and Territories,* edited by Janet Maybin and Nicola J. Watson, 168-182. Basingstoke: Palgrave Macmillan.

Sadker, Myra and Sadker, David. (1985) "Sexism in the schoolroom of the '80s." In *Psychology Today,* March, 54-7.

Salmon, Edward. (1888) "Boys' and Girls' Reading, 1884." In *Children's Literature: Approaches and Territories,* edited by Janet Maybin and Nicola J. Watson, 119-130. Basingstoke: Palgrave Macmillan.

Sarah, Elizabeth. (1980) "Teachers and students in the classroom: an examination of classroom interaction." In *Learning to Lose,* edited by Dale Spender and Elizabeth Sarah, 155-64. London: Women's Press.

Seelinger Trites, Roberta. (1997) *Waking Sleeping Beauty: Feminist Voices in Children's Novels* Iowa, IA: University of Iowa Press

Smith, Bonnie G. (2013) *Women's Studies: the basics.* Abingdon: Routledge

Spender, Dale. (1982) *Invisible Women–The Schooling Scandal.* London: Writers and Readers Publishing Cooperative.

Stevenson, Robert Louis. (1894) "My First book: 'Treasure Island'." In *Children's Literature: Classic Texts and Contemporary Trends*, edited by Heather Montgomery and Nicola J. Watson, 53-60. Basingstoke: Palgrave Macmillan.

Stinton, Judith., ed (1979) *Racism and Sexism in Children's Books.* Bristol, J.W. Arrowsmith Ltd.

Stoney, Barbara. (1986) *Enid Blyton. A Biography, 2nd ed.* London: Hodder and Stoughton

Suico, Terri. (2017) "History Repeating Itself: The Portrayal of Female Characters in Young Adult Literature at the Beginning of the Millennium." In *Gender Identities: Critical Re-readings of Gender in Children's and Young Adult Literature*, edited by Tricia Clasen and Holly Hassel, 11-27. Abingdon: Routledge

Swacker, Marjorie. ((1975) "The sex of the speaker as a sociolinguistic variable." In *Language and Sex: Difference and Dominance*, edited by Barrie Thorne and Nancy Henley, 76-83. Rowley, Mass: Newbury House.

Talbot, Mary. (2010) *Language and Gender 2nd ed.* Cambridge: Polity Press

Vygotsky, Lev S. (1986) Revised and translated by Alex Kozulin *Thought and Language*. Cambridge, Mass: MIT Press

Weizman, Lenore, Eifler, Deborah, Hokada, Elizabeth and Ross, Catherine. (1972) "Sex-Role Socialization in Picture Books for Preschool Children." In *American Journal of Sociology* 77, 1125-50

Zimmerman, Don and West, Candace. (1975) "Sex roles, interruptions and silences in conversation." In *Language and Sex: Difference and Dominance*, edited by Barrie Thorne and Nancy Henley, 105-29. Rowley, Mass: Newbury House.

APPENDIX A:
LIST OF PRIMARY TEXTS

Date of first publication

M.E. ATKINSON

August Adventure	1936
Mystery Manor	1937
The Compass Points North	1938
Smugglers' Gap	1939
Going Gangster	1940
Crusoe Island	1941
Challenge to Adventure	1942
The Monster of Widgeon Weir	1943
The Nest of the Scarecrow	1944
Problem Party	1945
Chimney Cottage	1947
The House on the Moor	1948
The Thirteenth Adventure	1949
Steeple Folly	1950

ENID BLYTON

Five On A Treasure Island	1942
Five Go Adventuring Again	1943
Five Run Away Together	1944
Five Go To Smuggler's Top	1945
Five Go Off In A Caravan	1946
Five On Kirrin Island Again	1947
Five Go Off To Camp	1948
Give Get Into Trouble	1949
Five Fall Into Adventure	1950
Five On A Hike Together	1951
Five Have A Wonderful Time	1952
Five Go Down to The Sea	1953
Five Go To Mystery Moor	1954
Five Have Plenty Of Fun	1955

Five On A Secret Trail	1956
Five Go To Billycock Hill	1957
Five Get Into A Fix	1958
Five On Finniston Farm	1960
Five Go To Demon's Rocks	1961
Five Have A Mystery To Solve	1962
Five Are Together Again	1963
The Island of Adventure	1944
The Castle of Adventure	1946
The Valley of Adventure	1947
The Sea of Adventure	1948
The Mountain of Adventure	1949
The Ship of Adventure	1950
The Circus of Adventure	1952
The River of Adventure	1956
The Secret Island	1938
The Secret of Spiggy Holes	1940
The Secret Mountain	1941
The Secret of Killimooin	1943
The Secret of Moon Castle	1953
The Rockingdown Mystery	1949
The Rilloby Fair Mystery	1950
The Ring O'Bells Mystery	1951
The Rubadub Mystery	1952
The Rat-a-Tat Mystery	1956
The Ragamuffin Mystery	1959

ELINOR M. BRENT-DYER

Fardingales	1950
The Susannah Adventure	1953
Chudleigh Hold	1954
Condor Crags Adventure	1954
Top Secret	1955

GWENDOLINE COURTNEY

The Grenville Garrison	1940
The Denehurst Secret Service	1940
Well Done, Denehurst!	1941

Mermaid House	1953
The Wild Lorings at School	1954
The Wild Lorings - Detectives!	1956

CAPT. W.E. JOHNS

Worrals of the W.A.A.F.	1941
Worrals Carries On	1942
Worrals Flies Again	1942
Worrals on the Warpath	1943
Worrals Goes East	1944
Worrals of the Islands	1945
Worrals in the Wilds	1947
Worrals Down Under	1948
Worrals in the Wastelands	1949
Worrals Goes Afoot	1949
Worrals Investigates	1950
The Camels Are Coming	1932
Biggles Flies Again	1934
Biggles and Co.	1936
Biggles Goes to War	1938
Biggles - Secret Agent	1940
Biggles in the South Seas	1940
Biggles "Fails To Return"	1943
Biggles and the Pirate Treasure	1954
Orchids for Biggles	1962
Biggles Looks Back	1965
Biggles Sorts It Out	1967

ARTHUR RANSOME

Swallows and Amazons	1930
Swallowdale	1931
Peter Duck	1932
Winter Holiday	1933
Coot Club	1934
Pigeon Post	1936
We Didn't Mean to Go to Sea	1937
Secret Water	1939
The Big Six	1940
Missee Lee	1941
The Picts and the Martyrs	1942
Great Northern?	1947

MALCOM SAVILLE

Lone	Mystery at Witchend	1943
Pine	Seven White Gates	1944
series	The Gay Dolphin Adventure	1945
	The Secret of Grey Walls	1947
	Lone Pine Five	1949
	The Elusive Grasshopper	1951
	The Neglected Mountain	1953
	Saucers Over The Moor	1955
	Wings Over Witchend	1956
	Lone Pine London	1957
	The Secret of the Gorge	1958
	Mystery Mine	1959
	Sea Witch Comes Home	1960
	Not Scarlet But Gold	1962
	Treasure at Amorys	1964
	Man With Three Fingers	1966
	Rye Royal	1969
	Strangers at Witchend	1970
	Where's My Girl?	1972
	Home to Witchend	1978
Marston	Three Towers in Tuscany	1963
Baines	The Purple Valley	1964
series	Dark Danger	1965
	White Fire	1966
	Power of Three	1968
	The Dagger and the Flame	1970
	Marston - Master Spy	1978

APPENDIX B:
ANALYSIS OF *FIVE GO ADVENTURING AGAIN*
(F5 NO 2)

character	list of modifiers	comments
George	fierce old George; awkward; sulky x 4 ; fierce x 2; difficult x 2; obstinately x 2 ; defiantly x 2; a huge frown almost hiding her eyes; scowled x 2; scowl; in a huff; shut the door with a bang; she tore out of the room; furiously; pale and sullen; [sensible - not what she is but what people keep advising her to be]; [face] dark and angry; perfectly impossible; disobedient, rude and defiant; her eyes gleamed angrily; rebellious; naughty girl; extraordinary [in A's opinion for daring to roam about the house at night]; quite fearless; [eyes] very blue and clear(= telling the truth); her boyish ways; old George [J]; old thing; marvellous - not afraid of anything! [J]; squealed (excitement); the little girl x 2 [+ his little mistress];	*negative: easily angry, sulks, defies authority, also in q violent/ aggressive ways like slamming doors* *positive: brave and truthful - tends to be greatly outnumbered by all the negatives* *still also some 'little girl' and 'squeal' things which link her w. Anne*

Anne	with tears in her eyes; terribly excited, rather frightened and ... afraid of falling; yelled; the little girl's chatter (nrly gave secret away); politely; with a giggle; giggled; beamed; eager to join in, eager to please; sticking up valiantly for her cousin; clever girl! [D]; her sharp eyes; her little mouth; squealed [excitement]; the little girl; darling [J]; poor old Anne [J]; her little fingers were not strong enough;	*negative: afraid, cries easily, can't keep a secret* *positive: happy and eager to please, also loyal and can be clever* *weak and small - is this negative or positive?*
Quentin	a very clever man, but rather frightening; he had little patience with children; frownier [A]; sternly; angrily; irritably; tall, cross and frowning	*variations on stern and angry - fairly negative - though he usually praises the kids at the end of the book, and admits his mistakes*
Fanny	a twinkle in her eye; with a laugh; very worried	*warm and smiling and affectionate - the worry is because she cares*
old farmer's wife	as lively as a bantam hen; bustling about; bustled off; the old lady + variants many times	
Dick and Julian	yelling ; obstinate [J]; politely [J]	*both boys and girls yell; both boys and girls speak 'politely' to adults they don't feel that comfortable with*
tutor (who turns out to be a baddy)	responsible and intelligent [Q]; his eyes were piercingly blue; seemed sensible and jolly; eyes very piercing; tough	*not what he seems - lots of positive at first*

| Anne's father | jolly and smiling | |
| Matron at boys' school | squealed [at mice] | |

INDEX

A

adolescence, 23, 67
adolescents, 145
Allan, Mabel Esther, 57
Armada paperback, 15
Atkinson, M.E., 5, 9, 10, 32, 34, 38,
    51, 59, 61, 67, 78, 85, 117, 126,
    129, 143, 158
    characters, 50
    cross-dressing, 153
    language, 119, 120, 123
    tears, 113
Auchmuty, Rosemary, 17, 22, 24, 33,
    146

B

Baines Reed, Talbot, 32, 115
Ballantyne, 28, 32, 101
Beale, Dorothea, 20
Beau Geste, 3, 53, 59
Blyton, Enid, 5, 10, 12, 14, 15, 18,
    32, 34, 35, 38, 41, 42, 43, 49, 50,
    58, 59, 60, 61, 67, 68, 69, 70, 71,
    72, 78, 79, 81, 82, 84, 94, 97,
    108, 109, 110, 113, 114, 115,
    117, 126, 127, 128, 133, 136,
    144, 145, 147, 158, 160
    criticism of, 11
    cross-dressing, 155
    farm life, 77
    imaginative girls, 143
    language, 119, 120, 123, 124,
        129, 135, 139
    language data, 124
    leadership, 90
    life, 11, 33
    male heroes, 104
    male privilege, 149

    parents, 128
    tears, 113
    wild children, 109
Boy's Own Paper, 29, 32, 38
Brazil, Angela, 1, 29, 30, 32, 38
Brent-Dyer, Elinor, 1, 5, 12, 13, 30,
    31, 32, 38, 43, 58, 59, 62, 63, 64,
    72, 83, 109, 113, 117, 126, 129,
    133, 144, 145, 148, 158
    books for girls, 43, 44, 70, 76,
        78, 131
    careers, 151
    language, 118, 120, 121, 123
    leadership, 90
    life, 15, 33
    male heroes, 103
    male wisdom, 149
    nightmares, 144
    parents, 76, 95
BSRI (Bem Sex-Role Inventory),
    124, 126, 127, 141
Buss, Frances, 20
Butler, Judith, 116, 140

C

Cadogan, Mary, 1, 5, 29
careers, 18, 23, 24, 33, 34, 66, 81,
    82, 83, 102, 151, 152, 159, 160
Carnegie Medal, 6, 36, 38
children's literature, second golden
    age, 5
climbing, 62
COBUILD language database, 117
cooking, 70, 71, 72, 73, 82, 93, 94,
    147, 159
Coral Island, The, 59
corporal punishment, 27, 35, 86
Courtney, Gwendoline, 5, 11, 13,
    16, 31, 38, 45, 51, 58, 59, 61, 62,

T

tomboy(s), 31, 42, 59, 64, 108, 111,
    121, 142, 147, 148, 153, 155,
    160
torture, 11, 12, 45, 109, 133, 160
Trease, Geoffrey, 3, 38
trousers, 21, 60, 79, 81

V

Vygotsky, Lev, 141

W

WAAF, 8, 54, 92
war, 9
wartime, 10, 14
Women's Royal Air Force, 64
World War One, 1, 4, 9, 16, 20, 21,
    22, 27, 70, 91, 101, 103
World War Two, 8, 9, 11, 21, 24,
    26, 28, 31, 34, 35, 37, 58, 91,
    102, 103, 122